A Buckeye Season

The Inside Story of the Glory and Heartbreak of Ohio State's 1995 Season

Jeff Snook

Masters Press

A Division of Howard W. Sams & Co.
A Bell Atlantic Company

Published by Masters Press
A Division of Howard W. Sams & Company, A Bell Atlantic Company
2647 Waterfront Pkwy E. Dr, Suite 300, Indianapolis, IN 46214

96 97 98 99 00 01   10 9 8 7 6 5 4 3 2 1

Library of Congress Cataloging-in-Publication Data Pending

Acknowledgments

First of all, I would like to thank everyone in the Ohio State football family for letting me become a part of your lives for the 1995 season.

From offensive coordinator Joe Hollis, who allowed me to infiltrate his meetings, to defensive coordinator Bill Young, who's as genuine and as hard-working as a guy can be, to Steve Snapp, to Archie Griffin, to Dr. E. Gordon Gee, I want to thank you all.

I want especially to mention John Cooper, whom I followed every day for five months. For the unwavering access you allowed me and for the time you took out of your schedule to help make this project a success, I sincerely thank you.

Finally, my most important debt of gratitude goes to Anne, whose unselfishness allowed me to take the time and effort to research and complete this project.

Contents

Foreword

First off, I need to preface the text of this book by informing you that I am a graduate of Ohio State University. I attended my first football game at Ohio Stadium on Sept. 30, 1972, Archie Griffin's coming-out party, and have been hooked on the seductive powers of the giant horseshoe and the team it houses on autumn Saturdays since.

However, I firmly believe you won't be able to detect any such bias as you read on. I wanted to present a clear, objective, behind-the-scenes look into a Buckeyes' season. In the end, I hope you have adopted a further understanding of Ohio State football, its players, its coaches and John Cooper.

I hope you enjoy the trip.

———————◆●◆———————

I remember it like it was yesterday.

December 30, 1987.

I was covering the Florida State Seminoles, about to play Nebraska in the Fiesta Bowl in Phoenix, Ariz., for a daily newspaper when word spread that Ohio State was about to name a new football coach to succeed Earle Bruce. So I walked up to then-Florida State Athletic Director Cecil "Hootie" Ingram to get his opinion. Now ol' Hootie was one of the best in the business at assessing coaching talent because he had played the game himself at Alabama.

"Tell me all you know about this John Cooper guy," I asked.

"Let me tell you, Buckeye (he always called me that for some reason), you got yourself the best coach out there, in my opinion," Ingram said. "You got a real good one. You watch, someday this guy will win a national championship."

For the next seven years, after the losses to Michigan and losses in bowl games, some Buckeye fans would have chuckled at Ingram's prediction. And now, after his eighth season in which he came closer than most people would realize, John Cooper's teams have won only one Big Ten co-championship and no national championships. His teams have finished second in the Big Ten in three of the past four seasons.

Of all the hundreds of conversations I had with John Cooper from Aug. 1 through Jan. 1, in researching this book, some were funny, some were educational, some were surprising and some were insightful.

But one stands out in my mind the most. And I believe it tells you what John Harold Cooper is all about.

During practice one day in October, the OSU women's field hockey team was about to play a game next to the football practice field. Music, if you can call it that, was blaring at jet-engine-like decibels from the field hockey sidelines and it clearly annoyed Cooper. Now if the music would have been Sinatra or Glenn Miller, that would have been one thing. But it sounded more like a mix of a reverberating base drum, two semis crashing head-on and four cats whose tails were caught in the door. The coach walked to the edge of the field and glared in the direction of the boom-box operators for several minutes, although he never made a move to have the noise stopped.

"You hear that crap?" he said. "You know what Woody would have done if he was here and heard that? Well, come to think of it, they wouldn't have been playing over there in the first place when practice is going on. I granted them permission to use that field, because we never used it."

Cooper then continued.

"Woody Hayes was a great football coach, but when you think about it, why did he have to be so mean? You don't have to be mean to the media. You don't have to berate the coaches and players. You don't have to be like that. You can still be nice to people and get their respect," he said.

Now since the day I left Ohio, I always have defended Wayne Woodrow Hayes to anyone who dared insult his memory, simply because I knew his other side — the one that spent as much time visiting hospital patients as he did drawing up the off-tackle play.

Furthermore, I knew Cooper respected Hayes' memory and the record he had accomplished at Ohio State. It wouldn't be easy to have a shadow of your larger-than-life predecessor following your every move, your every step. But that is what Cooper, and before him, Bruce, have gone through.

When you consider that dealing with fellow human beings is the most common form of communication, you have to realize that Cooper's opinion was honorable and more importantly, legitimate. He probably won't be happy that I recounted his thoughts, simply because Hayes' fans will deem them unkind to his memory. That certainly was not how he had meant them to be taken and that is not the point to be made here. My objective was to show a side of John Cooper, not Woody Hayes. Yet, it became obvious to me that as coach of what represents the most revered and cherished past-time for all Ohioans, he has been as misunderstood as Hayes.

Another time before a crucial game, as Cooper was about to lead his team out of the tunnel at Wisconsin, he walked up to me. The wind was blowing hard, the temperature had dropped into the 40s and my ears were red. Unprepared for the 30-degree drop in just 24 hours, I was shaking from the cold. "Jeff, want me to get you a hat, another sweatshirt, some gloves?" he asked.

What I thought then was — aside from "Why is he not thinking of the first series of plays?" — "Is this guy for real?"

He is.

I know one thing for sure — the people who say they don't like John Cooper have never met John Cooper.

Since Cooper became a Buckeye, I believe he would have been better served as a head coach to shed his nice-guy approach at times. To tighten discipline, to yell, to scream, to motivate better and to fire an unqualified coach once he realized he made a hiring mistake. He has fired only two assistants in 19 years. But his loyalty, like that of Hayes, is unparalleled.

In other words, at times, perhaps John Cooper should stop the music.

Still, I have no doubts that he is a better human being than he is a football coach. Take that either way you want, either as a compliment or as a criticism, but think about it nonetheless.

And in the end, how could anybody ever fault him for that?

1.

"I want to stay at Ohio State, but does Ohio State want me?"

John Harold Cooper sat in the Marriott next to Atlanta's Hartsfield Airport, his heart in one place and his head another. He felt anger and he felt betrayal. He also was somewhat confused. He was 57 years old now, and this wasn't the way it was supposed to work out for the final stage of his coaching career. Across from him sat Louisiana State Athletic Director Joe Dean, who, having fired Curley Hallman two weeks earlier, needed a coach to turn LSU into a winner after an unprecedented sixth consecutive losing season. The Tigers had just finished a 4-7 season, and fans were turning away from the program in droves.

Cooper? He just wanted to be wanted.

It was Nov. 29, 1994.

Ten days earlier, he had been carried onto the field by his players and then accidentally dropped into a sea of bedlam at Ohio Stadium. His Buckeyes had finally beaten Michigan, 22-6, his first win over the hated Wolverines since he had arrived in Columbus seven seasons earlier. His team had a 9-3 record and was headed to the Citrus Bowl to play Alabama.

Then Dean called. The timing was perfect, but for whom?

Cooper had just met with Ohio State Athletic Director Andy Geiger for his year-end evaluation, the result of which the coach wouldn't have placed proudly on his resume. He had only a year remaining on his contract, and Geiger had offered a two-year extension.

"Two years, can you believe that?" Cooper said later. "I can't recruit with a contract that totals three years. I can't keep my assistant coaches the way it is. My receivers coach had rented an apartment for the last three years. He was afraid to buy a house because of the fear they would fire my ass."

Losing assistant coaches wasn't a new thing at Ohio State. With rumors flying about Cooper's insecurity every fall, assistant coaches always were looking for good jobs with security. Receivers coach Mike Stock had just been the latest. He would soon leave to work for the Kansas City Chiefs.

So Cooper left Geiger's office at St. John Arena in a huff and accepted Dean's invitation to meet in Atlanta. The coach's daughter, Cindy, had interned one year in Baton Rouge and loved the place. A close friend, Mike Ferris, was a prominent LSU booster and served as a contact between Cooper and Dean.

1

Yes, things were shaping up for Cooper to leave his third head coaching job in his rearview mirror. He had exited Tulsa after eight seasons and a 57-31 record to go to Arizona State. He departed Arizona State after leading the school to their first Rose Bowl. And now, he was ready to leave Ohio State after beating Michigan for the first time. The past seven seasons had been a pinch of heaven and a dose of hell, anyway. His family loved Columbus when things were pleasant — in other words, when Ohio State was winning. Following the losses, it could be the worst place on earth for a coach and his family, as the Coopers had discovered.

To start with, fans hated Michigan, and Cooper's teams had an 0-5-1 record against the Wolverines until Nov. 19. That meant they had finished five seasons feeling miserable and another feeling nothing more than relief. Illinois had beaten Ohio State four consecutive times in Ohio Stadium. You think Woody Hayes ever lost four consecutive times to an opponent at the famed horseshoe? Not in his 28 years at OSU. Earle Bruce? Nope. None of their teams ever gave up 63 points, either. Penn State had walloped the Buckeyes 63-14 earlier in the season. Most Ohio State fans agree that their team shouldn't allow 63 points in a month, let alone in four quarters. And the Rose Bowl? It had become just another game that Ohio State fans watched on television as some other Big Ten team played. Six classes of Buckeyes had signed, completed four years of eligibility and departed without seeing Pasadena, California.

Critics found plenty to pick at off the field, too. Soon after he had arrived in Columbus, Cooper made a few too many commercials for their liking, one of which was filmed with him sitting in a hot tub. Conservative fans figured the coach was just out to make a buck off the Buckeyes. After all, Hayes disdained commercials and repeatedly turned down salary increases.

"There are some things I would do different," Cooper said. "For one, I wouldn't have made as many commercials, but that's the way coaches around the country do it. Every thing here that you do, you are compared to Coach Hayes. He didn't make commercials — he wrote books. The hot tub thing was stupid on my part. Here's what happened — I was building a house, and some guy was putting a hot tub in it. He shot a commercial with me in it. Now this comes under 'you live and learn.' What I should have done is say, 'Hey, you can use the commercial one time or five times or whatever,'"

Instead, the commercial wore out the airwaves in Central Ohio. To make matters worse, the coach wasn't even paid for the humiliation, either.

"People out there were saying 'This guy isn't coaching football, he's doing commercials,'" Cooper said. "Well I've never done a commercial in my life during the season. I did them in July. I should have followed my own advice, which is: Don't give people a reason to get after you."

Others disliked Cooper not because of where he was from, but where he wasn't from. In other words, he wasn't a Buckeye. He grew up in Tennessee and played at Iowa State. "I've heard people say he wasn't a member of the Ohio State family, so he isn't popular," Geiger said. "That's pretty petty, isn't it?" However, in his seven years in Columbus, Cooper felt he had become a Buckeye. He even carried one in his pocket for luck. He gave them to players and recruits. He had a portrait of Hayes, right under his family pictures, in his office.

Nonetheless, some Buckeyes fans believed they had their reasons to dislike John Cooper and were willing to pay his moving tab to the Bayou. The coach, feeling unwanted by his own administration, was ready to take them up on it, too. He had discovered he was one loss from being fired at least twice in his career anyway — the first time when the Buckeyes rallied to tie Michigan 13-13 in 1992. The second time had come and gone just ten days earlier with the win over the Wolverines.

Joe Dean tossed a wrench in the entire scenario — he didn't offer the job to Cooper that day in Atlanta. It was a move, or a lack of a move, that Dean later would regret. "The mood I was in, I would have taken the LSU job that day — if Joe Dean had offered it," Cooper said. "But he never did. He had one more candidate to interview, and then he was going to get back to me. And Ohio State just wasn't as committed as I thought they should have been."

Dean flew back to Louisiana to interview the school's defensive coordinator. Cooper flew home to Columbus to meet with Geiger again. This time the athletic director, in his second year since arriving from the University of Maryland, had changed his stance. Perhaps it was the knowledge that someone else wanted his football coach. Or perhaps he realized that stability in the football program was needed more than ever. Whatever, he was offering a five-year extension. That, Cooper thought, was more like it. He called Ferris. "Call Joe and tell him not to offer me the job," he said. "I am going to stay here."

* * *

Eight months and one week later, Cooper awakened from an afternoon nap on his office couch at the Woody Hayes Athletic Center and chuckled at the whole episode. It was a forced laugh. Some undeniable bitterness remained. His eighth season as Ohio State's head coach was to begin in 20 days with the Kickoff Classic against Boston College in East Rutherford, New Jersey.

He had agreed to a new five-year contract, which amounted to $130,000 in salary and another $370,000 in ancillary pay from outside the university. However, a key clause had Cooper being paid $250,000 for each of the first three years if he would be fired. It gave him the financial security he wanted. It also gave him the recruiting security he needed. The contract also would roll over one year if the Buckeyes finished in the top 10, beat Michigan or won nine games or more.

"It really wasn't the money for me. Hey, I got enough money to live on the rest of my life," he said. "I wasn't born on third base you know. I am comfortable with a good pair of jeans and cowboy boots, but you need a contract like this for your assistants and to recruit. Once they made it clear they wanted me, the decision was easy."

Still, after seven years, 84 games and now three contracts, he admitted that he still couldn't seem to figure the place out. "I came close, real close to leaving," he said. "But ol' Joe never offered the job. I really wanted to stay, and once Andy made me feel wanted, I was happy. Hey, I like it here. My wife likes it here. We didn't want to leave."

But if he was going to leave, he wanted to leave on his own terms. Cooper pondered aloud all the coaches that have walked in his shoes. Paul Brown. Fired. Woody Hayes.

Fired. Earle Bruce. Fired. Those coaches accounted for 314 of Ohio State's 667 victories in 105 years of football.

"Name one coach they haven't fired," Cooper challenged. "The thing that gets me about this place is that all the coaches I can name, all the athletic directors I know, have left here bitter. All of them. I don't want to leave here bitter. The first lesson you learn at Ohio State is that you aren't going to please everybody.

"One of the best things about this place is that it's 'Ohio State University.' But you know at the same time one of the worst things about it is that it's 'The Ohio State University.' It's almost like Ohio State never lost before. Everything has changed in college football, but the expectations. You can't win them all, especially with the (NCAA) scholarship limit dropping to 85. Look around the country. Look at USC, Oklahoma, Texas. They all had valleys."

It seemed the more Cooper talked, the more frustrated he became. He admitted it wasn't so much the pressures of winning and losing that got to him, but the expectations of the fans who lived in the past that made it difficult. His record, 54-26-2 in seven seasons, wasn't bad. But it wasn't Hayes-like either, and that's usually who any coach at Ohio State was compared to. It wasn't even Bruce-like. He would need to win 28 consecutive games to match his fired predecessor. If he had a fair chance to recruit good players, he believed, he would win at Ohio State. But, like Bruce before him, the rumors of his dismissal and the insecurity of the job itself made recruiting more difficult. Cooper would be the first to tell you that when he arrived in 1988 to take over for Bruce, the Buckeyes' cupboard was bare. It turned into the school's only losing season, a 4-6-1 team, since 1966.

"It was extremely tough because we weren't very good," Cooper said. "Earle was 6-4-1 the year before and the nucleus of that team had left. We were not very talented. The quarterback (Greg Frey) was inexperienced. We had no defense whatsoever. We couldn't stop anybody."

Cooper said he never blamed Bruce.

"Let me tell you — Earle Bruce was a great football coach," he said. "He got the most out of his talent, but he was put in a difficult situation because of the uncertainty surrounding recruiting."

It was, as Cooper found out soon, a catch-22 he would experience himself. He loathed the fact that the school's administration didn't lend their support at every turn. "They can stop the rumors by somebody saying, 'This guy is our football coach, and he's going to be here.'" Cooper said. "I haven't always had that."

Cooper said he expected the support, though, following his 10-1-1 team of 1993. The Buckeyes had lost to Michigan with a Rose Bowl berth on the line, but then turned around and beat Brigham Young 28-21 in the Holiday Bowl.

"We win 10 games in 1993, and I win a few coaching awards and that kind of stuff," he said. "I thought then that this ought to shut most people up, but I guess I was naive. Andy comes in and at his press conference (the day Geiger was hired) somebody asked him about (a contract for) John Cooper, and he made a point to say that nothing would be done until the season was over. It was almost like that 10-win season didn't count. The slate was clean. Then we just lost 13 out of our top-21 players, and nobody picked us in the top-five in the conference. We beat Michigan and finish second. Now that I look back, if we had not beaten Michigan, I wouldn't be here today."

Cooper sighed and gazed out his window at the rain, shaking his head and forcing a laugh.

"Tommy Prothro once told me, 'John, as you get older, the peaks don't get any higher, but the valleys get deeper,'" he said. "You know, it's true. We used to go out after all the games. Now, I go home, get a pizza, take a few Tylenols and go to bed. I am a loner on Saturday nights."

The coach stretched out on his couch and yawned. It was raining pretty good outside. Behind his desk was the framed game plan from that win over Michigan. A few drops of blood, now turned a rusty brown, were splattered on the page. His blood. "I smashed the blackboard at halftime with my fist," he said.

Just like Woody would have.

When he watched the tape of the ABC telecast of that Michigan game, Cooper couldn't figure out why Brent Musburger harped on Ohio State needing to win or Cooper would be fired. He figured it was the normal TV-induced drama. "The theme through the whole thing was that if we don't win that game, Cooper won't be here," he said. That's all Brent Musburger talked about.

"Then I found out later — he probably was right."

Nobody knew for sure if that's the way it would have been, except for Andy Geiger himself, and of course Archie Griffin — the athletic department's associate director who oversees football. The only man ever to win two Heisman Trophies and the player Hayes said was the greatest to ever play at OSU was essentially John Cooper's boss. He helped evaluate the coaching staff. That, too, mystified Cooper.

"I've told Archie this — I don't understand why the head football coach at Ohio State University doesn't report directly to the athletic director," Cooper said. "It doesn't make any sense."

Anyway, some still believe that Geiger was set to fire Cooper after that Penn State debacle if the Buckeyes lost one more game. But they beat Wisconsin, Indiana and Michigan for the first time under Cooper. Geiger won't say, but he admitted the loss to Penn State left him stunned and puzzled.

"It was possible," he said. "Nothing was a done deal at that point. We want to be powerful here. Football is very important to this university. But you have to be supportive of your coaching staff while they are your coaching staff. The thing that was impressive to me was the response to a disaster. They found their feet and their intensity after that, but I try to look at the whole package. I wasn't happy with the unevenness of their performance. Still, when you get humiliated on national TV the way we did at Penn State, I've seen teams throw in the towel. I think I saw then the potential of this (coaching) staff."

A theory has permeated Columbus for years that Cooper would have been fired twice already if not for the poor national publicity the university received when it fired Bruce. "I subscribe to it," Geiger said. "You can be rolling through coaches like the Grim Reaper, or you can try to build the program. Stability is important."

Geiger said he didn't mind Cooper talking to LSU's Joe Dean.

"John was frustrated," he said. "John wanted to put his toe in the water and see how it felt. Then I read where he said, 'I want to be at Ohio State.'"

Geiger, by all accounts a good man with a proven track record as an athletic administrator, was optimistic for Cooper's eighth season. "I have high hopes for it," he said. "This is a good football team. They have a good attitude. I like what I see."

———————————— ◆ ————————————

So did the coach.

"I feel better about this season than I ever have any other," Cooper said. "This team worked harder in the off-season than any I've had. Then again, I feel good every year."

Cooper was facing his 19th year as a head coach, his 33rd year in coaching overall, but none as tumultuous as the past seven. The critics can wear you down in Columbus. Cooper painfully discovered that fact as his hair grayed with each trying moment and with each lonely Saturday night. But he was determined not to be dismissed as other Ohio State coaches before him. His goal was to get the Buckeyes to the Rose Bowl again. Make a run at the national championship. Get the program back among the top 10 in the nation. And then retire on his own terms in a few years, living in Columbus as an admired and beloved former coach.

"I'll say one thing, and I may be boasting when I say this," Cooper said, "but I am a good football coach. My teams are always (fundamentally) sound. I don't cheat. They may fire me someday, but it won't be for cheating. There has never been a day since I've been here when I didn't think we would win. There has never been a day when I didn't think we would get the program back to where it should be.

"And this season, I think we can prove that to everybody."

A student manager knocked at the door, wanting to know which practice field Cooper wanted to use. It was three o'clock and the rain had finally let up, but the fields had to be soaked.

"Bring the cart around, and let's go check it out," the coach ordered. The manager nodded and closed the door.

Cooper sat up on the couch.

"If I didn't coach, I would have to get a real job, and I don't know what I would do," he said. "I guess I would kick back and hunt, fish and play golf, but there's only so much golf you can play. I am 58 years old now, and I feel like I am 38. I guess you could say it's a special time for me."

He slipped into his coaching shoes, straightened his crumpled hair, put on his glasses and headed down the steps.

Another season was near. And John Cooper was still a Buckeye.

2.

"You're only as good as your assistant coaches."

John Cooper always has believed strongly in that statement. Unlike others before him, namely Hayes and Bruce, he allowed his coaches to coach while he handled the peripheral duties of a head coach at a program like Ohio State: administrative decisions, speaking, discipline, dealing with the media, setting team rules and policies and coordinating the staff. Game plans and play-calling were left to Joe Hollis on offense and Bill Young on defense.

He often would say, "I let my coaches coach, and I handle all this other (fill in the blank)..."

Yet, it wasn't as if Cooper was uninvolved, either. When he watched film with his assistants, he possessed an uncanny talent for immediately spotting the opponent's defensive back who could be picked on, a defensive lineman who could be shoved around, or a linebacker who could be attacked because he played out of position. And naturally, when it came to crucial game-day decisions, such as fourth-and-inches when the game was on the line, Cooper made the final call.

Therefore, his most important job since Jan. 2, 1995 — when the team left Orlando, Florida following the Citrus Bowl loss to Alabama — until spring practice began, was to reassemble his coaching staff. Three coaches had left for other jobs, and he had fired another.

Cooper had lost tight ends coach Lee Owens, who was named head coach at Akron. He had lost receivers coach Mike Stock, whom the Kansas City Chiefs hired to coach special teams. He had lost Larry Coker, who had coached the Buckeyes' defensive backs but was scheduled to move to offense to coach quarterbacks. Coker then became Butch Davis' offensive coordinator at the University of Miami in mid-January. Coker's original move to offense was to replace quarterbacks coach Ron Hudson, whom Cooper had fired following the Citrus Bowl.

What Cooper came up with, a little by accident and a little by design, was his finest staff of his career.

It was a dream team of coaches, truly one of the best staffs in college football. A mix of experience, talent and knowledge. A perfect blend of feistiness and calm. And as a whole, it was a group of great communicators. Players heard their message and believed in it, which always hadn't been the case in recent years.

How did it all come about?

First of all, following the bowl game, Cooper agonized over the decision to fire Hudson, but realized it had to be done to improve the offense. Every quarterback Hudson had coached since 1988 had played brilliantly at times, average at times and awful at others. Cooper had discovered that Hudson wasn't exactly the best at relieving pressure from a 20-year-old who already had the weight of the world on his shoulders. There was enough pressure in being a quarterback at Ohio State without a coach telling him, "If you keep playing like this, you will get me fired!" Which is exactly what Hudson did through his headset to several quarterbacks during games.

"I almost went and told (Cooper) about it, but I just figured he knew," said Greg Frey, the quarterback from 1988-90.

"It was only the second time in my 19 years as a head coach that I had to let a coach go," Cooper said. "But it had to be done."

Once Coker decided to leave for the coordinator's position and more money at Miami, Cooper now had to go outside the staff to find a quarterbacks coach. It would be a crucial hire, given the importance of the position. "I was going to recommend this guy named Walt Harris when I walked into John's office one day, so I asked who he was thinking about as a quarterbacks coach," Geiger remembered. "He answered, 'Well, Andy, I really like this guy named Walt Harris.' I said, 'Whatever it takes, you got it,' and walked out."

Harris, the quarterbacks coach of the New York Jets for the past three years, had been dismissed along with the entire staff when team owner Leon Hess fired head coach Pete Carroll. Harris, once the head coach at Pacific, had to choose between another NFL offer and the Ohio State job. He moved to Columbus.

Cooper hired West Virginia offensive coordinator Mike Jacobs, a Cleveland native, to replace Owens when he was named head coach of Akron. Jacobs would coach the tackles and tight ends. It was a trade that upgraded the staff tremendously — Jacobs having 15 years experience as a coordinator while Owens had been only two years removed from high school coaching.

When Stock decided to leave, Cooper called Chuck Stobart, whom he had interviewed earlier for the quarterbacks job, to become receivers coach. Stobart, who had 13 years of experience as a head coach, had just been fired as head coach at Memphis, where he had put together three consecutive winning seasons. In coaching circles, it was well-known the firing was unjust. A new president had just wanted to clean house. Stobart, who grew up in Ohio and played at Ohio University, had also been the head coach at Toledo and Utah.

Cooper then hired Lovie Smith, for the secondary job which Coker originally vacated. Smith, who played for Cooper at Tulsa, had been coaching at Tennessee and was known as one of the nation's best recruiters.

When the transition was complete by the time spring practice started, he had replaced four departed coaches with four coaches totaling 88 years of college or NFL coaching experience. He would never say it publicly because he respected Stock and Coker, but Cooper probably had improved his staff at each of the four positions.

Such an all-star staff couldn't have been assembled at Ohio State since Woody Hayes' glory years — simply because of the school's archaic stance on salaries. Ohio

State had the second-largest stadium in the Big Ten and one of the nation's largest athletic budgets at about $31 million. The team played on national television more than not and in a bowl in 21 of the past 23 seasons. Still, staff salaries had lagged behind most conference teams.

"Just backward thinking," Cooper said. "There is no reason we shouldn't pay near the top of not only the Big Ten, but the nation's pay scale."

Previous athletic director Jim Jones was regarded as old-fashioned and hardly progressive enough to keep Ohio State competitive, but it wasn't entirely his fault. Hayes himself had turned down raises for years, settling for the $37,000 that he earned through his final year. Nowadays in college football, the lowest-paid assistant at a top program makes much more than that figure. Anyway, through Earle Bruce's nine-year tenure, his salary had been relatively low, too, since he made up the difference from television and radio shows. Naturally, his assistants' salaries lagged behind, too. It was just the way it was done.

It didn't mean everyone liked it, though. Cooper had lost 14 assistant coaches since he had arrived, something he was often criticized for by fans. "One reason — they all took good jobs that paid more money," Cooper said. "Why wouldn't they leave?" For example, until defensive coordinator Bill Young's salary was updated in recent seasons, he was making $63,000 — about $22,000 less than the defensive coordinator at Michigan. Geiger, a progressive-thinker who believed in taking a hands-on approach, changed it all, bringing salaries to the top of the Big Ten.

"You have to reflect the marketplace," Geiger said. "Thinking that coaches will want to coach at Ohio State because it is Ohio State, regardless of the money — that doesn't happen. John has lost some fine assistant coaches in the past, and we are doing something about it."

———————•◆◆◆•———————

Ohio State fans, no different than fans in other parts of the country, grew to disdain the conservative offensive approach that Hayes, and Bruce for the most part, had favored. For starters, the game had changed, and the pass-only-on-third-and-long approach didn't win many championships anymore. That was mainly true because, since NCAA scholarship cuts had evened the playing field, running games weren't as dominant as they had been in Hayes' heyday. And for whatever reason, the Buckeyes had not had a quarterback capable enough of enabling them to contend for a national championship since Art Schlichter's final season in 1981.

Until Bobby Hoying came along from tiny St. Henry, Ohio.

Hoying surely had all the ingredients to be among the best in the country: the needed size at 6-foot-4, 223 pounds, talent, good arm strength, and he was more than smart enough since he was an honor student. But offensive coordinator Joe Hollis and Cooper had decided long before the Citrus Bowl that they needed better performance from him, and the quarterbacks that would follow him, if they would ever get to Pasadena. He had completed 56 percent of his passes for 2,335 yards and 19 touchdowns in his junior season, but he still had thrown 14 interceptions — including three in the home loss to Illinois.

"I think Bobby needs to do the easy things better," Cooper had said. "He will make the great throw, then all of a sudden he has a back wide open, and he'll overthrow him. He needs to do the little things better, in my opinion."

Soft-spoken, articulate, and an excellent communicator, Harris was exactly what Hoying needed. He was exactly what Ohio State's offense needed, as far as coaching and recruiting. With him on the staff, luring a blue-chip quarterback to Columbus — which hadn't happened in some time — would be easier. And most ironically, he probably was exactly what Hollis needed, too. Hollis always had favored a balanced offense, but his expertise was the running game. A new perspective wouldn't hurt, especially if it meant better play from the quarterback, and he knew it.

Harris had learned a passing game similar to the so-called "West Coast Offense," which Bill Walsh had originally installed to turn the San Francisco 49ers into a dynasty. Essentially, it was a ball-control passing system that gave the quarterback plenty of options, usually receivers short, medium and deep. The system put plenty on the quarterback's ability to read defenses and find the open receiver, but with Hoying a fifth-year senior, Hollis, Harris and Cooper felt the timing was perfect to bring it to Ohio State.

"The feeling that I get from Joe is that they need the quarterback to play better," Harris said, "and that's where I come in."

Harris was such a high-profile addition that it was just a matter of time before the media would probe into any such power struggle among the offensive coaches. Would Hollis' role in decision-making be reduced?

When Tim May of the *Columbus Dispatch* brought up the subject three days into August camp, Hollis bristled. "Now, Tim, dammit, don't start a controversy," he said, rolling his eyes. "I am calling the plays, but we're all involved. It's just like last year. I will get on the headset and ask for ideas — 'Hey guys, what do you like here?'"

Hollis, who had coached under Cooper at Tulsa and was brought in from Georgia when Jim Colletto was named head coach of Purdue in 1991, was entering his fourth season as offensive coordinator. He realized the issue would be raised by someone, either fans or the media, but he sincerely believed there would be no problems.

"I am not the least bit insecure about it," he said. "Believe me when I say that, because even my brother asked me the same thing. I was in on the process of who we hired and I had input. If he helps us win, it benefits us all. We could have hired a high school coach, and I could have said, 'Alright, I am running the whole show.' But I did not want that. We wanted somebody to fit in with what we are doing."

Harris, too, didn't have time for any speculation over potential controversy. He was too busy teaching Hoying, the other quarterbacks and receivers the new system.

"My philosophy is to have a ball-control passing game, and I think I have come up with one without always needing a great quarterback," he said. "This system is the secret to the 49ers. It is a simple system really. Heck, they may have just 25 pass plays, but they do them all well. That's what we need to do. We will use more personnel, more formations, but the same plays."

Hollis, 47, like most assistant coaches, yearned to become a head coach. He had that title one year, in 1984 at Jacksonville State, before moving on to Georgia. The next time around, he figured, he would get a shot to coach a larger program. But timing is everything for coordinators when making the jump. The normal procedure in coaching circles was to parlay a great season into a head coaching job, and by December there were always jobs open in college football. Hollis felt he was ready, especially after learning how to deal with pressure from Cooper.

"This place is no different than anywhere else — there is always pressure to win," he said. "But you can't anticipate it before you get here. Coach Cooper tried to warn me and tell me what it was like. I got here four days after the Liberty Bowl (in 1990), and the media was saying some not-so-nice things about Coach Cooper."

Hollis once told a story of a loss during his first season in Columbus, a 10-7 heartbreaker to Illinois in which the offense stumbled, fumbled and bumbled through the entire game. "Now, my little boy, who was eight years old at the time, is watching the game on TV and starts crying. He asks mom if we were going to get fired," Hollis said. "Now, that's the kind of pressure I am talking about. I feel it every year."

Others would say that Hollis absorbed the pressure of coaching at Ohio State more than anyone else. It rarely bounced off, although he did an admirable job of hiding it until it grew late into the week when game day neared. He usually sat calmly in his office, chomping on a huge cigar, going over possible plays for that week's game.

As the man who called the plays, it was a natural that Hollis would be second-in-line when it came to being criticized. Cooper seemed to get a kick out of it all. He often played off Hollis' tightness, pulling his chain whenever he sensed it could be pulled. "I'll walk into Joe's office after my press conferences and say 'Well, I just guaranteed a win (to the media)', and Joe will say, 'No you didn't. No you didn't. Did you?'" the head coach said once. However, nobody liked to rib Hollis as much as linebackers coach Fred Pagac, who would tie a noose around his neck and walk into Hollis' office, as if the outlook was so dismal that there remained only one option. "I am always busting Joe because of all that 'pressure' shit," Pagac said. "There should be pressure to win. If you don't like it, get another job."

Still, the ten-member staff got along well for the most part. Cutting up and practical jokes were just a part of the routine.

Joking aside, the addition of three offensive coaches who already had impeccable careers, impressive resumes and reputations had to ease Hollis' burden. Especially since he hadn't had the utmost confidence in the offensive assistants who had departed. From the start of spring practice, he realized that wouldn't be a problem now.

Harris, 48, had coached at Tennessee, Illinois, Michigan State and California before becoming head coach at his alma mater, Pacific, in 1989. Following three seasons there, where his record improved each year, he believed the administration hadn't supported the program enough to guarantee its future. When the Jets called, he couldn't pass it up. Harris said the job became a three-year cram session of constantly discussing football and its strategies with the best minds in the game. And it allowed him three years to coach Boomer Esiason, whose signed picture hung on his office wall.

Thus, there was little doubt he was qualified to mold Hoying into one of the Big Ten's better quarterbacks. "He has a world of talent, it's just a matter of being consistent," Harris said. "He has a good, strong arm, and he is smart. I just want him to get rid of the ball quicker. I want him to make quick reads and get rid of it. It's a tough job being the quarterback here, but he doesn't have to carry this team on his shoulders. It's just great for me to be coaching a fifth-year senior.

"I told Bobby that after all he's been through, what was left to come would be easy. He had been through some rough times, and now I think only good times are ahead for him."

3.

Camp Cooper Begins

Nobody really knew exactly what to expect from the 1995 Buckeyes, not even Cooper. Fourteen starters and plenty of talent returned from a 9-4 team, but how can a team possibly be improved when six of its players were taken in the first three rounds of the NFL draft, including three in the first round?

Receivers Joey Galloway, the seventh selection of the entire draft, and Chris Sanders had accounted for 79 of the team's 181 receptions and 15 of its 19 receiving touchdowns. But they were seniors who left on schedule.

Korey Stringer, a bruising offensive tackle, Lorenzo Styles and Craig Powell, starting linebackers, on the other hand, left the program after their junior seasons — adding to Cooper's frustration with the NFL's rule to admit underclassmen. Defensive tackle Dan Wilkinson had departed following the 1993 season with two years of eligibility remaining. He would have been a senior now. Tailback Robert Smith, the fastest running back the Buckeyes have ever had, also left early two years earlier. "Nobody's been hit by as many juniors leaving as we have," Cooper said. "What we've got to do is get these guys to stay, but how do you compete with millions of dollars?"

Still, Cooper realized he had his most experienced players at the right positions since Hoying was a fifth-year senior and Eddie George, who rushed for 1,442 yards in the previous season but was hardly noticed nationally, was a senior. So was tight end Ricky Dudley, whose sculpted 6-foot-7 frame and excellent agility already had NFL scouts' attention even though he had played only one season of college football. Sophomore Nicky Sualua had already shown he could be an excellent blocking fullback, which is all Cooper had wanted from his fullback anyway. The entire offensive line returned, except for Stringer at right tackle.

When camp would begin, filling Stringer's position would become a priority. Sophomore Eric Gohlstin, who played only a handful of downs the previous season, and redshirt freshman Brooks Burris would begin battling for the job. "It's the only spot on the offensive line where we feel we don't have a proven Big Ten player," Joe Hollis said. "In fact, we feel we do at every other position on offense." Cooper expected a larger drop-off there than at any of the 22 positions in the lineup. "Players like Korey Stringer just don't come along very often," he said.

Defensively, every linemen — especially All-Big Ten ends Mike Vrabel and Matt Finkes and underrated Luke Fickell at nose guard — returned. So had cornerback Shawn Springs, who was as good as any defensive back in the league, even though he was just a sophomore. Greg Bellisari, a small but instinctive and tough linebacker, would be moved inside to replace Styles. Ryan Miller, who the coaches felt made as many big plays as Powell did the previous season, returned at weakside linebacker.

"This isn't the most talented team I've had," Cooper said. "The 1993 team probably had more talent, but there is no question they have worked as hard in the off-season as any I've ever been around."

Strength coach Dave Kennedy, who had arrived from Nebraska in 1989, had placed the Buckeyes on a tough voluntary summer program, but there was only so much coaches could do according to NCAA rules. Coaches can't force players to work out in the summer, but the players who did not stay did not earn many points with their position coaches, either. Usually each summer, a good percentage of the starters had remained anyway, but this summer had been especially satisfying for the coaches. Almost the entire team had put in extra time running and lifting weights since spring football ended. "Dave Kennedy has worked their butts off," Cooper said. "We had every player on scholarship working out this summer. That is what has me excited about this season. It's the attitude of these players. They want it. They want to be successful."

Kennedy had worked to take the school's strength program to where it should have been in the 1980s, and now others had noticed. In the spring, the University of Florida offered him a job for $67,000 — a $27,000 raise over what he had been making at Ohio State. "Andy called me up one day and said, 'Do you want to keep him?'" Cooper recalled. "I said, 'Yes. He does a great job.'" Kennedy's salary was bumped to $69,000, another example of Geiger's effort to bring the Buckeyes into the '90s.

———————◆·◆·◆———————

When the freshmen checked into their rooms at Morrill Tower on Aug. 2, every assistant coach was there to greet them while Cooper was spending the day in Chicago at the annual pre-season Big Ten meetings.

"We just want to make sure they don't get that faraway look in their eyes," defensive coordinator Bill Young said. "We encourage them to call home now and then."

Of the 17 freshmen, perhaps just a few had a chance to play immediately — punter Brent Bartholomew, maybe an offensive lineman and whatever defensive back showed he was ready. Bartholomew, by all accounts, had a major-college leg which was needed immediately since Scott Terna had graduated. "I think I can win the job," Bartholomew, recruited from Apopka, Fla., where he averaged 46 yards per punt as a senior, said while checking his bags with a team manager. "I don't have any doubts about my ability to punt with anyone."

Two days later, the first practice of the season began. The sun had been up an hour, but not long enough to burn off the dew of the grass at the Woody Hayes Athletic Center. Freshmen ran around in their new gray shorts and scarlet jerseys. Upperclassmen weren't scheduled to arrive for two more days.

Cooper watched, twirled his whistle as he always did, and visited with a few friends on the sideline. "I don't want to prejudge any of them," he said of his first-year Buckeyes.

"If that was the case, I wouldn't have ever played. We had five teams in college, and I was the fifth-team running back when I started. Archie Griffin, too. When he came here, he was the sixth-team running back. We don't even have six running backs. It's a numbers game now."

In essence, so was an important meeting between the morning and afternoon practices. He had been summoned to his lawyer's office, since he still hadn't signed his new five-year contract, which had been agreed to by both parties more than eight months earlier. The meeting was just to ensure the university had come through with what had been promised back in December.

The next day, as Cooper watched Lovie Smith work with the freshmen defensive backs, he laughed and thought back to his days in the same position. "Hey, feel this," he said, grabbing a reporter's hand and placing it on his right shoulder. "See, Lovie does it right. He has a G.A. (graduate assistant) throw to the defensive backs. All those years I threw to them when I coached the secondary and now my shoulder clicks. Hear it?"

There was no reason for the coach not to be in a good mood. He was about to welcome a team that had worked harder in the off-season than any he had ever coached. He was about to sign a deal that rewarded him with financial security for life, what would most likely be the final contract of his career. And he had a coaching staff not only made up of good coaches, but happy people.

"Who knows? We haven't played a game yet, but what I already like about these guys is they are great people," he said. "Life's too short for me to go home miserable every night after hearing people bitch about something. I want a happy group. I am getting too old for all those headaches."

Sunday, Aug. 6, brought nothing but smiling faces to the Woody Hayes Center. It was media/fan/picture day — a day before all the hard work would begin for real. As fans gathered on the artificial turf, Shawn Springs walked out of the locker room, lifted up his scarlet jersey and shouted, "The saga begins!"

For the next two hours, players and coaches posed, signed and smiled for fans while answering questions from the media. The crowds around such prominent players as Hoying, Vrabel and George swelled like high tide. At one point, following hundreds of autographs, Hoying, coming off a finger injury from the spring game, said, "My finger is fine, but I am getting a sore wrist."

The favorite topics for the day? Playing Notre Dame for the first time in 60 seasons, the possibility of not only earning a Rose Bowl trip but winning a national championship, and the team's brutal schedule.

"If we stay healthy," receiver Terry Glenn said, "we can go all the way. We can win it all, especially if we go 13-0 with our schedule."

There was little doubt that the schedule would be their main obstacle. Of their 12 opponents, which included an extra game with the Kickoff Classic just three weeks away, eight had winning records in 1994. The 12 had a combined record of 75-57-6 the season before. Before the Big Ten schedule would begin — which meant games at Penn State, at Wisconsin and at Michigan — they had to face Boston College, which whipped Notre Dame 31-11; Washington, which beat them 25-16 the year before in Seattle; Pitt and the Fighting Irish.

One three-week stretch from Sept. 30 through Oct. 14 translated into Notre Dame, at Penn State, at Wisconsin. It was a frightening trifecta, one that had coaches concerned that their hopes for a Big Ten championship would be wiped away by Halloween if they didn't get off to a good start.

"There's nothing we can do about it, but play them all," Cooper said. "So there's no sense complaining about it."

That was Cooper's public response to the schedule. Privately, he wondered why in the world a knucklehead athletic director would put together such a killer schedule. Geiger wasn't to blame, since football schedules usually are comprised at least five years in advance. "If I had my way," Cooper said, "we would never play a road non-conference game. Why should we? This will be the third time we have been to Pittsburgh since I've been the coach. That's ridiculous. They won't even fill the place, unless our fans do it for them."

Cooper did, however, want and need the Kickoff Classic as a late addition to the schedule. The team originally wasn't supposed to open the season until Sept. 16 against Washington, which opened Sept. 2 against Arizona State. That would have given the Huskies a two-week advantage in the number of practices allowed by the NCAA. And Washington would have had played a game already, so Ohio State had to accept the Kickoff Classic invitation in order to prepare for September.

The players themselves didn't mind the severity of the schedule. In fact, they didn't care if they had the Bears, Steelers or Packers in front them. The tougher the games appeared to be, at least on paper, the better. Washington? Revenge from last year. Notre Dame? Bring 'em on. Penn State? That 63-14 humiliation was on their minds.

"All anybody wants to talk about around here is Notre Dame," Hoying said. "They don't realize we have to play three games before we can get to Notre Dame."

Sept. 30 had been anticipated for some time in Ohio, mainly because the two powerhouse programs with all their tradition hadn't met since 1936. Campus bookstores' hottest-selling item was anything to do with the Notre Dame game at Ohio Stadium. It had become more than a game. It was now an event. And even with the event more than seven weeks away, tickets were selling for $300 for end-zone seats and $600 for seats between the 40-yard lines.

"I have a stack of requests for tickets for that game this high," Cooper said, holding his hand to his chin. "All people I supposedly owe favors to."

When a reporter asked Springs about Notre Dame, he just shook his head.

"We have to be up for every game this year," Springs said. "Not up and down, up and down like we have been in the past. Anyway, don't we play Boston College first?"

Only one destiny, however, would satisfy all their goals. They had been to Anaheim, California. They had been to San Diego. Orlando twice. They had never been to Pasadena.

"You wonder what it's like," George said. "I want to know what it's like to play in the Rose Bowl. You hear about it so much, I want to see it for myself."

"I don't want to look back on my career someday," Hoying said, "and not have the Rose Bowl be part of it. I don't know if I could accept that. That's why we have to work as hard as we can every day to get there."

The next morning, Aug. 7 at 8 in the morning, the entire team began its quest for that lone goal, practicing together for the first time. There were no photographers, no autograph seekers and no babies to kiss. Just 11 coaches hollering, encouraging and chastising and more than 90 players sweating in the early morning humidity.

During one agility drill for the guards and centers, Joe Hollis screamed: "Man, you're so stiff — your mother must have been a statue. Hey, anybody having any fun yet? Let's have some fun out here."

With that, the 1995 season had begun.

4.

A Hot Time In Columbus

Through July, it had been the hottest summer in Ohio in years and Mother Nature wasn't about to let up just because the Buckeyes had started camp. The temperature climbed well into the 90s, as players moaned and groaned through three practices each day. During breaks, they resembled cows to a trough, circling the water jugs until summoned back to the field.

Mentally and physically, they grew weary in just a couple of days, as the coaches had come to expect over the years. "They are making a lot of mental mistakes right now because they are tired," Cooper said. "The backs are blocking the wrong guy. The quarterback makes a wrong read. Defensive backs are in the wrong coverage. It's just a lack of concentration." Cooper had a special reward for those mistakes — 10 push-ups.

As coaches prepared for the first scrimmage at the end of the week, Cooper placed the sloppiness in perspective. It was normal. "This time of year, you can't get too high on them, and you can't get too down on them," he said. "They're plugging away, and that's all I ask."

The team would scrimmage at Ohio Stadium for several reasons, one of which was to give the coaches a chance to operate with headsets for the first time since there were four new assistants. "We need to work on game tempo," Cooper said. "Like using the 25-second clock and having Big Ten officials. Getting the players in and out of the huddle, on and off the field. I'll tell you right now — it will be ragged."

And hot. The temperature had climbed to 95 degrees at the stadium, Saturday, Aug. 12. The giant horseshoe sat empty, except for a few of the players' family members who had straggled through an open gate. As the team dressed in the locker room, Hollis, Harris and Mike Jacobs sat on a bench on the visitor's side of the stadium and gazed at the perfectly manicured field as Cooper was being interviewed by a television reporter.

"I remember being right here in 1980 when I coached at Illinois when Ohio State had Schlichter and that bunch," Harris said. "Our coach, Mike White, was real conservative then. I kept saying, 'Let's put it up a little' but he wanted to run the ball. Finally, we are down about 28-0 and he said 'What the heck, let's throw it.' It became a real track meet. Man, that was some game." Ohio State won 49-42. "Yep, there'll be some football played on this grass this season," Harris said, walking across the field to head to the press box, where he and Jacobs would watch the season unfold.

Hollis walked across the field to put on his headset. "What do I want to accomplish today?" Hollis said. "I don't want to get anyone hurt — that's what I want to accomplish."

From the beginning, Cooper was right — the play was ragged. But several things were evident: Tight end Ricky Dudley was improving quickly and the new offense would utilize short passes to the running backs as well as Terry Glenn's excellent speed. After one completion, in which Dudley broke two tackles, Hoying came to the sideline smiling. "Ricky's going to be a rich man a year from now," he said.

Dudley had arrived on a basketball scholarship, but it wasn't as if he didn't know football. He was named Texas' Class 4A Player of the Year, and after three years of basketball with the Buckeyes, he realized his professional future would involve wearing shoulder pads and a helmet. He impressed Jacobs from the day the coach arrived from West Virginia. "He can make some money in football and he knows it," he said. "He's doing the right thing. I mean, just look at his body." With D.J. Jones, 1994's starter who was an excellent blocker but an average receiver, sidelined for the season after undergoing open-heart surgery, Dudley had the starting job all to himself.

"I really wanted to compete with D.J.," Dudley had said before the scrimmage. "But whether he was here or not, I knew I was going to play a lot. I worked hard in the off-season. I used to go out and be shooting the basketball all day. Now I go out and catch 75 balls a day." Still, Dudley was raw, needing to improve his recognition of coverages and his blocking technique. Harris and Jacobs already had told him he would be featured in the offense. "It's scary," Dudley said, "and it's exciting."

Hollis got his wish. Nobody was injured during the scrimmage. "That's the best thing about it," Cooper said, looking into a television camera afterward. "Thank goodness we have two more weeks to prepare. We couldn't beat anybody today." Cooper loved the new offense, though. "We are hitting the backs more as opposed to taking a sack," he said.

What was the big deal? For starters, an Ohio State running back had caught one touchdown pass since 1991. There were worse things to do with the football than swinging a pass to Eddie George when other receivers downfield were covered. George's desire to have a special senior season had been obvious to the coaches since winter conditioning began. His 6-foot-3, 230-pound body was more sculpted than it had been in the past. His leg muscles were rippled like a bodybuilder, having run twice a day during the off-season instead of once as his teammates had. "I can't think of a player I've ever coached who has worked harder than Eddie George," Cooper said. He was faster, too. If there had been one knock on George, it was his elusiveness and speed in the open field. "You can tell he's worked on it," Cooper said. "He looks faster to me."

The next day, on Sunday, the team practiced only twice.

"The new coaches told me we work harder than any place they have been," Cooper said proudly. "They said they have never practiced on Sundays before. I'll practice any time I can, any time I am allowed."

On the Monday following the scrimmage, Cooper had an appointment with a reporter from the *Boston Globe*, which planned a feature story on him leading up to the Kickoff Classic. When the reporter walked into his office, Cooper was watching the O.J. Simpson trial on television, as he usually did while eating lunch during camp. The reporter asked Cooper if he could name the Big Ten's coaches during his first season at Ohio State. Cooper, who usually contends he can't remember last week let alone years gone by, took a few minutes but named them all correctly. Only two — Indiana's Bill

Mallory and Iowa's Hayden Fry — were still coaching in the conference (not counting Penn State's Joe Paterno). "That counts for something, doesn't it?" he said. "Hey, coaching's been very good to me. I've been in every state and I bet I have taken teams to 80 of the stadiums in the country. It's a great profession. You get to be around kids every day and watch them mature."

Asked about pressure to win at Ohio State, Cooper turned and pointed out his window. The temperature was in the 90s on the other side. "Now why worry about what you can't control?" he asked. "I know it's hot out there right now, but I don't want to talk about how hot it is. You can't control it. I told the kids that I could call (Boston College Coach) Dan Henning and say, 'Dan, it's hot. You give your team off today and I'll give mine off.' But it doesn't work that way.

"Sure, you have to win. You have to win every place. But look at the coaches who are out of it. They want back in. I get a call from (former Texas and Purdue Coach) Freddy Akers about three times each season, looking for a job. In my first coaching job, I made seven thousand dollars a year, got three hots and a cot. Our assistant coaches now make good money and get country club memberships. The game has changed, huh?"

So had Bobby Hoying's outlook. He arrived on campus four years earlier as an all-state football and basketball player from St. Henry, Ohio. He had played in the state's smallest division and some wondered if he was good enough to play quarterback at Ohio State. In just his sophomore season, he proved he could. As the Buckeyes finished 10-1-1, he started all 12 games and completed 54 percent of his passes for 1,570 yards. The numbers were even better during his junior year, but coaches believed Hoying had to be more consistent.

Now with Harris coaching him, he felt like a new man. None of Ohio State's quarterbacks were especially fond of Ron Hudson, and now that he was gone, Hoying was about to experience a new, positive approach. Twelve days before his final collegiate season would begin, he finished his dinner at Morrill Tower, where all players lived during camp, and headed for a lounge chair in the lobby. He slipped a pinch of snuff under his lip.

"I don't want to say anything bad about Coach Hudson," he said. "I am sure he had his reasons for doing things. Let's just say that I have learned a lot more about the game already. There was so much I needed to learn, like blitzing situations. Last year, if they blitzed, we would throw a 10-yard out and that was it."

Hoying, his blond hair cropped short, rubbed his right elbow. "My arm is a little sore right here," he said. "I've thrown a lot of balls during three-a-days, but hey, I am a fifth-year senior — I am not going to go complain about it."

The team had a 19-5-1 record and had won a Big Ten co-championship with Hoying as a starter and yet, it felt like something was missing for him. What was lacking from his career was obvious. "I guess it's not good enough yet because we haven't gone to the Rose Bowl," he said. "Isn't that how quarterbacks around here are measured? We've won a lot of games the last two years, but not enough. It seems if you finish in second place at Ohio State, it's not good enough. Let's just hope we don't feel that way at the end of the season. But I have no regrets coming here. It was here or Illinois, and I am real happy with my choice."

Hoying had experienced the tough times. In fact, he was booed during the 24-10 home loss to Illinois, ironically, the previous season — a game in which he threw three interceptions and the offense went scoreless in the second half. "I probably would have booed me too," he said. "But when I remember going to games here as a kid, I don't ever remember them booing anybody. It's a weird experience. I guess not everybody is as nice as you would like them to be. It really, really humbles you. I don't know of any other position that you get booed."

The fans' treatment of Hoying angered the coaches and his teammates, who knew that if they spent one hour around Bobby Hoying, they would never boo him. He was a three-year starting quarterback at Ohio State. He had been picked on several preseason All-Big Ten teams. He had every right to be cocky and arrogant. Yet, he was probably the most polite, well-mannered player on the team. He was a genuine team player, and he didn't care who received the credit for winning.

"He's just a good kid," Harris had said earlier. "He's been through so much here already. How can you not like Bobby?"

Hoying knew this was his last chance at Ohio State. His last chance to go to the Rose Bowl. His last chance to win a national championship. As he sat there, 12 days before it all began, he admitted he felt something special about this team. It had been 27 years since the school had won a national championship and 11 since it had played in the Rose Bowl and yet, Hoying knew all those goals were more than possible. Deep down, he expected them to come true.

"I have to admit I am really pumped for this season," he said. "I just hope we get off to a good start. We can't be turning the ball over and making mistakes in the first game." He stood up, yawned and headed for the elevator. "Time for my nap."

The next day, Hoying, George and defensive tackle Matt Bonhaus were voted team captains by their teammates. "It's awesome," Hoying said. "It means everything to me. You look back at the names of the captains, and you just hope that someday you can be in position to be a captain."

One week before the Kickoff Classic, defensive coordinator Bill Young leaned back in his office chair and glanced up his depth chart. He had six starters coming back from a defense that surrendered 318 yards and 16.2 points per game. Take away the 63 that Penn State scored and the defense's scoring average would have been 12 points per game. The defense gave up 400 yards or more only twice — to Penn State and Alabama.

"We have an outstanding first unit," he said, "but if we lose one or two guys...."

Young and linebackers coach Fred Pagac had moved outside linebacker Greg Bellisari inside. He felt good about weakside linebacker Ryan Miller, who played often the previous season. The other linebacker, however, was redshirt freshman Jerry

Rudzinski. He needed only experience. The secondary could be a problem, since it had three new starters — cornerback Ty Howard and safeties Anthony Gwinn and Rob Kelly.

"We need the defensive line to dominate until these young guys rise to another level," Young said. "The thing we are trying to do this year is create turnovers. We had 27 last year, and we need to do better than that. I want them swarming to the football. We've never been a big blitzing team here, but I hate to use the term 'bend but don't break.' We want to play field position football and not get beat deep."

Wherever Cooper had gone since becoming a head coach, he made sure he took Bill Young with him. The two were that close. He had been on Cooper's staffs since 1981 at Tulsa. A native of Texas who grew up in Oklahoma and played at Oklahoma State, Young would just as soon wear a flannel shirt, drink a beer and put his feet up on the desk. He was unpretentious, modest and yet he always had a bubbling personality. "If you know Bill Young," one assistant said, "you like Bill Young. Right away."

"Bill Young is as hard-working and unassuming as any coach you will ever meet," Cooper said. "He puts in more hours here than anybody on this staff. As the old saying goes, he's just an 'old ball coach.'"

Young qualified as a workaholic. He often watched film of NFL defenses to pick up fresh ideas, but usually, he knew exactly what he wanted to do on game days by the time he was finished viewing film on the previous Monday. He was that good at finding an offense's tendencies and weak spots. Naturally, Ohio State usually stayed near the top of the Big Ten's defensive statistics.

Young figured to be the next assistant coach to move on. In fact, Cooper came close to losing him in the off-season. He had been a finalist for the Oklahoma State job, which ultimately went to Colorado assistant Bob Simmons. "I thought I had a chance, but ultimately, I guess I didn't," he said. Ohio State's defensive players would have been crushed if he had left. Young, the only coach on the staff without children, regarded his players as his family. He always took a personal approach with them, even bringing in small cakes for their birthdays.

"Not only is he a great guy, but he always has a great game plan," nose guard Luke Fickell said. "He puts us in position to make the plays. I love him for it."

───── ◆ ─────

Aug. 22, five days before the game against Boston College, Hollis and the offensive staff met at 6:50 a.m.

By that afternoon, as they would on every Tuesday throughout the season, they had finalized a game plan. Also, as they planned for each game, they had scripted the first 15 plays in advance — that is, until third down anyway, when distance dictated the call. The advantage was simple — coaches in the press box could get an early indication of how defenses would react to certain formations. That would make calling plays easier as the game progressed.

In the first game, they expected Boston College to blitz often and from all angles. "We want to throw it downfield," Hollis said. "That is, if we can protect Bobby. They are going to blitz us a lot. We'll pick our spots with the run, but I think we can run the football on anybody."

Harris and Jacobs would be upstairs on headsets, with receivers coach Chuck Stobart, running backs coach Tim Spencer and Hollis, of course, on the sideline during the season. Harris' job, other than dealing with Hoying on the phones when the quarterback came off the field, would be to recognize the secondary's coverages while Jacobs recognized defensive fronts.

"I know it will be a real comfort for me," Hollis said. "We need to get everybody's input, and these guys know what they are doing."

The confidence in his new colleagues eased Hollis' mind, since he hadn't always had it with other assistants in recent seasons.

Throwing it downfield, as Hollis and Harris wanted, was one thing. Completing it downfield, now that receivers Joey Galloway and Chris Sanders were in the NFL, was a question yet answered. Their replacements, juniors Buster Tillman and Terry Glenn, had potential but were generally unproven even though Tillman caught 33 passes as a sophomore. Glenn had caught only seven in relief of Galloway, but had been impressive in camp. He had repeatedly blown by Ohio State's defensive backs, even Shawn Springs, and hadn't dropped a pass yet.

"Terry has had an outstanding camp," Cooper said. "If he plays like he has in practice, he will make people forget Joey Galloway. He's just as fast."

Reporters who covered the team rolled their eyes when Cooper continued to praise Glenn. They had heard it all before, yet Glenn had 15 career receptions and no touchdowns. How could he be mentioned in the same breath as Galloway, who left with 108 career receptions, 1,894 yards and 19 touchdowns?

"I think Terry offers the same things Joey did," Tillman said. "He has tremendous speed. He can jump, and he's a natural athlete. I think he'll surprise a lot of people, but he's not going to surprise me."

Or Stobart, either, for that matter. The first-year receivers coach realized he had a real talent on his hands "from the first day I saw him. He's right there with the best I have seen."

This week, however, Glenn wasn't at his best, "He's got a cold, a migraine and everything else," Stobart told the other coaches. "We're just lucky to have him out there (during practice)."

What worried the coaches even more was fullback Nicky Sualua, who was obviously overweight and out of shape after spending many practices in summer school to remain eligible. Sualua, who stood 5-foot-10, was listed at 245 pounds. He weighed closer to 265. As Cooper always joked, Sualua didn't like school and didn't like football. Other than that, he liked anything to eat. "He's like me," Cooper joked. "There isn't a meal he doesn't like."

It wasn't as funny to Hollis and Spencer. There was a huge drop-off in talent to backup fullback Matt Calhoun. Hollis rarely called Sualua's number — he carried the ball only 25 times the previous season but he had become a punishing blocker, and his position was a crucial part of the offense. After all, it was similar to having another guard in front of Eddie George.

"Tim, what are we going to do about Nicky?" Hollis asked.

"He'll be good for 20 to 30 plays," Spencer replied.

"Yeah," Hollis said, "but what we going to do about the other 50?"

The day before the team, ranked No. 12 in the Associated Press preseason poll, departed for Newark, New Jersey, Cooper was feeling good about the opener for his latest edition of Buckeyes. Very good, for that matter. Perhaps more so than for any season-opener since he had arrived, and that's saying something. He hadn't lost one yet, winning all seven as Buckeyes coach. "You always have questions," he said. "This time last year, we were wondering who was going to play left tackle and how Eddie would do at tailback." Of course, those questions were answered by Orlando Pace, the Big Ten's Freshman of the Year, and George's 1,442 rushing yards.

For starters, he didn't think Boston College matched up even though the Eagles returned 13 starters from a 7-4-1 team, which had beaten Notre Dame 30-11. For another, he believed his players were in the best shape possible because they had practiced in intense heat.

Players, too, thought they were ready to play a game. As always, they grew to dread practicing in August and looking across the line of scrimmage at the same faces. This camp had been perfect in one respect — there had been no disciplinary problems. Nobody had entered into any trouble. There wasn't even a curfew violation, or at least none that was discovered.

"Yeah, it usually seems that something happens in fall camp," Hoying said. "We've all behaved well. We've all made bed check, and we've all concentrated on nothing but football. I guess that's the way it should be."

"I just want to play a game," Bonhaus said. "We had winter conditioning, then spring football, then summer conditioning. I am tired of seeing the same faces. I am ready to hit somebody else."

In less than four days, he would get the chance.

5.

A Classic Start

Archie Griffin paced the lobby of the Meadowlands Hilton waiting for the team to arrive from the airport. It was 9:45 p.m., Aug. 24, three days before the Kickoff Classic. The room keys for players and coaches were neatly arranged on a table by the lobby's door. A cameraman from a local television station waited nearby, not realizing who the anxious guy in the suit and tie could be.

He was just the man Woody Hayes called the greatest football player he had ever seen, and he still looked as if he could pick up the first down on third-and-six. And Lord knows, in the days when a running play was called on that down-and-distance, he usually made Wayne Woodrow Hayes happy. But this was Archie Griffin the athletic administrator who handled the advance planning on all road trips. The season would mark the 20th anniversary since Griffin's senior season, in which he won a still unprecedented second Heisman Trophy. His hair had receded with the years, unlike his loyalty to Ohio State.

"From the very start — I mean I was born at University Hospital, and played ball here in Columbus before Ohio State — this place has meant a great deal to me," he said. "My life is built around this university."

If anything has changed from the day in which he wore number 45, it is that Griffin has had to adapt his standards to those of college football today. He played on teams with a combined record of 40-5-1. He had played in four Rose Bowls. The Buckeyes haven't been to one since Jan. 1, 1985. It was no secret that Griffin evaluated the head football coach now, and that he also represented the past. Those factors naturally could cause friction between his office and the coaching staff.

"There is a standard to live up to here," he said. "We want a coaching staff that looks after the kids, that teaches them to be productive citizens, and at the same time produces winning football seasons."

The 11-year absence of visiting the Rose Bowl naturally agitated Griffin, as it did fans and coaches. Amazingly, as a player, he didn't know what it was like to spend New Year's Day anywhere but Pasadena, California. "It's been too long," he admitted. "I guess I was a little spoiled as a player, but it's still been too long."

Griffin sensed something special about the school's latest team, however.

"This team doesn't have any real superstars," he said, shuffling his feet, "but you know, I really like their chemistry. And they have worked pretty hard this fall."

Shortly after 10 o'clock, more than 90 players and coaches burst through the lobby doors. Cooper was smiling. He had reason to be — his contract would be signed before the team flew home. School president, E. Gordon Gee, who had been on a belated honeymoon, was flying in for the game and the deal would be sealed.

Security.

"When do you ever have it, really?" Cooper asked. "They can still fire me at any time. All I got now is a guarantee. If they fire me now, they have to pay my ass."

Helen Cooper, the coach's wife of 38 years, watched her husband chat away with friends and reporters and finally grew impatient. "John Cooper!" she said. "Let's go. Will you get over here?" The coach may have signed a new contract, but he still realized who was boss. The two, with daughter Cindy and son John Jr. in tow, headed to their rooms.

The next morning Cindy, John Jr. and John Sr. climbed out of a courtesy car and headed into the press conference at Giants Stadium. Cooper avoided an awkward moment when he was introduced as the coach of Ohio State's 1986 team, which lost 16-10 to Alabama in the Buckeyes' only other Kickoff Classic appearance. Earle Bruce, present as a radio analyst for a Columbus station, shuffled in his seat in the audience.

"Just wanted to correct you — it wasn't me in '86," he said, pointing into the crowd. "Coach Earle Bruce over there was here then." Bruce smiled, as Cooper began describing what he liked about his team.

For Bruce, it was another moment he had to endure if he wanted to live in Columbus as he chose. Especially if he worked as an analyst and attended every Buckeyes game, home and away. He truly loved Ohio State and felt bitterness over his firing toward only one man, former school president Ed Jennings. He will never understand having been fired with an 82-26-2 record. His teams had won five-of-nine games against Michigan and five-of-eight bowl games and had been to the Rose Bowl twice.

"John's been able to do something no other coach has done — lose to Michigan more than anybody else and still keep his job," Bruce told reporters as Cooper gave television interviews. "It used to be, if you lost to Michigan three times in a row, you lost your job. Hell, I think Coach Hayes would still be there if he had beat Michigan those final three times. I give credit where credit is due — John is a hell of a negotiator."

Whether it was a backward compliment or a shot at his successor or perhaps the university, only Bruce knew. But he had been fully supportive of Cooper on the air. Indirectly, Bruce admitted he thought he himself was one reason Cooper was still in Columbus. "People have told me that my situation changed the way people think about firing people," he said. "Maybe that has helped him. At least that's what my friends tell me anyway."

A few feet from Bruce sat Eddie George, flanked by a few reporters. George expected 35 friends and relatives coming to the game since he grew up in nearby Philadelphia, where his mother sent him to Fork Union Military Academy. "Basically, she did it to straighten me out and give me some discipline," he said. "I wasn't a bad kid, but I got into things like all kids do. Maybe I was running with the wrong crowd." His mother, Donna, who worked as a flight attendant and a part-time model, flew everywhere to watch her son play. "I sent him to Fork Union not as punishment, but as something I knew he needed," she said. "I call it tough love. He needed discipline. And look, I think he turned out just fine."

He had. For a guy who wasn't a so-called blue-chipper, Eddie George had become a model citizen, the hardest-working player on the team and a 1,000-yard rusher. He was as respected by his teammates as any player or coach at Ohio State. "Hey, when Eddie talks," guard Jamie Sumner said, "you listen." George had his sights set on even more.

After the reporters had moved on, he picked up a magazine that listed a preseason All-Big Ten team. He wasn't on it. "It's just someone else's perspective," he said. "I know my ability. But yes, it does motivate me."

The day before the game, the coaches watched Michigan rally to beat Virginia 17-16 in the Pigskin Classic in Ann Arbor. The Wolverines won on the final play, and as the coaches walked out on the artificial turf at Giants Stadium for the final practice, it was all they were talking about. "Can you believe Michigan?" Cooper asked. "They got lucky, didn't they?"

Walt Harris looked around as if he was seeing an old friend for the first time in a long time, which he was, since he had spent the past three years coaching at Giants Stadium.

"This is the worst stadium in the NFL for a quarterback," he said. "The wind is treacherous. You get all kinds of wind, but that is not until about November."

On this day, it was 90 degrees and sunny, as it would be on game day, too.

As Cooper watched his team warm up, he shook his head when fullback Nicky Sualua trotted by. Or waddled by, to be precise. "Nicky's not close to being in shape," Cooper said. "He thinks he is, but he isn't." The coach looked up at one of freshman Brent Bartholomew's skyrockets for a punt. "The kid's got a big-time leg," he said. "Now let's see if he pees down his leg during the game."

Bartholomew walked to the sideline, plunked himself down on the bench and gazed up at the 78,000 empty seats. "Man, I've never seen a stadium like this," he said. "It's a long way from Apopka. If I just catch the ball, everything will fall into place. Coach Cooper told me he just wants hang time, but I want to see the return man turning around and chasing the ball."

It had been one month since Bartholomew, like all the freshmen, had left home, and he was experiencing the typical freshman blues. "He's going through a lot of stuff right now," kicker Josh Jackson said. "He's homesick. We all went through it. I hated this place my first year. I wanted to go home, too, but you get over it."

As the team practiced, Cindy and John Cooper Jr. watched intently from seats in the end zone. The coach's daughter and son never missed a game, home or away. "We are a very close family," said John Jr. "The biggest thrill I get is standing behind Pop during games, holding his headset cords." The Cooper children had seen first-hand how some fans' verbal abuse had hurt their father over the years. Yet, it had hurt them much worse than it did John Cooper. Following a home loss to Illinois once, John Jr. went after an abusive fan. "Man, it just kills me when I hear some things that some fans say to him," he said. "If they saw him like we saw him, they couldn't help but love the guy."

Like the days when Cooper coached at Tulsa and John Jr. worked construction during the summers. "He would wake up and make me a fried egg and bacon sandwich," John Jr. said. "While I was eating it, he would be packing my lunch. Or like this past summer when I come home to my house and he is bent over, sweating up a storm, cleaning out the window well."

Cindy wrapped her arm around her brother. "He probably wouldn't want you telling all these stories, John," she said.

Her brother smiled and continued, "I want Pop to be the first coach to win the Rose Bowl from both leagues. We like Columbus, and we want to stay there. Heck, Pop wants to be liked. He's aged a lot since we got to Ohio State. He takes the losses much harder now than he used to."

———————————————————

Aug. 27, 1:50 p.m., 15 minutes before the opening kickoff, Cooper gathered his players in the locker room.

"In 33 years of coaching, I've never been more proud of a football team than I am of this one today," he said. "You're a better football team than Boston College. Now you just have to go out and prove it. I know every player on this team is going to lay it all on the line today. I know it. I hope it's hotter than hell today, I really do. We will wear this team down. Are we going to play a perfect football game? No. We won't play a perfect game all season, but let's try. No penalties. No stupid mistakes. Wouldn't it be great to score on defense today? Let's return a punt for a touchdown. Or a kickoff. Let's carry the fight to B.C. all afternoon, get them down, and finish their ass off. Put them away. I am proud of you, now let's go win!"

Upstairs in the ABC booth, Keith Jackson was telling the nation, "We've had one-sided affairs the last two years here, but today, we think we've got an evenly-matched game."

And with Mike Malfatt's short kickoff, the 1995 season began.

Boston College, ranked 22nd, began doing what it did best — taking a physical, smashmouth approach to the running game. Running back Justice Smith carried six consecutive times to begin the game, until an offensive lineman jumped on fourth-and-one, forcing the Eagles to punt.

On the Buckeyes' first offensive play of the season, they were penalized 10 yards for holding. It didn't matter. After George gained three on his first carry, the offense got into gear. Hoying completed his first three attempts for 30 yards and Matt Calhoun, starting in place of the overweight Sualua, rambled 27 yards to set up George's first touchdown of the season — a 12-yard run around right end in which he broke two tackles and dived into the end zone.

Eight plays, 80 yards and it took just 3:47. It was the beginning of a long day for Boston College, although the Eagles responded with two drives that resulted in only a field goal.

With the score 7-3, Shawn Springs took the ensuing kickoff, ran toward the right sideline and followed two crushing blocks — one by backup defensive end Jeff Wilson and the other by Terry Glenn — 97 yards to the end zone.

"I was just trying not to run out of gas," said Springs, whose father Ron was a running back at Ohio State in the 1970s. "I could hear my dad watching TV back in Dallas laughing at me huffing and puffing all the way down the sideline. I thought I was going to run out of gas."

Springs' return made Cooper a prophet, since he had predicted such a play before the game.

With 2:18 remaining in the first half, Boston College had downed a punt inside the one-yard line, where on first down, an Ohio State offensive lineman had moved. The ball now was no more than an inch from the Buckeyes' goal line. Two plays later, they faced a third-and-ten from the same spot. This was Boston College's chance to hold, receive good field position and get back into the game before halftime.

This also was where Harris' influence became apparent. Ohio State teams in the past may have ran off tackle to get some room for the punter. But not now. As Hoying dropped into his own end zone, and a linebacker headed for him, everyone was covered. Everyone but George, who glided out of the backfield into the left flat. Hoying turned and delivered the ball perfectly in stride, leading to a 14-yard gain. Hoying got flattened. After George gained 19 more on a draw, Hoying threw deep to Glenn who twisted to catch the ball over his shoulder at the Boston College 20-yard line. Two plays later, Hoying threw a short out to Dudley, who was mismatched on a linebacker when he turned the reception up field for a 12-yard touchdown that made it 21-3 at the half.

"We can't get a longer touchdown drive than that," Cooper said. "What was it — 99 and seven-eighths yards? The key play was the swing pass to Eddie. We've worked on it enough to know how to use it."

If there was any chance that Boston College would come back, it was crushed on the Buckeyes' first possession of the second half. Eighty-two yards in 18 plays. It amounted to only three points, but it ate 7:35 off the clock and wore down Boston College's defense for good.

Later in the quarter, Glenn displayed what Cooper had been raving about for some time. Hoying threw a pass deep, high and what appeared to be overthrown, but Glenn caught up with it. The receiver left his feet and stretched parallel to the ground, cradling the football with his fingertips as he came crashing to the artificial turf. It was a spectacular catch for 46 yards. Problem was, Glenn's reaction. He raised his arms high in the air, drawing a penalty under a new rule to prevent individual celebrations.

The catch didn't lead to a score, but Glenn had made his point. "He went and got it, didn't he?" Hollis said. "I thought Bobby threw it a mile over his head, and he just turned on the jets and caught up with it."

"Awesome," Hoying said. "Simply awesome."

George's second touchdown, a nine-yard run, made it 31-6 before Cooper cleared the bench. With less than three minutes remaining, Tommy Hoying fired a 12-yard touchdown pass to Dimitrious Stanley. The scoring pass was the first of his career. When the carnage was finished, Ohio State had a 38-6 victory.

"When we needed a play," Springs said later, "it seemed like we made it. That's the way it was all day."

Cooper's team had been impressive, balanced and in excellent physical condition to withstand the heat. Boston College had worn down. Hoying had completed 17-of-26 passes for 269 yards and one touchdown. He did not throw an interception and showed that this Ohio State team would pass at any time from anywhere. George rushed for 99 yards and caught three passes for 44 more.

"In the past, running backs here really weren't part of the passing game," George said. "They said they wanted it all last year, but nothing really happened."

Sort of like Glenn's potential. Glenn had finished with 105 receiving yards on only three receptions. He totaled 110 yards the entire 1994 season. While watching the pregame warm-ups, Cooper and Hollis immediately could tell that freshman cornerback Billy Gustin, listed as a starter, would be no match for Glenn. "When we opened the game, we knew number 15 wouldn't be able to cover Terry," Cooper said. When the game ended, Cooper walked up to Boston College cornerback Daryl Porter and said, "Don't worry. You are not going to play against too many receivers better than Terry Glenn."

"He can fly, can't he?" Hoying asked. "And Eddie was running over people. Going into it, we were anxious because we didn't know what to expect. Now we feel pretty good." The quarterback was as happy for his brother's first career touchdown pass as he was for himself. "I told him he would never forget the first one," he said.

What also was new and improved was the communication between the offensive coaches. Upstairs, Harris and Jacobs recognized everything Boston College threw at the offense. Hollis, in turn, responded. And Cooper, always listening, had noticed. "We had great, great communication from the press box to the sideline," Cooper said.

If there was a downside to the game, the defensive front was pushed around at times in the first half when Smith gained 110 yards on 21 carries. He gained only nine more in the second half, but only because Ohio State had a huge lead. "I am concerned," Cooper said. "From tackle to tackle, we've got to shore it up. You cannot have vertical holes in your defense when you get back to play in our league."

Once the team reached the locker room and sang "Across the Field" as it does following each victory, Cooper gathered his troops and held up a game ball. "This one goes to Rose Hill, Billy's wife," he said. Billy Hill, the school's head football trainer since 1974, had died suddenly in February from a heart attack. He was just 48 years old. "Remember, we dedicated this game to him."

Hoying walked into the training room, where Hill's successor, Bill Davis, had summoned him. Blood dripped from a gash on his chin. "You think I need stitches for this?" the quarterback asked. Davis glanced at the wound and nodded. The battle scar would be a reminder of Boston College's blitzes. The Eagles came after Hoying from all angles, and usually knocked him down following his release.

As Cooper headed down to the field for his postgame radio show, he said, "Well, now we have plenty of time work on Washington. Tomorrow, we'll see New York."

The previous two winners of the Kickoff Classic — Florida State in 1993 and Nebraska in 1994 — had gone on to win the national championship. That fact, even though perhaps just a coincidence, wasn't lost on Cooper or his players. "We know it," Hoying said, "but we also know we got Washington and 11 other games next. With the teams we play this year, there's no room for that (talk) now."

As scheduled, the Buckeyes remained for two more days since their next game was three weeks away. On Monday, the team toured the World Trade Center, the New York Stock Exchange and the Empire State Building. As the bus rolled on and happy football players gazed out the windows at the nation's largest city, Cooper grabbed a microphone and narrated the day's events. That night, they took in a Yankees game, and someone from the Columbus Clippers (the Yankees' AAA farm team) had arranged for Cooper to throw out the first pitch. Before he headed onto the field, he chatted with Yankees manager Buck Showalter, who noticed Cooper was wearing one of those cheap Yankees caps that the vendors pedaled.

"You can't throw out the first pitch in that," Showalter said, summoning a bat boy to fetch a genuine hat from the clubhouse.

Cooper, now with an authentic Yankees hat on his head, walked to the mound. Yankees catcher Mike Stanley told him to take his time and not try to throw the pitch too hard. The coach wound up and threw a strike.

"From tiny Powell, Tennessee, to Yankee Stadium," he said. "I've come a long way, huh?"

6.

"I lived so far in the country, I had to go toward town to hunt."

The line is one of John Cooper's favorite sayings. Then again, he has about a million of them. Another is, "I wasn't born on third base." It was a baseball analogy for a football coach, but it got the message across. As he said following his pitch at Yankee Stadium, he had come a long way from the hills of east Tennessee.

In his own words...

"I was born at home, not in the hospital. Heiskell, Tennessee is where we lived. We liked to say it had a four-way stop sign and two of 'em didn't work. It was out in the boondocks, where I went to elementary school. I went to high school in Powell, about six miles away. My graduating class had about 80 in it, maybe. When we took the bus to school, I was the first getting picked up and the last to be dropped off. I was picked up at seven in the morning and wasn't dropped off until five in the afternoon. I had two older brothers, two younger sisters and a younger brother. My daddy, Averil Cooper, was a union carpenter. He worked half the year and then would get laid off. He never worked a whole year. My mom, all she ever knew was hard work. Mom's name was Mildred. She was the hardest working person I ever knew. She raised six kids, milked cows, cooked, washed, ironed, gardened, and worked at the post office on Saturdays. Nobody worked as hard as she did.

"We lived on a 65-acre farm and we farmed about 15 acres of it. We farmed it with mules. I used to get out of grade school and instead of waiting on the bus some days, I would run home a mile and a half to help my granddad. He was a sharecropper, and I would plow more from after school until dark than he had plowed all day. That was a big deal for me. I would bale hay in the summer for 50 cents an hour. The first real job I had was helping build a house for 40 cents an hour when I was about 12 years old. I was the mud man for the bricklayer. I got paid 17 dollars in cash the first time. Seemed like I was rich. I guess we were poor then but didn't know it. We always had clean clothes and plenty to eat. My favorite meal then and to this day is pinto beans, cornbread and fried potatoes. That's what I was raised on. I don't know of a morning that went by that Mom didn't get up and make sausage gravy and eggs for breakfast. We canned beans and corn and picked blackberries. We shared everything we had. We gave away tomatoes. It was just country living, that's all it was. But we were happy.

"My first football game that I remember... me and a buddy hitchhiked into Knoxville and saw the Volunteers play Kentucky in 1946. Walter Slater was a running back at Tennessee, and he returned a punt and scored right in front of us. We had seats in the end zone. Later on, I would go to town just about every Saturday to watch the game. If I didn't see the game, I would listen to Lindsey Nelson's broadcast. That was a big deal in my life, watching the Volunteers play.

"My first memory of playing football was at halftime of Powell High games. It was a big deal for us as kids to go out on the field and tackle each other. The first time I went out for football, I was in the ninth grade. They gave me a pair of hip pads that were way too big for me. They told us to run a lap around the field, and my hip pads were falling down as I ran. My coach said I was too little to play, so he made me the manager. I was just a little shit. By the time of my senior year, I was a quarterback and defensive back. I think we were county champions about every year I had played. They used to have a city-county all-star game and after my senior year, my high school coach was picking the team, so I was invited. I was the MVP of the game, and I wasn't being recruited by anyone. Nobody from my family went to college anyway. You just got out of high school, you got a job in Oak Ridge, either with Alcoa or pumping gas at a service station or whatever. But everybody kept telling me, 'Johnny, you ought to go to college.' So I went to college. I walked on to play football at Tennessee.

"Once I got to Tennessee, I would wait in those long lines, stand in one line a half an hour and get up there and realize I was in the wrong line. I didn't want to be there anyway, but people talked me into it. I got discouraged and got me a job at a manufacturing plant. Then I started dating Helen Thompson. She had been a cheerleader at my high school and was a year behind me. Anytime we had a date, we usually double-dated with other friends. She was smart and attractive, and came from a good family. So then I got me a car. The next year — and I will never forget this as long as I live — my cousin Ralph and I were working remodeling houses. He said, 'Let's volunteer for the draft.' I remember it like it was yesterday because it was the day that Don Larsen pitched a perfect game in the World Series. Recruiters always wanted you to sign up, but that amounts to four years. If you volunteered for the draft, it was two years. So I went and told these recruiters, 'If you convince my cousin to sign up, I'll sign up.' We called Ralph 'Worry' as in 'Worry Wart.' Then one day, he is putting up Sheetrock in a back room, and this army recruiter comes over and starts talking to me. I said, 'Buddy, go talk to my cousin. He's the one you have to convince.' Now Worry's got a hammer in his hand, and he's putting up that Sheetrock. He's on a stepladder. This guy is standing at the door telling him about the buddy system. My cousin says, 'Listen here, we're going in the G.D. army for two years. If you got anything less than that to talk about, keep on talking. If you don't, then get the hell out of here.' I never will forget it. We volunteered, got drafted, and we were in the army.

"I spent the first six months in Arkansas. That Christmas, I went home and got married to Helen. I was 19. Then I was transferred to Fort Benjamin Harrison in Indianapolis for eight weeks. I could type so they taught me to be a stenographer of all things. Then they shipped me to Germany for 15 months. Anyway, two guys off my high school team got football scholarships. I felt I was as good or better than them. Even most of the players in that city-county all-star game got scholarships, and I was the MVP of that game. So when I was ready to get out of the army, I wrote letters to several colleges. I sent one to Phil Dickens, the head coach of Indiana. The coach at East Tennessee State wrote back and offered me a scholarship. Then one day I get a letter back from Phil Dickens. He had turned the letter over to Lou McCollough and wrote that Lou will be in contact. Then I get a letter from Lou, and he is coaching at Iowa State. He said if I get out of the service at a certain time, he would give me a scholarship for one quarter. I just pitched the letter up into my locker because I was going to East Tennessee State. A week later, I get a letter from my mother saying Lou had contacted her and had offered a full scholarship and wanted to know why I didn't get back to him. Then I get a letter from him that said if I could make it by September the fourth, 1958, I would get a full scholarship. I went to Tennessee to pick up Helen — I haven't seen her for 15 months — and we drive to Ames, Iowa. We didn't have any money, just what Helen had made while I was in the service. We lived in married housing there, and I never will forget this: It started raining the first night and we had to put boxes on the kitchen table because the roof was leaking. Helen was miserable. She was almost 20 years old and away from her mother and dad for the first time.

"My goal then was to graduate and get a high-school coaching job back home. I don't think I ever missed a class in college, and I bagged groceries in the off-season. Back in those days, it seemed like there was 60 freshmen on the team. The first day of practice as a sophomore, they put me on the scout squad so I was the fifth-team tailback. We scrimmaged the varsity every day. On the first day of spring practice, head coach Clay Stapleton stopped practice and took my scout-team jersey off me and put it on another kid and put his on me. That's how I was promoted to the varsity. So now I am the fourth-team tailback and the third-team tailback quit. Then the second-team tailback got his girlfriend pregnant and dropped out of school. Now I am the second-team tailback. The first-teamer, Dwight Nichols, was a 1959 *Look* All-American. It seemed like players kept leaving and finally, we had only thirty football players — "The Dirty Thirty." By the time I was a senior, I was voted captain and named MVP of the senior class.

"But the thing I remember most was, in those days, you never went around the coaching staff when they were in their offices. I was in the head coach's office two times in my college career. Then when I am a senior, I made an appointment to go talk to him. I was as nervous as I could be. I bought me a tie. I didn't even own a tie then. I walked in there and I told him, 'Coach, someday I want to be sitting in your chair. Someday I want to be a head football coach like you are. What kind of advice can you give me?' He loosened his tie as he always did, and said, 'John, I think you would make a heck of a coach. Matter of fact, if I had an opening, I would hire you. If you go to grad school, I will move my freshman coach up to the varsity and you can coach the freshman team, but I can't pay you any money.' I told him I would do that if he treated me like a coach, if he would let me sit in meetings and be a part of the staff. He agreed, and I started my coaching career.

"At Christmas, I went home to Tennessee and talked to the county superintendent about a high-school coaching job. He didn't give me the time of day. Then one day out of a clear blue sky, Clay Stapleton asked me, 'John, how would like to coach at Oregon State?' I said I would love it. Then my next thought, although I didn't say it was, 'Where the hell is Oregon State?' Here Helen is waiting for me to get out of school so we can go home to Tennessee, and now we're heading farther away. Clay used to coach at Oregon State with Tommy Prothro, and he knew he was looking for a young coach to hire. I called Coach Prothro, and he wanted me to fly up. Helen bought me a coat and a hat for the interview. He offered me a job. It was early February of 1963. My first salary would be $7,000, and I was tickled to death. We packed up everything and drove to Oregon, and Helen cried all the way out there. As soon as we got there, I went to California to recruit for two weeks. You know, it rains in Oregon all the time. So Helen was by herself in the rain, and I am down in the California sunshine. I coached the receivers and one of them, Vern Burke, led the nation with 69 catches. The next year, we go to the Rose Bowl, and Michigan killed us.

"Tommy Prothro was a giant of a man, an all business-type guy. He played chess and bridge — those are the only things he did out of football. He was the most intelligent, most sound football coach I ever knew, and he had the most influence on me. And he gave me the best breaks in my career. After two years, he went to UCLA and took me with him. In the first year, 1965, I was making $9,000 and coaching the defensive backs at UCLA. One of my defensive backs was Bob Stiles. We won the conference and beat Michigan State in the Rose Bowl. Michigan State that year had the greatest talent I had ever seen assembled. Anyway, my little defensive back was the MVP of the Rose Bowl. He had his picture on the cover of *Sports Illustrated*. I have been coaching now three years and been to two Rose Bowls, so I am thinking there's nothing to this business. The next year we are 9-1 and we beat Southern Cal 14-7, but the faculty representatives picked USC to go to the Rose Bowl. The next week, Southern Cal got beat 51-0 by Notre Dame. Here we were 9-1 and staying home. You talk about being disappointed.

"After that game, (UCLA assistant) Pepper Rodgers got the Kansas job, and I went with him to coach the defensive backs. Bobby Douglas was our quarterback, and we played in the Orange Bowl that season. Pepper probably was the best offensive coach I've ever been around. I stayed at Kansas for six years. When my dad died of a heart attack at 67 years old in 1972, I wanted to get back closer to home. So when Fran Curci got the head coaching job at Kentucky, he hired me and I stayed there for four years. By then, I knew I wanted to be a head coach. I came to realize it's all timing in the coaching business. When we had the good teams, like at UCLA and Kansas, you move on to a better job. You are not going to get a job when you are coaching a losing team. We are 9-1 at Kentucky, and we beat North Carolina in the Peach Bowl that year. It was 1976. I saw the Tulsa job was open, so I called and told a secretary that I wanted to talk to the person that was hiring the head football coach. She put me through to the head of the search committee, and I arranged to fly out to Tulsa to interview. I remember Helen telling me, 'You don't have a chance to get that job.' She's always been on the pessimistic side. When I get there, I pick up all the sports pages to find out everything I can about the school and the search committee. The write-up in the paper mentioned all the candidates. There was Larry Lacewell and Bill Pace. The last sentence said, '...and John Cooper, the defensive backfield coach at Kentucky, will also be interviewed.' I interviewed that night at 5:30, and two people dominated the interview. I figured these two guys would be making the decision. Buddy LaFortune, an oil company executive, was one. The other one was Mickey Whitney, the head of the school's fund-raising club. I had a great interview. When I've always interviewed, I never let them ask the questions.

I always go in and take the bull by the horns and present my case. I was staying at the Sheraton at the airport, and I told them on my way out, 'If anybody wants to come out and talk football before I leave in the morning, you are more than welcome.' Well, nobody called me. I couldn't sleep that night. The next morning, I get up bright and early, and I call Buddy and tell him that I want this job. Then I call Mickey and tell him the same thing. Pretty soon, Buddy sends his driver out to get me at the airport and takes me downtown to his offices. Now you talk about a very impressive place. He has the whole floor of a bank building, so I figure I am talking to the right guy. We talked football all day. When I leave to go home, he told me the president would be calling me that night. Sure enough, the president called me and offered me the job. Helen couldn't believe it. But I was right, those two people did the hiring.

"We were 3-8 in our first year. It would be our last losing season. We had winning seasons our next seven years, went 9-2 once and 10-1 once. Then when the Arizona State job came open, I wanted it. I got it. I put together a good staff. The first thing we got going was a good weight program. We could have won the Pac-10 the first year but got beat 16-13 by Arizona. We had some good players — a lot of them are still in the NFL. Then the next year, 1986, UCLA had lost an afternoon game and we were playing Cal that night. If we win, we're in the Rose Bowl. The place was electrifying. People are bringing roses to the game and everything. We were beating them 21-0 at halftime, and we returned the second-half kickoff for a touchdown and that place absolutely exploded. It was the first time and only time a team from Arizona has gone to the Rose Bowl. What a memory that Rose Bowl was. There was so much interest in the game in Arizona that they moved the Fiesta Bowl to January 2. I bet you we had 60,000 Sun Devil fans there. The thing I remember most was when we are getting ready to take the field. It's a gorgeous day, the place is packed, and all of a sudden it dawns on me — this is it. This is the Rose Bowl. This is the ultimate. That's when I start pinching myself. I am thinking 'Boy, I've come a long way.' I am just a country boy from east Tennessee. All the hard work and all the stops have paid off. Then we go out and win the game on top of that. Once we settled down, it was a mismatch. We had the ball 12 minutes in the third quarter and there was absolutely no question we were better than Michigan, even though we won only 22-15. It's got to be the highlight of my career.

"At the end of that season, but before the Rose Bowl, the athletic director from Texas, DeLoss Dodds, came out to visit me. Their job was open, but I was not going to pass up coaching in the Rose Bowl. The next year, the North Carolina job was open, and I gave it some thought. At that time, I wasn't sure that I wanted to live the rest of my life in Arizona. Our roots are in Tennessee and a lot of people don't realize that Helen was really close to her mom and dad. It was time to make a career decision. Cindy was a freshman at Arizona State and Johnny was out of school. I figured if I stayed out there a couple of more years, the kids would have their roots established and that's probably where we would live the rest of our lives. We didn't know if we wanted to stay that far from where our roots are. The next year, they announced the (NFL's) Cardinals were coming to town and I realized it might be difficult to give the people the type of program they wanted to have every year. I could have had the North Carolina job that year, although I didn't think it was a better job than the one I had. But it would have put us back in the vicinity of where we wanted to be.

"Then the Ohio State job came open. The Ohio State people talked to (then UCLA Coach) Terry Donahue about this job. Terry and I are very close, and he called me or I called him, I really can't remember, to talk about it. It got me interested in it. Bill Myles was on the selection committee, and he's a former football coach so I called him. He invited me to Dallas. I flew there to meet with him, (Athletic Director) Jim Jones and (OSU President) Ed Jennings. It was early December, 1987. I am supposed to meet them in the Hilton Hotel at the airport, but I couldn't find Bill or anybody when I got there. I called Bill Myles' home, and his wife said she didn't know where he was. I guess he didn't even tell her where he was going because everything was real hush-hush. Anyway, about 15 minutes later, they come walking in. We interviewed. After I got back to Phoenix. Jim Jones then called me a few days later and said I was the guy they wanted as coach. I said, 'That's fine.' I had an agent I had arranged...what's his name? One of the big guys in Los Angeles. Oh, Marvin Demoff. I told him what I wanted in the contract, and I told him to handle it. I never even met him. On the night we played in the Freedom Bowl — December 30, 1987 — I told the athletic director and my staff that I was leaving. I told the players before the game. We got the contract worked out about noon that day, and we beat Air Force that night. After the game, Bill Myles was outside with a limo and took us to the airport. We got on a jet and flew to Columbus, arriving about four in the morning. I had been to Columbus once in my life — one time when I was coaching at Arizona State, we came and watched spring practice. When we got to town, we went to Dan Galbreath's house and then met the trustees and had a press conference. It was an opportunity to get a better job back in the part of the country where Helen and I grew up. That was how I became a Buckeye."

7.

Three Long Weeks

The 20-day layoff between the Kickoff Classic and the season's second game against Washington Sept. 16 at Ohio Stadium was the longest in Ohio State history — other than those leading to bowl games, of course. "That's a long time between games," Cooper said. "It's a good time to spend on fundamentals. It's almost as if we are beginning the second phase of camp."

That may not have been exactly what the players wanted to hear when they returned from New York, but there was hardly anything they could do about it but return to work. They had paid their dues by working hard in camp, playing very well in the rout of Boston College, and now they wanted to suit up and play another game. Instead, they had to grind their way through practice for almost three weeks before entering Ohio Stadium for the first time. "It's a long time," nose guard Luke Fickell said. "Too long. We are ready to play. Now."

Especially since they had the memory of a 25-16 loss to Washington in Seattle from a year ago. Now they possessed a new-found confidence, they had jumped to tenth in the polls and would be playing at home.

On their first Saturday off, most of the team watched Northwestern shock Notre Dame 17-15 on television. The Big Ten's lowliest team the past three decades had gone into South Bend as a four-touchdown underdog and upset the ninth-ranked Irish — Ohio State's fourth opponent. The result gave Cooper a little vindication for trailing Northwestern 9-0 at the half on the road the year before, although the Buckeyes had rallied to win.

"It's exactly what I have been talking about — anybody can beat anybody," Cooper said. "Look what we went through up there last year. Anyway, better Lou (Holtz) than me. They would have booed me out of the stadium when we came home if we had lost to Northwestern."

That game the previous season had marked one of the few occasions in Cooper's career that he had lost his temper, but it had nothing to do with an official's call or a player not hustling. Encountering a verbally abusive Ohio State fan when the team headed toward the locker room at the half, he grabbed the hat off the fan's head and spiked it. A television camera had caught the whole thing. "I really don't remember what he was saying — 'Cooper's no good' or something like that," Cooper said.

While watching practice on Sept. 5, Cooper said Notre Dame's loss was more than just an upset — it was indicative of the big picture in college football. "I am convinced there aren't any great teams in college football anymore," he said. Still, top-ranked Florida State had beaten Duke 70-26, and second-ranked Nebraska had clobbered Oklahoma State 64-21. Washington, on the other hand, had slipped by Cooper's former team, Arizona State, 23-20 in its opener. "Washington didn't look that good on film," Cooper said. "If we play like we should, we should kick Washington's ass."

But it wouldn't happen without a little so-called butt-chewing of their own first. The coaches realized that the next day while watching a lackluster practice in disgust. After the players were put through their usual 200-yard conditioning sprints following the workout, Bill Young gathered his defense at one corner of the field. There, he sent them off running in two more sprints for emphasis. Now they were tired enough to only listen.

"You guys aren't practicing worth crap," Young screamed. "You aren't working hard. You're lazy, and you are not focused."

Defensive ends coach Bill Conley stepped in to add his thoughts, "You had better start focusing on Washington. These guys were on probation last year, and they beat you good. Don't you want to pay them back?"

Once they dismissed the defense, Young and Conley repeated the scene with the scout teams. It is normal for scout teams everywhere to lack talent, but this scout team hadn't been giving much effort. As a result, the first teams usually prepared poorly, also. "This isn't to punish you — it's to make you better," Young said. "It's to make the team better. You guys aren't working hard enough. You have to help us make this defense better. You need to give us a better look. You need to give 100 percent. We want to get to the Rose Bowl. Don't you want to go to the Rose Bowl?"

Young turned and walked toward the locker room, still seething, although the outburst was a little calculated.

"They are just looking at the big picture right now," he said. "It's 100 percent mental. The talent level of the scout team is pitiful, so they can only do so much. The other guys just aren't focused. We want to be tough on them now when we are winning and ease off later if we lose. I really believe the secret is to coach hard when you are winning."

Still, the second of the third practice weeks presented a quandary for the coaches, since there was no game for the players to set their sights on. The win over Boston College had provided enough buoyancy the previous week. The next week, they would be able to look forward to a game. But this was a week in between, a week in limbo. "This week is a bitch," Hollis said. "It's a bitch to the coaches and to the players. Do we push them, or do we ease off? Are we going to be in shape? Is the edge going to come off? You worry about it more because we played so well."

The next day, the defensive coaches were presented with a tangible problem when starting strong side linebacker Jerry Rudzinski was diagnosed with a fractured foot. The injury had occurred five days earlier, but the pain wouldn't go away.

"It was a simple drill with the tight ends last Friday, and I felt it. I guess I planted wrong on it," Rudzinski said, leaning on crutches after practice. "It was sore, and I iced it down over the weekend. Then the first thing when I got out there, I felt it again."

Linebackers coach Fred Pagac figured he could promote junior-college transfer Kevin Johnson in his place. Or maybe Marc Willis, another junior-college transfer. Or maybe junior Obie Stillwell. "It hurts us right now," Pagac said. "It's not good news. I don't know what I am going to do right now, to tell you the truth."

Told the news, Young sighed and shook his head. "Now I guess we are glad we have the extra week of practice. We feel we have guys who can play there, but they are just young and inexperienced. The question is, how long is Jerry going to be out?. They told us six to eight weeks, but will it be longer?"

Coaches, however, told Rudzinski he would probably miss no more than four weeks. Thus, they hoped he wouldn't become depressed if he expected such a long layoff of inactivity.

Friday, Sept. 8, it was 4:45 p.m. when Walt Harris called his wife to tell her he would be a little late. It was the annual night of skits and songs at the team's training table. Each year, upperclassmen forced the freshmen and team managers to act out skits, while first-year coaches had to sing "Across the Field," one of the school's two fight songs. Harris glanced at a song sheet. "I don't know the words yet," he said.

Just then, Larry Petroff, the staff's administrative assistant, ducked his head into Harris' office. "Don't let anything keep you from getting over there at five," Petroff instructed. "You can't get out of it. You have to do it. You *have* to sing."

Harris listened, rolled his eyes and went back to work. If he had to do this with every new job, he would know half the fight songs in college football by heart. His wife had grown tired of the relocating that went with the coaching business. Since 1977, they had moved from California to Michigan to Illinois to Tennessee, back to California to New York and now to Columbus. And once he arrived, the media speculated how long he would stay.

"I don't know, but if you talk to my wife, we might be here 15 years," he said. "She is tired of moving. She wants to be a mother (to the couple's two children) and settle in one place for a while. That experience in the NFL was very difficult on my family."

Harris longed to become a head coach again. He was older now and much wiser than when he coached at Pacific. And as tough as coaching three years with the Jets was, the experience was invaluable. If he just could get another chance.... "Somebody will take a chance on me again," he said. "It's just a matter of paying my dues and waiting, and this is as good of a place to be as any." He went back to preparing for Washington. "The problem Washington poses is that you are usually one man short against their front," he said. "You have seven to block eight. Picking up the blitzes will be the key, because we think we can get open against their defensive backs." After a while, he turned out the lights in his office and headed across the street to the Fawcett Center for Tomorrow where the team was eating dinner. He arrived twenty minutes late.

Over dinner, the coaches discussed the Arizona-Georgia Tech game played the night before. Lovie Smith's son was a defensive back for Arizona, a team Cooper would just as soon forget. While at Arizona State, he had not beaten Arizona in three attempts, so it could have been written that his teams had a 1-7-2 record against its arch rivals since he left Tulsa in 1984. "Never beat 'em. Tied one and lost two," he said. "One year, we're better than them but it's tied late in the game. If we win we go to the Rose Bowl. Then we turn it over, and they kick a field goal in the final seconds to beat us 16-13." He shook his head and dug into some ice cream covered with strawberries.

From another table, Mike Vrabel overheard Cooper. "Telling old war stories again, coach?" the defensive end asked, winking. Cooper just nodded and continued to eat his ice cream.

It was typical Vrabel, the team's best at riding teammates, or even coaches when he felt he could get away with it. When dinner concluded, Vrabel, Matt Finkes, Hoying and Fickell arranged their seats so they would be front-and-center when the talent show, or lack-of-talent show, began. Then they began to hoot and howl, ordering the freshmen to get on with it. "That Vrabel, Finkes and Fickell — they love to have fun," Young said. "Man, they are tight. You don't see them go anywhere without the other guys."

Once the show started, freshman tackle Drew Elford crawled out on his knees, barking instructions for stretching exercises. It was a pretty good imitation of strength coach Dave Kennedy, who stands well below six feet. Kennedy blushed and chuckled. After a few rap numbers, which were so awful that they brought boos and debris, a manager walked out wearing a shirt with the slogan "I love Boomer" written on the back. He was mocking Harris, a self-proclaimed fan of the Jets quarterback whom he had coached the past three years. The players, even Hoying, roared with laughter. A final skit listed the top ten reasons "why Ohio State will go to the Rose Bowl." Number five was, "Because Coach Cooper wants his $50,000 bonus." Cooper raised his arms, smiled and nodded repeatedly.

Finally, when it was time for the four new coaches to sing the fight song, Harris, Jacobs and Smith unenthusiastically lip-synched the lyrics. Chuck Stobart, however, stole the show. A native Ohioan, Stobart bellowed the words to "Across the Field," pumping his fist with each verse. By the time he was finished, the entire team had jumped to its feet to join him.

"Ah," Stobart said, sweat pouring off his forehead, "I always wanted to be a Buckeye."

And now that he was 60 years old, two years older than Cooper, Stobart had become one. A year earlier, he never imagined he would be coaching in Columbus. But the president of Memphis had cleaned house, firing Stobart, after three consecutive 6-5 seasons, as well as the athletic director. The experience left him rightfully bitter.

"It turns you off as far as coaching on that level," Stobart said a few days later. "It was a whole lot of hard work without much appreciation, and it was frustrating. We broke school records, we had three straight winning seasons after they hadn't had two in seventeen years. When I got there, they were on probation for god sakes."

Stobart took some solace in the fact that those in the business — coaches, athletic directors and NFL scouts — realized he had done an excellent job. It wasn't easy to recruit at a non-football power like Memphis. But once a coach is fired, restoring public perception is another matter. Still, unlike most others who go through it, Stobart wanted to coach again immediately.

"My friends told me to take a year off, but I wasn't crazy about staying out a year," he said. "I was afraid I would play golf and do all that other stuff and not want to get back. I had a chance to scout for NFL teams, but I really didn't want to do that. My first choice was to get with a top program like Ohio State, a place where football is important and you have a chance to be successful. Now that I am here, what I would like to do is coach ten more years and then retire with a place here and a place in Arizona or Florida."

Stobart was hoping to take a national championship ring with him into retirement. Under Bo Schembechler, he had coached on three Rose Bowl teams at Michigan and another later at USC. He knew the ingredients of a great team and he knew talent when he saw it. And he knew, too, that Ohio State now had both. "This team is very capable," he said. "In fact, I'll say this — I would be disappointed if we didn't go undefeated and play in the Rose Bowl for the national championship."

Already, after just one game, fans were beginning to feel that way, too. The letters-to-the-sports-editor column of Sunday's *Columbus Dispatch*, a barometer of fans' feelings toward Ohio State football, bubbled with optimism. An example: "Ohio State's magnificent effort against Boston College brought back memories of performances from years past. The intensity and emotion forced a good team into early submission. Simply, the team was well-prepared and the intensity level never wavered. Now that Coach Cooper has apparently found the right formula, let us hope it will continue. Maybe then the program will be back to normal" — John G. Neal.

Since he arrived almost eight years earlier, the weekly column had become a favorite forum for Cooper-bashers. And the coach, although he wouldn't admit it, read it each Sunday.

"I went to the library once to check this out and found out it's true...," John Cooper Jr. said. "The same people have been writing the negative letters over and over again."

Things appeared to be changing though, and perhaps Cooper was finally winning over the John G. Neals of the world.

———————◆•◆•◆——————

Monday morning, Sept. 11, Cooper walked into the offensive meeting shaking his head. He had just watched fullback Nicky Sualua get off the scales. "Guess what Nicky weighed?" he asked, taking guesses from around the room. "Yep, only 266. I asked him what happened. At least he's honest. He said there's a pizza place across from his place and he ordered a large the other night. The guy threw in some breadsticks." The coach laughed, even though he had to act perturbed in front of Sualua.

"I'll bet he's not over here working out today either, is he?" Tim Spencer asked. When Cooper shook his head, Hollis told Spencer, "Let's put him at second team until next week. Guys, we can't be joking around about this all the time. We have to get him in shape."

Cooper left and then walked back in after a few minutes. He held a piece of paper.

"This just off the high-speed sports wire — Lou Holtz has a compression of the spinal cord, is in the hospital for an operation and will be out three to four weeks after that. Bob Davie will be the head coach."

Hollis said, "I don't like that — that's all they need to fire them up."

"No, No," Harris said. "He runs the show. The rest of those guys stand around while he does everything. Then again, he'll have a (film) projector in the hospital room and be telling them what to do."

Holtz's surgery just added another twist to the impending Notre Dame game that was more than two weeks away. Would the coach be back by then? Would the injury inspire Notre Dame for another "win one for the Gipper" sort of thing? Once Ohio State's coaches realized the injury wasn't life-threatening, those questions popped into their minds.

Finding the answers would have to wait. "Come on you guys," Hollis said, "we've got to worry about Washington. What about Jim Lambright? That's who we have to worry about. Is he going to be there Saturday?"

Following practice, it was the offensive coaches' turn to be disgusted this time. Hollis shouted and screamed at his players, who had missed assignments and appeared uninspired: "We could be very good or we could be average. It's up to you. Which way do you want it? You guys just aren't practicing worth a shit."

Later, he said, "They're just unenthusiastic. They are not being pushed (by second-teamers), and they know it. It makes me mad. It makes us all mad."

The next morning, film of the practice revealed what the coaches had seen in person — it was awful. Everyone looked tired and run down. Hollis thought it was the perfect time to ease the physical requirements for some key players.

"Coach," he said when Cooper walked in, "we have a bunch of guys with banged up knees. Orlando (Pace) is one of them. Eddie, too." As the film continued, Harris said, "Look what (tight end) Bobby Houser did. He did something nobody did — he broke to the ball after a play. We have to talk to them today about this. We need linemen breaking to the ball."

Hollis mumbled, "We wouldn't have had them breaking to a plate of food yesterday. I think too many of them are banged up. We may need to ease up after practice today."

Harris believed the grass practice fields weren't giving enough for the players' legs. "They need to do something to make the field softer," he said. "With 20 days between games, that field will get to their legs. When you are a head coach, you pay attention to stuff like that. When you are an assistant, you go with the flow."

Once they turned their attention to Washington's defense, it was as if they were seeing part of Boston College again. Only better. And quicker. Much quicker. The Huskies liked to blitz often, too, but they had better athletes than Boston College. At times, protecting Hoying might be a problem. When Hollis complained of his sinus pain, Harris replied, "Joe, that's Washington's front causing your sinuses to go bad. Mine, too. The speed of their defense makes it tough. We need to hit two bombs to get up on them right away. That would make it easier."

Hollis chuckled as he scribbled something, "OK, I'll put that in the script."

When Cooper walked in and overheard the conversation, he referred back to another of his common sayings — "Don't make your opponent better than they are." He put his feet up on a chair and blurted, "Aw, you guys, they aren't the same team on the road that they are at home. You'll see. Don't make them better than they are, right Chuck?"

Stobart nodded and smiled.

The next night, when Cooper addressed a booster meeting, he was keeping his confidence to himself. It was one thing for him to talk that way around his coaches and players, but quite another to do it in front of fans and the media. For them, obviously, he had to throw around the praise as if the Buckeyes were playing the Dallas Cowboys every week.

"Washington is a real good football team," he told the boosters. "We will have our hands full. But I want the same atmosphere in the horseshoe that we had for Michigan last year. If we get that, I'll assure you we won't lose a home game this season."

About 200 fans, mostly elderly, attended the bi-weekly booster meetings, hanging on every word from the coach. Being the first gathering of the season, Cooper introduced the entire team. Usually, he would pop in a game tape and explain a play or two. As he talked, Sports Information Director Steve Snapp, who has worked at the university since 1973, watched from the hallway.

"These booster meetings probably go back to the '50s," Snapp said. "Woody used to get up and talk and talk and maybe never even mention football. Earle (Bruce) did it because Woody did it, and he knew what it meant to him. John's really not that big on it. He does it because it was done before he got here."

Since the first home game was nearing, Cooper had to lecture his players on selling their game tickets, which was an NCAA violation. At Ohio State, where each game is a sellout, tickets were always in demand. There had been players in the past who made a buck by unloading their game tickets for a tidy sum.

"Just don't do it," Cooper instructed them following Thursday's practice. "They're no free lunches. There are all kinds of people out there trying to buy them and resell them and make a buck off you. You'll lose your eligibility if you do it. (Former running back) Vince Workman did it, and he got caught. You'll get caught. Just don't do it."

Minutes later, when the team changed to gather for its usual Thursday night meeting, he gave them the weekly grooming lesson for Friday night's dinner at the university golf course. Cooper always ordered his players to dress up during team gatherings or road trips.

"Wear a coat and tie. Some of you need to clean your act up," he said. "Look sharp, be sharp, play sharp. There is a football game tonight — Kansas versus TCU. Get off your feet and watch it. Get your fluids. I don't want to see anybody cramping up on Saturday if it's hot."

Then he turned inspirational.

"Get your focus. I challenged our fans — I want the loudest crowd ever here. We got beat up there last year. It's payback time! A lot of people in the country are wondering — how good is this Ohio State team? They will find out Saturday at 3:30 on ABC, won't they? If they want to make it a hitting contest, that is fine with us. Now let's get ready to kick their ass!"

———————————◆◆◆———————————

The next day, Friday at 5 p.m., as his 18th-ranked team practiced at Ohio Stadium, Washington Coach Jim Lambright kneeled down to run his fingers through the grass. It appeared to be in need of a lawn mower. An old football trick for years called for groundskeepers to let the grass grow to slow a visiting team that had more speed. But Ohio State's groundskeepers said the length of the stadium grass was normal.

"I always appreciate long grass," Lambright said. "It would scare me to death if it was real, real short. But going into a stadium like this, you are always going to be the underdog anyway."

Eddie George didn't care what surface he would run on Saturday, just as long as he had the chance to be on the field. The inactivity of his freshman and sophomore years as he waited behind first Robert Smith and then Raymont Harris whittled at his patience, although Harris became one of his closest friends. Until his junior season when he gained 1,442 yards, George was more known to Buckeye fans for two crucial fumbles as a freshman in a home loss to Illinois. That day still ate at George's gut. But the Boston College game, in which he was named the Kickoff Classic MVP, showed that he had prepared himself to have an excellent senior season. While Cooper regretted not getting him one more carry to surpass 100 yards (he finished with 99), it didn't bother the running back.

"A year ago, I just wanted to get back out on the field since I hadn't played much in my first two years," he said. "I had to be patient and wait my turn. Now I know what to expect, and I see my own improvement from one year to the next. I am trying to be the best. That's what I want."

Coaches had waited for George to show more elusiveness, as well as patience when following his blockers. Now he was. Ironically, in a story in the game day program for the Washington game, he was quoted: "Everyone else doubted me. They said I couldn't do this, or couldn't do that. I couldn't break the long run. I wasn't quick enough. I just had to sit back and laugh and keep working hard."

There was little doubt to Young Saturday morning that Washington would do what Boston College did — run right at the interior of his defense. The front seven, despite having two All-Big Ten ends, was relatively small as a group. But this time, the Huskies didn't have Napoleon Kaufman, who rushed for 211 yards against his defense the year before.

Young had tried to keep things simple against Boston College, which may have accounted for the Buckeyes' trouble stopping the run. At least he hoped that was the reason. "I was disappointed in myself, because I had a real limited package," he said. "We had no zone blitzes or anything like that. I should have called for more substitutions and we needed to do more line stunts to shut them down."

Young and Pagac also decided to start Kevin Johnson in Rudzinski's place. Thirty minutes before kickoff, Rudzinski sat on the bench as his teammates warmed up. He tried to smile, but the heavy cast on his foot was weighing down his mood. "I am pretty bummed out right now," he said. "It's killing me not to be out there. Good thing I have three more years left. If I were a senior..." His voice trailed off.

In the first quarter, Washington tailback Lorenzo Neal showed that the Huskies didn't miss Kaufman all that much. Neal ran for 18 yards on the first play, and on the next series, he cut back against the flow for 66 yards that set up a touchdown as the Huskies took a 7-6 lead. Earlier, Hoying had scrambled before heaving a desperate pass to Sualua, the 266-pound guard-in-the-backfield, for a 22-yard touchdown. Josh Jackson's extra point had been blocked.

George then took a pitch, ran left and began a day he would never forget. He gained seven, four, ten, five, five and eleven yards leading to a 19-yard field goal by Jackson. On the next series, he gained three, three, fourteen, and then on a fourth-and-11, the coaches sneaked him into the left slot in field-goal formation without Washington's defensive players noticing. On the snap, George turned and looped around to the right to take a pitch from holder Brian Heinen. He sprinted outside, cut upfield and dived for the first-down marker as the fans roared. Two plays later, Hoying passed six yards to Glenn to give the Buckeyes a 16-7 lead.

On their next possession, George showed that the off-season work on increasing his speed had paid off by darting for 51 yards. He then faked out two tacklers on a seven-yard touchdown run to make it 23-7 late in the second quarter. As he reached the end zone, Brent Musburger told ABC's audience, "Folks, Eddie George deserves serious Heisman consideration."

Early in the third quarter, safety Rob Kelly recovered a fumbled snap that preceded George's next big run, a 16-yarder through a huge hole opened by tackle Orlando Pace for his second touchdown. As he jogged back to the bench, the crowd began to chant "Eddie! Eddie!"

Washington's defense, and the crowd of 94,104 for that matter, had been awed by George's broken tackles and third- and fourth-efforts. Simply, he refused to be taken down. When it was all over, he had carried 36 times for 212 yards and two touchdowns to lead Ohio State to a 30-20 win. He had become the first player in school history to rush for 200 or more yards three times in his career, something that not even the great Archie Griffin had accomplished.

He had impressed everyone, even Washington's All-American safety Lawyer Milloy. "George is in a class by himself — a guy that big and that fast," he said. "We tried to get him down on the first pop, but he wouldn't go down."

The day caught even George by surprise, not because of any lack of confidence, but because he remembered Washington as having a relentless, tough defense.

"After watching Washington on film, I was wondering if I could get 50 yards against these guys," he said. "I just told our guys to maintain their blocks, and I would make the best decision (which way to cut)." Asked if he deserved to be a Heisman Trophy candidate, George responded as he would the entire season — in true modesty. "That's something the media picks, guys they feel are deserving of it," he said. "If I am deserving of it, that's great. But I am still focused on the team goals. I am just going to try to go out and win games. That's what my job is."

Steve Snapp's job, on the other hand, was to promote Ohio State's players for awards and All-American teams. As the school's sports information director, he now had the evidence needed to justify promoting George for the Heisman Trophy. Snapp later designed a postcard that he would mail to each Heisman voter following every game. "We're not big on huge campaigns and things like that like other schools are," Snapp said. "This is just to make people aware of his statistics."

George's big day had overshadowed some obvious problems. Freshman punter Brent Bartholomew froze in his first game in front of the home crowd. His two punts wobbled off the side of his foot for 28 and 12 yards — the second giving Washington excellent field position when the lead had been cut to 30-14 early in the fourth quarter.

The defense got pushed around somewhat, too, as Neal gained 135 yards and Washington totaled 401.

"When you give up that many yards, you can't be happy," linebacker Greg Bellisari said. "We've got plenty to work on, because everybody we play against is going to try to do the same thing."

Young wasn't satisfied with anything but the win. He walked up the steps inside the locker room and headed for the interview room, already sweating through his shirt even though he had just showered.

"We played like a defense that hadn't played in three weeks," Young said. "It's tough when you are used to playing against our scout team. We just made too many mistakes and didn't tackle well, either. It's back to work tomorrow."

When he finished, he walked by Joe Hollis, who was still being interviewed. Young nodded toward the offensive coordinator and said, "Yes sir, the best defense is a good offense."

On this day, however, the best defense was not having to face Eddie George.

8.

Terry Glenn's Big Day

Eddie George awakened the next day, feeling as if he had been hit by a truck and dragged the length of a football field. He hurt all over. "I feel horrible," he said. "Horrible." Thirty-six carries translated into getting tackled 36 times — or 34 since he had scored two touchdowns. Still, when it was time for the team to run sprints on Sunday night, guess who led the pack? "He always wins the sprints," Cooper said. "That's just Eddie being Eddie."

"I will be fine in a few days," George said. "It just takes time to get over the normal bumps and bruises."

The wounds went much deeper for the run defense and the kicking game, representing potential danger for the team.

In two games, the defense had allowed 119 yards to one running back and 135 to another and appeared vulnerable to a good running team, of which Notre Dame and the Big Ten favorites usually qualify. When Bill Young examined the film, he knew what went wrong on every one of Washington's big plays. "It's not the team, it's an individual thing each time," he said. "A guy tries to help a teammate and gets burned. One time on the long run, a linebacker got too far inside. It's one thing here, another thing there."

Defensive end Mike Vrabel felt as if the layoff had hurt the defense. "I think 20 days without a game might have had something to do with it," he said. "We won't have to worry about that now — we're back into a routine where we practice, play a game, practice, play a game."

The tackling had been awful, which Young attributed to the hitting limitations during practice. The Buckeyes hadn't held any scrimmages between the Kickoff Classic and the Washington game, simply because they couldn't afford any injuries. Now it had showed. Until the 1990s, coaches would hold full-speed scrimmages when they wanted because they had 105 scholarships. If anyone got hurt, they always had another talented body at each position. "Not anymore," Young said. "You just can't tackle anymore because you are so thin. We can't tackle Eddie George in practice."

And the opponents couldn't tackle him during games.

The kicking game's problems included Mike Malfatt's erratic kickoffs, but the main worry was Bartholomew's freshman funk. It would be corrected as soon as he graduated from his severe case of nerves. At least that's what the coaches figured, or better yet, hoped. Cooper fretted that his poor punting would cost the team a game. When he bumped into Bartholomew and his father Sunday in the hallway, he joked, "Hey, you're still on scholarship aren't you? Now you just got to start kicking like it."

Later, he wasn't as lighthearted about it. "I've never seen such a horrendous kicking game in my life," he said. "Our kicking game is like my golf game. I am great on the range, and then I get out there and you don't know where it's going. I know he can do it. I've seen him do it, so he gets as long as he needs." It angered him simply because the team spent countless hours practicing the details of the kicking game.

Bartholomew didn't have any real answers. In practice, he had been nothing less than awesome. In two games, he had punted horribly. He even hinted that he was too relaxed. "Mentally, it was one of those bad games," he said when interviewed by a local television station. "It is not going to happen again. I promise. Coach talked to me about it. I promised him, too."

Monday afternoon, Marc Katz of the *Dayton Daily News* asked Cooper what he thought about the weekend's avalanche of points from around the country. Five of the top-ten ranked teams — No. 1 Florida State, No. 2 Nebraska, No. 4 Florida, No. 7 Penn State and No. 9 Colorado — had scored more than 60 points each. Since the bowl alliance would match the nation's No. 1 and No. 2 teams at the end of the season, excluding the Big Ten and Pac-10, many coaches and writers wondered if teams were running up scores.

Cooper took all sides of the issue — he believed certain coaches were running up scores yet didn't blame them, yet said he would never do it and also blamed their weak schedules.

"Hey, don't blame the guy scoring points — blame the defense," he said. "I worry about getting experience for the young guys in those situations. I just hope I have to worry about it some time. But look who those teams are playing. Who does Auburn play? Who does Florida play? Tennessee? They all play weak teams outside their conferences. Why don't we run up the score? Because we don't play Tennessee-Chattanooga.

"You go back in the history of football and check out all those great teams, look up who they were playing. Look at Ohio State's last national championship season. Who did they beat?"

For the record, in 1968 when each team played only two non-Big Ten games, the Buckeyes defeated Southern Methodist 35-14 and Oregon 21-6. The issue seemed to raise the coach's ire, perhaps because his team was facing a murderous schedule. It irritated him to see other teams ranked above the Buckeyes, now No. 8, beating patsies silly when his team already had played two ranked teams in two games. And more were to come.

Cooper shook his head and turned to answer his telephone, "Hey, Jim, how you doing? How many do you need? You got 'em. Ten tickets." He hung up and turned back to Katz. "An old buddy from high school who wanted some tickets for Saturday. He's from Knoxville and I know he knows Johnny, but I don't care who he roots for. Now where was I?"

The impending game at Pittsburgh pitted Cooper against a friend, Johnny Majors, who had played and coached at Tennessee. So naturally, the two coaches had plenty in common, including dozens of mutual friends.

Pitt had just lost 38-27 at Texas after starting with two wins. The Panthers had beaten Washington State 17-13 and Eastern Michigan 66-30, and it appeared Majors was turning the program back into a winner in this third season. It was just the type of game that would be dangerous for Ohio State, since it was on the road, Pitt was improving and it was sandwiched between emotional games against Washington and Notre Dame. So all the ingredients for a letdown existed. Cooper didn't buy it.

"I don't," he said. "All that letdown talk is overrated. I would be shocked if that's the case with this team. I think our guys are smarter than that. Pitt has got a lot better team than last year, I know that. They could have beaten Miami last year and should have beaten Texas."

The next morning at 7 o'clock, Harris walked into the offensive meeting holding a sheet of paper. On it, he had written 10 passing plays he thought would work against Pitt's defense. "We want to make them disperse their coverage, obviously," he said. "Terry Glenn is going to get a lot of balls thrown his way."

"We probably didn't throw it downfield enough Saturday," Hollis said. "We need to make a more conscious effort to do it. What were we? Forty-percent pass?" He grabbed his calculator. "Yep, 39.7."

"That's good," Harris replied. "Right where we want to be. The way number 27 was running...well, nobody thought we would run the ball that well on that front."

Once the coaches had viewed Pitt's three game films, they felt confident knowing Ohio State had twice the talent. Maybe three times as much. They just had to avoid mistakes and turnovers and they would be 3-0 returning for the showdown with Notre Dame. "I think the only way they can beat us is if we do something stupid and turn the ball over a bunch of times," Hollis said.

Harris had coached for Majors at Tennessee from 1983-88 and knew a little about the coach. That wouldn't hurt. As they watched film of Pitt's defense, he said, "Johnny's involved with this side of the ball. The secondary is his forte, you know. But look how they give up the middle. I've never seen a team give up the middle like this." That prompted Hollis to respond, "I don't think Johnny's doing much football stuff anymore. No meeting time. He must be out raising money."

When Cooper joined them, Hollis summarized the game plan for Saturday — they would throw it short, medium, long and often. Once Cooper glanced at a few minutes of film, he saw why. "They put a lot of heat on their defensive backs," he said. "Man-to-man with no help."

In between films, Cooper complained of the training table food at the Fawcett Center. "Last night, the regular patrons were in there eating with the players," he said. "I was signing autographs while I was eating. Can you believe that?"

At his weekly media luncheon, Cooper was asked if his tailback deserved to be in the Heisman race. "Eddie's not flashy," he said. "He's the old workhorse. He puts in eight hours a day, works hard and goes home. But it couldn't come to a more deserving winner if it does come his way. My attitude is if he keeps doing what he's doing, it all will take care of itself."

Following the day's practice, the coach wanted to make sure his players took care of their academic requirements. "Tomorrow is the first day of classes," he told the team. "Go to class! Go to study hall! If you miss class or miss study hall, you won't practice. If you don't practice, you don't play. It's as simple as that."

With that said, Cooper hurried into his office to change before driving downtown to his weekly radio call-in show. The show, carried on 73 stations in Ohio and West Virginia, lasted from 7-9 p.m. "It's two hours and that's probably an hour too long," Cooper said, "but it goes fast because we get so many calls." The show, part of his contract, also had a seven-second delay in case a caller wanted to verbally abuse the coach or toss in some profanity. And following a few losses, such as the 63-14 drubbing at Penn State a year earlier, the seven seconds had come in handy.

On this night, however, all but one caller was completely positive and ingratiating. The caller had asked Cooper why he criticized his players publicly early in his Ohio State career. "I don't think I've ever gone out of my way to criticize any of my players," Cooper answered. "But if you want me to apologize on the air, I will do that now."

It was as nasty as it would get, since most simply praised Cooper and thanked him for the 2-0 start.

Afterward, he said, "That's about normal. You don't get many bad calls when you win. I've said this all along — only five percent of the fans are that way. You are not going to please them no matter what you do. That one guy — sometimes they act like it is wrong if I say a player had a bad game. Let's face it — a lot of people resent me because I am not from Ohio. They all say, 'Woody wouldn't have acted like that.' Usually, I will get constructive criticism. That doesn't bother me too much. I get more of the hatred in the letters. It's never a dull show, anyway."

Once again, it had not been a good week of practice and by Thursday night, Hollis was frustrated with his offense's poor concentration. "We just haven't practiced very good this week at all," he said. "I wanted to bite my f— lip today. Thursday's just not the day to blow up. It concerns me. It's all mental. This stuff we're doing isn't new. They can't beat us, but we can beat ourselves."

Minutes later, Cooper began his Thursday address: "The busses leave tomorrow at 11. Don't be late. If you have a class that gets out at 10 or 10:30, go to class. Don't use that as an excuse. Anybody who has to miss a class, get a letter here.

"Now let's get focused and go over there and kick their ass. I don't feel that you have practiced that well this week. It would be a shame to let somebody beat you when they are not in the same class as you. We can't go over there and fumble and have penalties and make mistakes in the kicking game. Johnny Majors is a friend of mine, and I know he likes to think he is a guru in the kicking game. Let's beat them in the kicking game. Let's protect the quarterback. I don't want to see our quarterback get hit. Now get your rest, and we'll see you tomorrow."

The road trip would be the first in Cooper's career in which the team would bus back and forth. "It would be about the same time if we flew, maybe 30 minutes shorter at the most," he said. "By the time we check our bags, get through security, board and fly — we would be there by bus."

It had turned cold and drizzly by the time the team busses rolled into Bellmont Country Club in eastern Ohio Friday afternoon for lunch. Heads turned when 64 extremely large young adults sauntered into the dining room. When the lunch crowd realized who was in their company, several applauded.

Chuck Stobart, finishing off a piece of cherry pie, chuckled at the differences of where he had been and where he coached now. Naturally, it seemed people anywhere in the state loved Ohio State football. It wasn't the case at Memphis, but he did have some fans in high places. "Yeah, Cybil Shepherd was one of our biggest fans," he said. "She give the team a pregame pep talk when we played at USC one year. She was good, too. We won that day.

"Now Elvis...it's too bad he isn't still around. He would have really helped that program. They said he loved football. He would have donated some money to that program. They used to tell me he would pay players 50 dollars to come out to his house to play football with him. Can you imagine that?"

But even Elvis wouldn't have been able to cover Terry Glenn. While Stobart was in charge of all the receivers, he always paid special attention to Glenn on and off the field. "God, is he good," Stobart said as the receiver walked by. "He's a special player."

During practice at Pitt Stadium three hours later, Hollis gathered his offensive linemen for a lecture on Pitt's blitzing tendencies. "You have to watch for the delayed blitz," he said. "They'll come late. They'll give us a few things we haven't seen yet." Mike Jacobs jumped in. "Guys, this is a no-sack game," he said. "A no-sack game."

Following the light practice, Cooper had replayed the three-hour bus ride and the movie that went with it for a television reporter. "We had to watch 'Dumb and Dumber,'" he said. "All those kids have seen it three or four times. Have you seen it? It's crazy."

The next day, as players milled around the lobby waiting to load the bus for the two-mile trip to Pitt Stadium, a television set was tuned to the Notre Dame-Texas game. Lou Holtz's weathered face, propped up by a bulky neck brace, appeared on the screen. Recently released from the hospital, he would wear headphones and watch the game from the coaches' booth in the press box. "I haven't seen a game from the press box since I was at Ohio State in 1968," Holtz said as the Notre Dame game was about to start. "It was that Rose Bowl game against O.J. Simpson and USC."

Ironically, it was the game in which Ohio State last won a national title.

In the next few hours, the Buckeyes would play as if they were capable of winning another.

Harris had predicted the middle of the secondary would be wide open. And Glenn filled it all day, streaking past helpless Pitt defensive backs as if they were standing still. On the second possession, Glenn ran free down the middle on a post pattern and Hoying found him. He broke a tackle and then sprinted to the end zone for a 75-yard touchdown. Near the end of the first quarter, he made a spectacular diving catch in the end zone over the middle, and yet, after field goals of 24 and 39 yards by Josh Jackson, the Buckeyes led only 20-14 at halftime.

The Terry Glenn Show continued on the first possession of the second half, as he ran another post and found himself alone, catching a 36-yard touchdown pass. It was almost too easy. A few minutes later, on third-and-goal, Hoying threw to Sualua for another score and it was becoming a blowout. On the next possession, Glenn streaked down the right sideline as no defensive back paid attention to him. Hoying lofted a pass into his hands for a 61-yard touchdown. Now it was a blowout — 41-14 heading into the fourth quarter.

When it was over, Ohio State owned a 54-14 win and Glenn owned the biggest day for a receiver in school history. His 253 receiving yards had broken Gary Williams' school record set 14 years earlier. His four receiving touchdowns tied another school record.

Cooper made it clear to his team when they reached the locker room that finally, the time had arrived to think and talk about Notre Dame. "Good win," he started. "You are a good football team. Nobody can beat you, but you can beat yourselves. I think it's been 50 years since Ohio State played Notre Dame..."

Archie Griffin, noticing the mistake from the back of the locker room, whispered to someone next to him, "It's been 60, hasn't it?"

Cooper continued...."We are going to spend little time on this film. This game is over. I want no stupid comments about Notre Dame. Keep your mouth shut. I am telling you right now — that stadium is going to be rocking next Saturday. I'll tell you another thing — Coach Cooper is going to be ready. So you be ready!"

If there was any relief, other than escaping a road game with a 40-point win, it was being able to finally focus on the Fighting Irish. Cooper had told his players since camp that Notre Dame was a taboo topic. Now it had arrived. "Finally," he said on his postgame radio show. "Let's talk about Notre Dame." When he was told Notre Dame had beaten Texas 55-27, he said, "Well, obviously, they are on track now."

As Cooper walked the maze through Pitt Stadium to meet the media, Sports Information Director Steve Snapp brought him up to speed on Glenn's day statistically. "A school record?" Cooper asked. "Really?"

Once there, Cooper knew it would be a good time to boast a little. He had predicted repeatedly how Glenn would become a great receiver, while others had been skeptical. Now he could rub it in. "I've been telling you all year long — if he keeps playing his game like he's played so far, he'll make you forget about Joey Galloway. I think you finally saw what I've been talking about."

Glenn, who was as quiet and as shy as any player on the team, wasn't about to boast that he was better than Galloway. After all, a year ago Galloway had caught 44 passes and Glenn hardly played. "Joey is a great player, I don't think people will forget him," he said quietly, swarmed by reporters after the game.

Harris had been correct, though. Pitt's defensive backs played as if they were lost at times. The middle of the field was vacant for most of the day. At other times, they tried to play Glenn man-to-man, and with his excellent speed, nobody in college football could cover him without help. So Pitt's defensive backs surely wouldn't be able to do it. "We knew if they played man coverage like we had seen in film," Glenn said, "then I'd be wide open a lot."

Hoying, too, figured he would have a big day after seeing Pitt's defense on film. And he had. He had completed 15-of-24 passes for 296 yards and five touchdowns, which also tied a school record. Except hardly anyone noticed because of Glenn's gaudy statistics. Tommy Hoying and Stanley Jackson also threw touchdown passes in the fourth quarter, giving the team a school-record seven touchdown passes. They had totaled 636 yards — the most for an Ohio State team in nine years.

"We were aggressive from the start," Hoying said. "We saw some things there we knew we could exploit. It's a fun day when it's like that."

Cooper felt better about two aspects of his team that went unnoticed — the defense allowed only 264 yards, and Bartholomew averaged 41 yards in two punts. With the offense appearing unstoppable, things couldn't have looked better heading into the Notre Dame game.

Before Cooper finished giving his postgame interview, a reporter started to ask, "Woody used to regard Notre Dame as another Big Ten opponent, that type of big game when...."

The coach interrupted, "Woody never played Notre Dame."

"I know, that's why he never played Notre Dame. That was his logic," the reporter said.

"I shouldn't even be answering that question," Cooper said. "I don't know what Coach Hayes thought about Notre Dame."

By the time the busses were loaded, Andy Geiger, who had his two sons on the trip, nixed a movie that had too much violence. "See what else they got," he told John Cooper Jr., who went scurrying off to another bus. A minute later, the first bus began to pull away from the stadium when the coach's son came huffing and puffing up the steps. "Guess what I got?" he asked, smiling. "Rudy!"

When the irony sank in, everybody laughed. It was perfect — they would watch a movie about a Notre Dame fan-turned-player. As the caravan rolled across the Allegheny River on their way back to Ohio, the sun was setting and the Notre Dame fight song was blaring over the video monitors inside the bus.

A week from now, they would all hear it in person.

9

Two Traditions Come Together, Finally

The coaches arrived at the office earlier than normal for a Sunday morning. First, they had to arrive at some strategy for keeping the team's attention in the right direction. Media scrutiny and hype for the game would be enormous during the week, all potential factors for deviating the players' focus.

"We're going to have to get all over them this week," Joe Hollis said as they watched film of the dismantling of Pitt. "Notre Dame will be saying how great we are. They will be saying we're the best team they've ever seen and all that other crap. By the end of the week, our kids will be believing it."

Cooper predicted the week would feel like Michigan week. Only it would be much warmer. "There will be a lot more players looking at film, the coaches will spend longer hours in here, and the adrenaline will be flowing a little thicker," he said.

While the coaches went over the Pittsburgh film with the players later that afternoon, Cooper stopped after one kickoff coverage play in which Alonzo Shavers had made the tackle. Of course, he usually made the tackle for the kickoff coverage team, totaling four the day before. And he also scored his first touchdown, catching a seven-yard pass in the final minutes from Tommy Hoying. "Alonzo, I just want to tell you in front of everyone that you deserve a scholarship," he said. "So you got one." The team erupted in loud applause.

Shavers had become one of the team's most popular players, despite his differences from the other players. How was he different? Just his route to Ohio State for one thing. It made his one of the most intriguing backgrounds on the team.

Shavers had played high school football at Columbus Eastmoor, which also produced Archie Griffin, but he had only small-college scholarships to choose from when he graduated. He then joined the army, served in Panama during the U.S. invasion and also in the Persian Gulf. When he left the army, he still dreamed to play college football. So he walked on at Ohio State.

Here he was, a 25-year-old with a wife, a three-year-old son, a job as a shoe salesman and memories of getting fired upon while in Panama. He even paid for his tuition and books. He wasn't your average college football player. But after dodging bullets and collecting bodies as part of his patrol in Panama, dodging blockers on kickoff coverage was easy. His teammates called him "Pancho," and his coaches called him "The Rat" —

because as Cooper said, "He weaves downfield on kickoffs like a rat, and he always gets the cheese."

Now, a day after scoring his first collegiate touchdown, Alonzo Shavers had a full athletic scholarship.

"Now I can quit my job," he said. "Man, I can't tell you how happy I am. It seems everything is falling into place. Can it get any better?"

The next day, at 11:45 a.m., Cooper rushed out of his office wearing a black and scarlet warm-up suit. He hopped into his Cadillac and headed for the Quarterback Club luncheon at the Elephant Bar in north Columbus. He had been asked about Notre Dame for months, and this would be his first chance to talk about it without feeling guilty. "That's all anybody's wanted to talk about for months," Cooper said, heading up Olentangy River Road. "It was like they almost forgot we had to play three other games first."

The Quarterback Club was the usual stop on the coach's Monday schedule. "I don't get paid for it, so I let them know a long time ago that I don't want to come out here and take any crap," he said. "The first time I went there, they wanted to know 'Why didn't you do this, why did you do this?' I said, 'Hey guys, I don't want to come out here for nothing and hear all this second-guessing.' I just usually talk for 10 minutes and leave. Sometimes I eat lunch. I don't want to sit around and bullshit."

Especially during Notre Dame week.

"That's just the thing," he said. "People ask me how I can keep it as a normal week. Hey, it's not a normal week. It will be a normal week in practice, but let's face it — the hype, the tension, the attention — it's not a normal week. What's it been since we played them — 60 years?" He now had the years correct.

As he drove, he wondered how the game would affect the fans' affections. Would all Ohio State fans remain Ohio State fans come Saturday? The question itself seemed preposterous. Sure, Catholicism was one powerful force when it came to the Fighting Irish, but nothing would erase years of loyalty from Buckeye faithful, would it? "I don't know," Cooper said. "Some lady came up to me the other day at Pitt. She had an Ohio State shirt on and said, 'Coach, I am a big Ohio State fan, but next week, I don't know who to root for.' Notre Dame has the greatest following in the country. That's why this week, we will find out who our real fans are."

Cooper then shook his head, adding, "You know, that's why I hate to play Notre Dame. Somebody told me that's why Woody never scheduled them."

Many theories existed as to why Ohio State and Notre Dame hadn't played since 1936. It was as if two big bullies had lived on the same block for years, but somehow they never fought each other. They just beat up on everybody else and ignored each other. After all, these were two of college football's most traditional powers, perhaps the two most traditional powers. They had 12 Heisman Trophy winners between them. They combined for more than 10 national championships. The tradition they provided college football — Touchdown Jesus, The Horseshoe, The Four Horsemen, Script Ohio, Gold helmets, Silver helmets, Rockne, Hayes, Paul Horning, Archie Griffin, The Victory March, Across the Field — was deep and unparalleled. And the fact they were located in neighboring states made it more than coincidence.

The story goes that longtime Notre Dame Athletic Director Moose Krause had tried for years to convince former OSU Athletic Director Ed Weaver to get the two teams together. Each time, Weaver would go to Woody. Each time, the coach would say "Are you kidding? Hell no, we don't want to play them. Get out of here!" Some speculated that Hayes figured he could get a team fired up to play only two or three big games each season. And he had the world's best rivalry in Michigan already.

Therefore, Hayes' firing indirectly led to the matchup. Once he was gone, Notre Dame tried again and new OSU Athletic Director Rick Bay eventually agreed to a two-game contract to play the Irish. A game in Columbus in 1995 and a game in South Bend in 1996. "The fan inside me said 'That's a great game, go for it,'" Bay told the *Columbus Dispatch*. Bay agreed to the deal in 1987 when the current players were in junior high, Holtz was in his second season at Notre Dame and Cooper was at Arizona State.

Now Bay was the athletic director at San Diego State.

And Cooper was left to face Notre Dame.

If he had his way, the two teams wouldn't meet — especially considering that Ohio State had to gather itself and go play at Penn State a week later in a game that would determine the early front-runner for the Big Ten title. As Cooper drove to the luncheon, however, he felt fortunate that this wasn't a typical Notre Dame team. He had spent the previous day studying film of the Irish with his assistants, and he was confident he had the better team. After that shocking 17-15 loss to Northwestern, the Irish had rallied to beat Purdue 35-28 before destroying Vanderbilt 41-0 and Texas 55-27. From all indications they appeared to be improving, but films, however, never lied.

"Let me tell you — they aren't a great defensive team," Cooper said. "We will play much better defenses than this one, but I can't say that this week. Offensively, they are pretty good. They will come in here and try to run on us. I know that." He also knew he was in for a week of Lou Holtz's flattering rhetoric. Holtz had a history of publicly building up his opponents and tearing down his own team.

"Shoot," Cooper said, "he does that if they are playing Navy. You watch what he says about us this week."

Sure enough, Holtz must have been getting predictable. "This is the best Ohio State team John Cooper has had," Holtz said. "This may be the best Ohio State team since '68 when they won the national championship. I looked at the Pittsburgh film and told my assistants I was feeling worse and was staying home."

The hype for the game had grown like a monster on steroids despite Notre Dame's one loss. It actually began in Columbus in the spring with ticket scalpers asking $300 for end zone seats. Two on the 50 required a second mortgage, or at least a credit card with a large limit. Cooper and all the other coaches had allotted their tickets a long, long time ago. "Anybody and everybody who has ever done anything for me has called," Cooper said. "Some guy got me tickets to the Super Bowl last year, and I couldn't even pay him back."

Although he had never coached against Notre Dame in 33 years as a head coach and as an assistant, Cooper, while at Tulsa, had faced Holtz, who was at Arkansas, seven times without ever beating him. "We would bus down to Fayetteville, get our $150,000, get beat, give the kids a bucket of chicken, and bus home. Everybody in the athletic department was happy but me," he said. "He's a good, sound football coach. His teams never beat themselves. He'll show the twin set (two receivers to one side) and just try to run on you all day."

But where would Holtz be on game day? Would he follow doctors' advice and sit calmly in the press box, or coach from the sideline, where his players might take his presence as a little extra incentive? Holtz had hinted that although his neck still was too sore, the excitement of the game would probably lead him to the sideline. "I promise you — Lou Holtz is still coaching that team," Cooper said.

Cooper pulled into a parking spot reserved for him and walked into the luncheon. Businessmen stood and applauded. After he ate he summarized the game at Pitt, Notre Dame's personnel and answered questions. Former All-American fullback Pete Johnson raised his huge hand and stood. If Cooper thought current fullback Nicky Sualua was big, he had nothing on Johnson, who had to be pushing 350 pounds.

"Coach," Johnson said, "I got a question. In the third quarter Saturday, when you are up 34-7, just give the fullback the ball three times in a row. That's all I ask. Three times in a row."

"Pete," he said. "When we're up 34-7, I am going to call you down from the crowd and give it to *you* three times in a row. But I don't think you can carry it that many times."

The crowd roared as Johnson chuckled and took his seat.

"Coach, are you getting a feel of the historical significance of playing Notre Dame after 60 years?" someone asked.

"It will sink in, believe me," Cooper answered. "But what the hell? It's only Monday. I haven't even seen all their game films yet."

With that, he waved, shook a few hands and headed for the door. It was time to go back to work.

By Tuesday morning, several Notre Dame players had been quoted in newspapers saying the game "was just another game." That didn't sit well with many Buckeyes, including Cooper. When a reporter asked him about it at his media luncheon, he bristled. "It is not just another game," he said. "Not to our players and not to me. The conference is the most important thing, but it is stupid to say this is just another game. It is a big game. It was a big game the day it was scheduled."

Cooper then gave the Irish their own black board material, criticizing Big Ten teams' willingness to schedule Notre Dame. In recent years, the Irish had series with Michigan, Michigan State, Northwestern, Purdue and now a two-game series with Ohio State. "With the addition of Penn State to this league, why play another top-five or top-ten team in the country?" he said. "I'll go even a step further, and you guys will love this one — if I was the Big Ten (commissioner), I'd say, 'If you want to play us, come into the league.' Why play them?"

Writers scribbled away, realizing the quotes would ruffle some feathers in South Bend.

Ohio State's players surely didn't feel they were about to play just another game.

"In high school you dream about playing in games like this," linebacker Greg Bellisari said. "You don't want to go somewhere and play 10 games that don't mean anything. You want to play every game like it means everything."

On this day Bellisari actually mentioned that the winner still would be in the running for the national title. Not many of the players had publicly talked of such a goal, until now. "I start out like that from week one — I think national title," Bellisari said. "You ask Florida State and they start out from week one going for it."

Assistant coaches, especially Hollis and Harris, didn't want the significance of the game to weigh on certain players, however. Especially Bobby Hoying. Harris had preached to his quarterback about trying to remain ignorant of all the hype, ignoring the emotion of the game in order to execute the offense. Naturally, it would be easier said than done. "I've got to be calm and above all the emotion," Hoying said. "The stadium will be like the Washington game here two years ago and Michigan last year. Even Coach Cooper told us this is a game we will remember the rest of our lives."

The afternoon brought another poor practice, especially defensively. Coaches fretted and screamed and when it was over, Cooper gathered his troops in one end zone for another lecture: "When you look at the film of this practice, I am sure you will feel like I feel — that it was a horsecrap practice. We play like that on Saturday, and Notre Dame will run the ball right down our throats. We would have gotten beat 28-7 today. (Notre Dame tailback) Randy Kinder would have had a big day on you today. The fullback would have run over you."

The tongue-lashing finished, Cooper marched inside as the team moped off behind him. It had become clear to him that he also had to change his focus and spend more time with the defense, and less with the offense. "Probably," he said. "This week and next week. I am not happy with the way we are playing over there."

Not that Bill Young wasn't rightfully concerned, but he had seen teams practice poorly early in the week and then play well on Saturday. He headed off to the weight room to relieve a little stress. "Look at this body," he said, glancing down at his ample stomach. "You can tell I don't work out enough. But you got to do something, you know? At least I try to do something."

Figuring how to slow the Irish's running game was something. Stopping it was quite another. He, Cooper, linebackers coach Fred Pagac and everyone else knew that Holtz's game plan would be to run the football down the defense's throat. Then, just when the linebackers would creep toward the line of scrimmage, quarterback Ron Powlus would sneak in a play-action pass or two.

"That's Lou Holtz," Young said. "He usually is one step ahead of everybody else. I was looking at their film and on one play against Texas, that wheel route is open. So on the next play, they came back and hit it big. That's how good they are. My worst fear are the long drives. They had a 21-play drive against Texas. We are not good enough to sit back and wait."

Young had noticed that Powlus, when he dropped back, usually looked for wide receiver Derrick Mayes, especially in crucial situations. If the defense could take Mayes out of the game, that would make passing situations easier. And he had just the cornerback to do it. He would assign Shawn Springs to Mayes in man coverage at all times and play zone across the rest of the field. He wouldn't blitz much, except for an occasional blitz from the outside. That way, if Notre Dame ran the option, Ohio State would be in the perfect defense.

"These guys are good and yes, I expect a new thing or two from them," Young said. "But hey, they are not the Monsters of the Midway."

The next night after practice, Cooper wanted to get exactly that point across to his players. It was from his "don't-make-the-opponent-better-than-they-are" mode. "We should score and score and score on them," he told them. "Let me tell you, Notre Dame isn't that good. They aren't a great football team. We should kick their ass. But we can't beat ourselves."

The speech was quite a contrast to the lecture the day before, but it was appropriate for a Wednesday. Coaches would yell, scream and lecture on Tuesdays, encourage on Wednesdays and inspire on Thursdays. By Fridays, a quiet confidence mixed with anxiousness usually permeated the building.

Springs had plenty of confidence as the good cornerbacks do. Thirty minutes after practice, he walked out of the locker room without a shirt and headed for some Gatorade. The matchup with Mayes would be no big deal, he believed. At least that was the party line, and he was sticking to it. "It ain't no different than going against Terry or Buster in practice," he said. "Who am I going to face that's any better than Terry? Derrick Mayes doesn't have 4.2 speed. He's bigger, but he's not faster. I have no problems with big receivers. He's a big-time receiver, and I want to show the nation I can shut him down. I am going to eat him up, kill him. You watch."

During Thursday's practice, a day when the team works on the two-minute drill, other special situations and the kicking game, former quarterback Greg Frey watched Harris instruct Hoying on a finer point of reading a linebacker's movement. "Look at how Walt Harris communicates with Bobby," said Frey, who passed for 6,316 yards (second on the school's career list) as a three-year starter. "Wish I had played for a quarterback coach like that. He talks, then he listens. You can tell that this is a good coaching staff."

What transpired next was simply surreal. It was part corny, part tradition and part nostalgic. Once practice concluded, the school's band lined the field and proceeded to begin the famed Script Ohio march. This version was something never seen at Ohio Stadium, though. Players had joined in, grabbing instruments and marching along. Matt Finkes and Mike Vrabel beat on drums. Cooper marched along proudly with a trumpet to his lips.

"That was fun," Cooper said afterward. "We looked good out there, didn't we?"

As the players joked, danced and cavorted back to the locker room, an outsider wouldn't have known the Notre Dame game was less than 48 hours away. If anyone had a case of the nerves, it wasn't showing. The team acted as if it was on spring break at Daytona Beach. "That's the way our players are," Cooper said. "They're always pretty loose. That's the way I like it."

Cooper pulled a statistic out of Notre Dame's press release to use for his Thursday night address to the team: "Notre Dame has not given up a touchdown on a punt return or kickoff return in 108 games. Let's beat them in the kicking game. Here's another kicking guru. Let's beat the kicking guru. I predict we'll take a return for a touchdown." He then lectured them on hydrating their systems, since the temperature had reached the mid-80s all week, and it wasn't supposed to change for game day.

"(Purdue) Coach Colletto told me that (Notre Dame) really got tired as the game wore on," he said. "If we pound them and pound them, we will own them in the fourth quarter. I am told there will be 500 ex-Ohio State players in the tunnel before the game. Jim Stillwagon will be an honorary captain for us. Let's show them how good you are!"

Holtz, arriving with his own car and driver, beat his team to Ohio Stadium Friday afternoon for a scheduled walk-through on the field. It was his first sight of the stadium since the 1968 Ohio State-Michigan game. Holtz then was the secondary coach in his only season under Woody Hayes, and his favorite story of Hayes derived from that game. When the Buckeyes scored in the final minutes to take a 48-14 lead over Michigan, Hayes ordered a two-point conversion. It was successful. "I asked him later why he went for two points," Holtz said. "Woody said, 'Because they wouldn't let me go for three.'"

Twenty-seven years later, he had returned to the famed horseshoe.

Holtz, who grew up in East Liverpool, Ohio, probably would have returned much earlier had Ohio State officials offered the job to him in January, 1979, after Hayes was fired — rather than asking him to interview for the job. At that time Holtz coached at Arkansas. They also had taken the same approach with Indiana basketball coach Bob Knight, an OSU graduate, when Fred Taylor retired a few years earlier. Ohio State could have had Knight and Holtz, regarded by many as the best basketball coach and the best football coach in collegiate athletics.

When Holtz's players arrived 20 minutes later, they simply milled around on the grass and sweated in their suits and ties. It was unusually hot for Sept. 29. Holtz, neck brace and all, gave a few television interviews. "I never believed you got anything out of practicing at someone else's stadium before the game," he said. "The only thing you learn is where the showers are." As his team left and headed toward the Marriott in north Columbus, Holtz stopped to greet Archie Griffin near the visitor's locker room.

"Arch, let me ask you," Holtz said, "...you are planning this tunnel of former players tomorrow, right?" Griffin affirmed that a human tunnel of former Buckeyes would be in place as Ohio State would run onto the field. Holtz then said, "Well, can you let our team run through it, too?"

A few minutes later at the Woody Hayes Center, Cooper asked Tim May of the *Columbus Dispatch* about Notre Dame's appearance. "How were they all dressed? You know you aren't allowed to issue them coats and ties anymore. The NCAA did away with it."

May asked Cooper for his "gut feeling." The coach smiled.

"I am confident. But I always feel good before a game," he said. "Don't print that now, but you know I feel real good." Just then, ABC's Bob Griese and Keith Jackson arrived for their scheduled interview with Cooper.

A few doors away, Hollis sat by himself in darkness, chewing on a big cigar as he watched film of Notre Dame's blitzes. "Look at that hole, if we get that in two-back (formation), Eddie will be into the secondary like that," he said, snapping his fingers. "I think they are going to blitz us a lot. On early downs, they'll blitz us and play man. On third, they'll blitz us and play zone behind it. We've got to protect. We've got to protect."

Hollis pulled the cigar out of his mouth and turned off the VCR. "If we run like I think we will, and protect like I think we will," he said, "we will kick their ass."

10.

It Was Worth The Wait

Saturday, Sept. 30 brought bright sunshine and temperatures that reached 80 degrees. Thousands of fans were eating and drinking their way into a good mood outside Ohio Stadium by 11 a.m. — four and one-half hours before kickoff. Later, 85-year-old Allen Murray stood at his usual post in Section C6 on the upper deck at the closed end of the giant horseshoe. A black Ohio State cap covered his white hair. Through thick glasses, he gazed down at the lush green grass on the playing field as his mind, still sharp after all these years, drifted back six decades to the day a Notre Dame team last stepped on this field. It was 1935, his first season as a stadium attendant.

"Remember it like it was yesterday," Murray said. "Ohio State out-played Notre Dame in that game. Had a 13-0 lead, but Francis Schmidt took some of his good players out in that first half. Remember back then, if you took them out, you couldn't play them again until the next quarter. It was a dumb move." Even then, six years before Pearl Harbor, Ohio State coaches were being second-guessed. Some things never change. "Anyway, I remember these Notre Dame students still wanting to bet that they would win," he said. "They were waving around five-dollar bills. I would have bet any of them, but I just didn't have five dollars in my pocket back then."

As every Irish fan knows now, Notre Dame stormed back to win 18-13 that day in the "Game of the Century." When the media recounted the game over the previous few weeks, enough pain remained for many of the Ohio State players from that game that they refused to discuss the loss — 60 years later. Even Murray still felt some hurt. "We should have won that game," he said. "No doubt about it."

By 2 p.m., the first gold helmet appeared when a few of the Irish's special teams players milled around near the south end zone. Murray's eyes caught the sun's glare off the golden domers. "I didn't think it would ever happen again," he said. "Never thought I would see this day. Today will be different. Cooper's got a good offense now. I think we will beat Notre Dame today." He read two fans' tickets, directed them to their seats and turned to look down at the field again. "Yep," he smiled. "It's sure hard to believe it's been 60 years."

A few minutes later, Larry Romanoff, OSU's director of NCAA compliance, looked up at the goal post at the south end. "They aren't taking these down today," he said. "They're the kind that don't come down. You could put 100 people up there, and it wouldn't budge. Plus, they're greased. Hopefully, nobody will get hurt in the celebration."

Like the coaches and players, everybody at Ohio State was just *that* confident.

Fifty minutes before kickoff, as players from both sides warmed up, former Ohio State players were beginning to gather near the end zone. There were current NFL players like Cris Carter, Robert Smith and Korey Stringer. There were stars of the '60s such as Rex Kern and Jim Stillwagon and stars of the '70s — Rick Middleton, John Hicks and of course, Archie Griffin.

And there was a relatively unknown ex-player named Fred Crow, Jr.

Crow, 80, had stuck his left arm up to block Notre Dame's extra-point attempt to preserve the Buckeyes' 13-12 lead during the 1935 game. Problem was, Notre Dame's final touchdown wiped away Crow's potential hero-like status. "For a brief time," Crow said of the blocked kick, "I was on top of the athletic world." But that was not the end of Crow's story. When the rematch neared, his health was failing, so he had the following clause written into his living will: "If I die before the Ohio State-Notre Dame game, my left arm shall be cremated, and the ashes shall be spread in the south end zone of Ohio Stadium." It was in that end zone where Crow had blocked the Notre Dame kick. But now, it was where he watched the pregame festivities, fortunately, making the clause in his will insignificant.

Geiger stood in the end zone beaming as all the Buckeye lettermen gathered. He had that look in his eyes as if he wanted to strap on a helmet. "Could this day be any more perfect?" he asked. Geiger gazed out to midfield to John Cooper, shooting the breeze with the guy whose head was propped up like a Titleist on the first tee — Lou Holtz. To nobody's surprise, Holtz now planned to spend the day on the field rather than in the press box. Cooper had back surgery a few years earlier, and the two coaches were commiserating about and comparing their ailments.

Cooper and his staff were finally giving Geiger what he wanted to see, the athletic director said. He believed he saw a change since the massacre at Penn State late during the 1994 season. "I see more intensity, confidence and competence," Geiger said, adding that a post-season talk must have hit home with the coach. "I told him 'You're the man. Take control. Do the job, and I will be there for you.' He needed it. This is a very good staff, and they are doing the job now."

It was almost as if Geiger wondered what took Cooper so long to get the message. Why hadn't he coached this way in his previous seven years here? Had he changed? Did he work harder now? "I can't answer that," Geiger said, clapping as players ran by. "You have to ask John. But I like what I see."

Five minutes before kickoff, a human tunnel of approximately 500 former players began to take shape. Only a few, who now were in their 80s, ever got the chance to play Notre Dame. The eyes of several of the former players said it all. They were ready to change places with the current Buckeyes, if they could have shed a few pounds and stepped back into time. They would have just scrapped the tunnel, suited up and beaten Notre Dame right then and there — beer bellies and all.

"Man, there is nothing like this atmosphere," said Carter, who had become of the NFL's premier receivers. "Pro football can't compare to this."

Finally, Cooper and his team emerged from the locker room, sending the largest crowd in Ohio Stadium history — 95, 537 — into a frenzy. The coach had that intense stare in his eyes, similar to a hungry dog who hovered over a steak bone. It was the look he usually saved for game day. "Hey Cooper!" a fan yelled. "We take the field last! This is our stadium. Let Notre Dame come out first!"

A new NCAA rule, however, called for the home team to enter the field first. And the coach was ready now, rule or no rule. Nothing was holding him back. He took off running as more than 100 wild-eyed youngsters in scarlet jerseys followed. Suddenly, he caught his shoe on the edge of the track and tumbled head-first onto the grass. Players were running over him and for a second, it appeared the head coach was about to be trampled by his own team. Some former Buckeyes smiled and even broke into a sly chuckle when they realized that the coach had survived the first hit of the day unscathed. Finally, a player helped him to his feet and he limped mildly to the sideline. "I thought I was going to get trampled," he said. "Our team was ready to play. They ran over me. I am not as fast as I used to be."

Would it be an omen, or a "Win one for the Tripper?"

As the Buckeyes failed to convert a fourth-and-goal at Notre Dame's three-yard line, it appeared to be the former. Bobby Hoying overthrew a wide-open Ricky Dudley in the end zone. "You get out there on the field, and you see those (gold) helmets and it's Notre Dame," Hoying said later. "It was awesome. I think a couple of us were so keyed up for this game — I was a little off early and I think that is why." Bill Young's fears were beginning to be realized after Hoying's overthrow when Notre Dame's running game kicked in late in the first quarter. The Irish moved 95 yards for a field goal and then 61 yards which tailback Randy Kinder capped with a three-yard run. Notre Dame led 10-0 four minutes into the second quarter, the crowd was stunned and the "Victory March" was blaring away. Holtz was pacing, but happily pacing.

Hoying then underthrew George on a screen pass that was perfectly set up. It would have been a large gain. So much for Harris' desire to have Hoying approach this as just another game, but the coach knew his quarterback would settle down sooner or later. Finally, he threw short to Buster Tillman who broke into the clear for a 51-yard gain. Four plays later, he found Glenn for a 10-yard touchdown.

Notre Dame's offensive line, however, continued to blow Ohio State's defensive line off the ball. After another poor kickoff by Mike Malfatt, who slammed the ball out of bounds — giving the Irish the ball at their own 35 to start — Notre Dame did just what Young had expected. Kinder gained three, fullback Marc Edwards gained 12, Powlus then play-faked and lofted a pass to Edwards for 18 more. Kinder then carried four more times, and on the fourth, he started left, cut back right and jogged untouched into the end zone to complete a seven-yard run. It was Notre Dame 17, Ohio State 7.

Things were getting worse, too, when the team's best offensive lineman, tackle Orlando Pace, departed the game with an upset stomach. While he was vomiting in the locker room, finally and fortunately, Hoying settled down into a rhythm.

He changed a bad play at the line of scrimmage into a quarterback draw that gained eight yards on a crucial third-and-four at Notre Dame's 43. Later, on fourth-and-2 at the Irish 27, he threw underneath to Glenn for a first down. One play later, he fired a pass into the right corner of the end zone that appeared headed for nothing but open grass. Suddenly, Dimitrious Stanley twisted to his right, turned back to his left and caught the pass over his shoulder. It was the most important catch of the season so far, and probably the most difficult one to boot. Most importantly, it cut Notre Dame's lead to 17-14 at the half.

Although he was relieved since the late touchdown whittled the deficit to just three points, Cooper was furious in the locker room. So was Young. The head coach hurled his hat across the room. "It would be a damn shame to let this team beat you when they are not as good as you," he shouted. "It would be embarrassing. Now let's get out there and win this game!" Young's tirade wasn't quite printable. "A lot of F-words," one player said. "He let everybody have it. Just what we needed, actually."

Still, the old-fashioned tongue-lashings couldn't stop Notre Dame's running game alone, as the Irish put together one of their best drives of the season to start the second half, from their own 20-yard line to Ohio State's two in 16 plays. There, facing third-and-two, defensive end Mike Vrabel made one of the most important plays of the game. As Edwards took a handoff, Vrabel knifed a gap and stopped him for a two-yard loss, forcing Notre Dame to settle for a field goal and only a six-point lead.

After Hoying couldn't move the offense on the next series, Notre Dame started to self-destruct when Emmett Mosley fumbled Brent Bartholomew's punt at his own 19. Ohio State long-snapper Dean Kreuzer recovered.

Two plays later on third-and-six from the 15-yard line, Harris and Hollis agreed that tight end Ricky Dudley would be open over the middle for the first down. After he used his large frame to wall off a linebacker, and Hoying put the football right in his lap, Dudley wasn't satisfied with just the first down. He turned and pulled two tacklers into the end zone. Jackson's extra point gave Ohio State a 21-20 lead. Then the Derrick Mayes-Shawn Springs matchup got interesting. Powlus, on third down from his own 12, threw a perfect pass into Mayes' hands as Springs trailed the play. In Springs' defense, he had been responsible for an underneath coverage while safety Rob Kelly did not get to Mayes in time. The play gained 56 yards and invigorated the Irish. But two plays later, when Notre Dame was threatening, Springs jammed Mayes at the line of scrimmage, turned and sprinted to make a diving interception.

"I am faster than he is. I just felt if I could get a good jam on him, I could make the play," Springs said later. "When I jammed him, he kind of stopped, and I just played." Springs' father Ron, on the sidelines, had another perspective. "He was probably so mad at getting beat, that he wanted to make up for it," he said.

Glenn's speed then put a dagger in Notre Dame's collective heart. Facing a third-and-three from the OSU 18, Hoying threw short to Glenn, who turned and saw an open field. He sped past the safety and outran cornerback Allen Rossum — the Irish's fastest player and former Texas high-school sprint champion. By the time Glenn reached the end zone, the Buckeyes had control of the game. "As I was running," Glenn recounted, "I was looking at number 15 (Rossum) out of the corner of my eye, saying to myself 'Well, this guy is supposed to have run a 10.02 in the 100 meters. I wonder how fast he really is?' So I turned my jets on. I knew my teammates would get on me if he caught me."

On Notre Dame's next play, Powlus fumbled the snap and Matt Bonhaus recovered. George then ran five yards to make it 35-20, sending the largest crowd in Ohio State history into madness.

It had turned into another huge game for George, whose 61-yard run later put Notre Dame away for good. After his 32nd carry gained seven yards, Cooper called him to the sideline for good. The scoreboard flashed: "Eddie George, 32 attempts, 207 yards, 2 TDs" — prompting the crowd to chant again: "Eddie! Eddie!"

The locker room was bedlam after the 45-26 victory. University President E. Gordon Gee hugged Cooper. Archie Griffin high-fived Hoying. Walt Harris hugged Joe Hollis. Geiger slapped everyone on the back. "What a day!" Geiger kept saying. "What a day!"

Following the Lord's Prayer and a rousing edition of "Across the Field," Cooper's tired and strained voice got the players' attention: "You know how proud we are of you? Particularly you seniors? That's a game you will remember for the rest of your lives. You are the first Ohio State team to ever beat Notre Dame. Conditioning was a factor. You know all that hard work really paid off. But let me tell you one thing — this doesn't mean a damn thing if you don't go to Penn State and win next week! Now watch what you say this week. I don't want to hear any of you making comments about the revenge thing and how you are going to beat Penn State."

A voice bellowed out: "It's payback time!"

Cooper climbed the stairway in the locker room to talk on his postgame radio show. Next door, hundreds of members of the media awaited.

When Cooper finished the radio show, he told Sports Information Director Steve Snapp: "I need to go talk to these recruits right now. Send Eddie in (to the interview room)." The running back appeared and the media swarmed him. The tiny interview room in the bowels of Ohio Stadium was hotter and more crowded than ever since a record 560 credentials had been issued. It was the first time all day that George had little room to run. "The electricity in the stadium was unbelievable," George said. "It wasn't even like this last year for Michigan. We got down 10-0, but we didn't panic."

Ten minutes later, Cooper entered. "At Tulsa," he started, "Lou beat us seven years in a row. Today made up for it. That game seemed like it lasted a week. I really didn't feel like we had the game won until they punted with five minutes to go."

Nobody had scored more points against Notre Dame in the decade since Holtz became head coach. In the visitor's locker room, he told the media how impressed he was with the Buckeyes' offense. "I thought their offense was outstanding," he said. "They didn't have a penalty. They didn't have a turnover. They converted on third down. They played a great game"

It was just as Hollis and Cooper had wanted. They had felt all along that only the Buckeyes could beat the Buckeyes — by committing turnovers, penalties and mistakes. And the way it started, with Hoying a little off his game, they had to wonder. "(Hoying) was a little tight," Hollis said. "But the good thing about having a fifth-year senior at quarterback, he settled down and made some great plays. We never panicked."

Hollis finished talking to the media and headed back to the locker room, wiping the sweat off his forehead. He was always thinking of the next problem to overcome, and now was no different. "You know the national media is going to make our players 'all-world' this week," he said. "The good thing is I don't think it will be a problem. We'll just have to preach to them a little more."

Young was facing his own onslaught of reporters, who wanted to know what he could do to improve his defense, which gave up 447 yards and its third 100-yard rushing game to a running back in four games. Kinder had gained 143 yards on 28 carries.

"You got any suggestions?" Young asked. "If you do, we could use them. We were just trying to get them stopped. Our offense is strong enough that we just have to get them the ball. Our offense is outstanding. Just outstanding." Young walked out of the interview room, turning his attention to the next obstacle, Penn State. Having allowed an average of 353 yards per game, he now had to face the Nittany Lions and the rest of the Big Ten. "Well, the preseason's over," he said. "This is the real deal now."

Finally, after another 200-yard day, George was earning serious consideration in the Heisman Trophy race. He had rushed for 640 yards, six touchdowns and averaged almost six yards per carry in four games. "If he doesn't jump in the middle of that Heisman race now," Cooper said, "then I don't know what it takes." But George wasn't about to politick. Again, he downplayed his desire for the award, and reiterated he cared only about the team.

Two hours following the game, he and Raymont Harris walked into a sports bar/restaurant close to campus to eat some ribs and watch the evening's college games. Diners cheered. And as he tried to eat, he was hounded by autograph-seekers and picture-takers as Harris ate in virtual anonymity. Two years earlier, Harris was the starting tailback while George was an unknown second-stringer who was somewhat depressed over a lack of playing time. Now, each had to realize the ironic twist.

Some Buckeyes had waited 60 years to repay Notre Dame. Eddie George had waited two years to start, and another to become a full-fledged star.

"All we heard about all summer was Notre Dame, Notre Dame," George said. "It was worth the wait."

11.

The Big Ten Begins

Sunday morning, once the coaches returned to work to watch the Notre Dame film, Cooper leaned down to rub a small abrasion on his right knee. It was a souvenir that resulted from his nasty fall when the team took the field. He really had thought, just for a split second, that he would be trampled by his own players. Now that would have made embarrassing headlines, and it would have prevented him from enjoying one of the most gratifying wins of his 33-year coaching career.

"I enjoyed it last night," he said. "Believe me, I enjoyed it."

Obviously, it had been far from another lonely Saturday night. But the ecstasy wouldn't last, and he knew it. It never did. Like every coach, he chalked it up, enjoyed it for a few hours and looked forward to climbing the next hill. Or in this case, the next mountain. Despite the 4-0 start and a gradual rise seven spots in the polls since August to become the fifth-ranked team in the nation, the Buckeyes had not done one thing toward accomplishing their main goal: getting to the Rose Bowl. In another words, they hadn't yet played a game in the Big Ten. "We can't get tied up with the rankings and all that," Eddie George said. "Our goal is to be number one at the end of the season. There are too many challenges ahead of us. Notre Dame doesn't mean anything as far as the Big Ten goes."

Penn State, on the other hand, meant *everything*.

The Nittany Lions had almost cost Cooper his job the previous season, walloping the Buckeyes 63-14 in the school's most humiliating loss in the modern era and most likely ever. Now Ohio State had to return to Happy Valley again, because of a quirk in the Big Ten schedule.

Soon after the players had filed out of Ohio Stadium the previous day, Penn State had been upset 17-9 by Wisconsin at State College, Pa. The upcoming matchup, which naturally had been singled out before the season as a game that would be crucial in determining the Big Ten champion, appeared to pit two teams headed in opposite directions. Ohio State's coaches and players knew that another loss would knock the Nittany Lions out of the Rose Bowl race. "I don't think there is any way they can lose two games and go back to the Rose Bowl," Cooper said.

Nevertheless, the 19-point win over Notre Dame didn't mean there weren't many problems to correct. Obviously, everyone was pleased with the offense, which scored its 45 points in the final two and a half quarters. But nobody was satisfied with Ohio State's defense or special teams. Somebody, especially somebody in Lou Holtz's position, could have made a case that Notre Dame had self-destructed. "Believe me, we've got to play better defense against the tougher teams in the Big Ten," Cooper said. "Giving up more than six yards per play is not acceptable to me."

Cooper may have been convinced more than ever that this would be a season in which the team could win every game with a consistent, explosive offense. It was an offense of great balance — averaging 230 yards rushing and 297 passing so far. And it was an offense that could strike quickly as it did against Notre Dame or drive 99 yards as it did in the season's first game against Boston College. Hoying now was an experienced, consistent and accurate quarterback, not the erratic player he had been in the past. Perhaps he was playing better than any quarterback in the nation. Already, he had thrown for 12 touchdowns while the season school record was 19. He had been intercepted only three times. It seemed nobody could cover Terry Glenn and nobody could stop George, who averaged 160 yards per game. Tight end Ricky Dudley was improving rapidly, although he wasn't being used often enough. And left tackle Orlando Pace mashed anything that got in his way.

"The way we're playing offensively, we don't have to shut people out to win," Cooper said. "This might be one of those years where the offense has to carry the defense."

Bill Young didn't prefer it that way, but he wasn't stubborn, either. He realized the defense could take a more conservative approach and play softer. "Sure, having the offense we do affects what we do on defense," he said. "If we jump out to a 14- or 21-point lead, we are not going to be blitzing and giving up the big play. If we don't give up the big play, we are going to win the game."

Comparisons were beginning to surface between the team and Penn State's perfect 12-0 team of the year before. The Nittany Lions had not lost a game despite having nothing more than an average defense, because they were so perfectly balanced and basically unstoppable offensively. Each had a great quarterback (Hoying/Kerry Collins), a great tailback (George/Ki-Jana Carter), a great receiver (Glenn/Bobby Engram) and a talented tight end (Dudley/Kyle Brady).

Cooper also knew that the humbling loss to that Penn State team the previous year would be rehashed over and over again during the week. He had to just prepare for it, and perhaps use it to the team's advantage. "I really believe that game last year has nothing to do with this year," he said. "It was embarrassing, what else can I say?"

Not much. Neither could the players.

"I just tried to forget it," Hoying said. "When I think about my junior year at Ohio State, I will think about that game and how bad it was. Now is the time to remember how bad we felt."

At 4 p.m., Cooper and the coaches gathered the team for the usual Sunday review of the previous day. "Now let's look at this tape and then bury this thing," Cooper said. "It's over." Hollis, in his usual way of attempting to gain the team's focus, said, "Let's wait 'till the end of the year before we start saying how great we are."

The tape rolled and it took only one punt coverage play for the coaches to get the players' attention. Assistant coach Bill Conley's voice exploded, "Matt Finkes! You are watching the play. That's not your job — that's what 96,000 people are doing."

The transition from ecstasy to enjoyment to focus had been made. Notre Dame, finally, was history.

On Tuesday, Oct. 3, America was captivated by the news that the verdict in the O.J. Simpson trial would be announced at 1 p.m. Cooper, who tried to recruit Simpson to UCLA 30 years earlier but lost out to Southern Cal, had followed the trial closely through the television set in his upstairs office. He, for one, wouldn't miss seeing the verdict even if the governor himself had summoned him to the state house.

During the usual 7 a.m. meeting, it was naturally the topic of the day. When Hollis yawned and remarked, "I am just not sleeping very well. I was up at 3:30 and couldn't go back to sleep," Mike Jacobs replied, "You and O.J. Neither of you slept last night."

Hollis had a good reason — he and his wife learned their adoption application for a third son had been approved the night before. "Went home and celebrated," Hollis said. "It's a done deal." Everyone offered their congratulations as Hollis pulled out a box of huge, expensive cigars. "And," he said, "see what you get when you beat Notre Dame. You get all kinds of gifts."

Conley stuck his head in the door with more good news a few minutes later. The Buckeyes also learned of a family addition. "The big tight end from Hamilton committed last night," he said, referring to 6-foot-7, 250-pound Mike Gurr, who announced he would sign a letter of intent in February. The win over Notre Dame, played in a loud and festive atmosphere, had to impress dozens of recruits, the coaches figured. Perhaps Gurr was just the first of many who would commit to the Buckeyes in the next few weeks.

When it came to recruiting, Conley, who along with linebackers coach Fred Pagac had played at Ohio State, was the man. He coordinated the staff's efforts to attract players to the school. One part of his job, in addition to coaching the defensive ends, was to push the other assistants to make recruiting calls and coordinate visits. At times, it wasn't an enviable position since most assistant coaches despised recruiting. Travel was one reason. Another was constantly praising mostly immature 17- and 18-year-old kids who may wind up at Michigan because of reasons as concrete as the Wolverines' fight song or at Notre Dame because of the Irish's golden helmets.

Conley, however, didn't mind.

"The other guys sometimes resent him when he asks for their phone logs and asks them how many calls they made," Cooper said. "But that's his job. That's why I put him in charge of it all. He's good at it. Recruiting anymore is the lifeblood of a program. When I go to hire a new coach, I want a good recruiter more than a good coach."

Conley, a disciple of Woody Hayes, was one of the best. He, too, knew that the perfect start not only gained the attention of the fans — but more importantly — the attention of the nation's top high school players. "We're going to have a good year," he said of the staff's pursuit of 25 top players. "I can tell that already."

One of the successful tasks of the day's offensive meeting was decoding the hand gestures of Penn State's defensive backs, who signaled the coverage that the secondary used on each play. As in baseball, it was football's version of stealing signs — a common and perfectly legal practice. "They're not a real emotional group, are they?" Harris asked after watching a Penn State player make a tackle and walk motionless back to the huddle. "They'll be wired Saturday, you'll see," said Jacobs, who coached against the Nittany Lions several times while at West Virginia.

Penn State's Big Ten schedule had been a hot topic among the conference's coaches since the school was admitted two years earlier. For example, the Nittany Lions played the three toughest conference opponents — Wisconsin, Ohio State and Michigan — at home. In the previous two seasons, they had a week off before playing Ohio State and a week off before playing Michigan. "Don't you know?" Hollis joked as film of the Penn State loss to Wisconsin rolled. "Paterno's got it in his contract that he doesn't play any conference teams worth a shit unless it's at home."

"But *this* game surprised him."

The Badgers' 17-9 victory which ended Penn State's 20-game winning streak surprised a lot of people, including Cooper. "Well yeah, who wouldn't be shocked when they lose at home?" he asked. "That's a tough place to play." More importantly, it made the ensuing game crucial for Penn State. If Ohio State would win, one of the conference's big three would be eliminated, leaving only the Buckeyes and Michigan as heavy favorites for the Big Ten title.

Hollis asked Cooper, who had spent most of the two previous days with the defensive coaches watching film of Penn State's offense, if the Nittany Lions' offense was as good as Notre Dame's. "Shit no," Cooper said. "Notre Dame is darn good on offense. Penn State is good, but last year they were great."

While the Temple-Penn State tape, from which the Nittany Lions won 66-14, rolled, Hollis said, "Coach, this is the worst team we've seen in a long, long time." Cooper asked, "Who is that up there?" Told Temple, he said, "You know what's wrong with Temple? They tell me Bill Cosby was supposed to put all this money in the program, and then he never did it. They don't have any money."

It was the usual banter in between agreeing on plays to write into the game plan, organizing the practice schedule and making personnel decisions for the week. As usual, Cooper, who at times popped in and out of meeting rooms like a jack-in-the-box, provided the laughs and a lighthearted approach to preparing for the next game. He would joke about one thing, and then pontificate on another, providing his insight and perspective on any subject from fans to officiating to the American legal system to movies to politics. All the while, the assistants laughed, listened and were entertained.

"You know what I am going to do?" Cooper asked his offensive staff. "I am going to write the Mid-American Conference and tell them what a good job their officials did Saturday. Three penalties in the whole game, can you believe that?" Someone mentioned that Lou Holtz didn't have quite the same opinion, and asked if either team got away with holding infractions. "Shit, they held and we held all day," Cooper said. "They just let 'em play. I like it that way."

Cooper had placed a call to Rutgers Coach Doug Graber, who had engaged Paterno in a shouting match two weeks earlier. Penn State had thrown a late touchdown pass in a 59-35 win over Rutgers, infuriating Graber. It is common practice for coaches in college football to share information on teams they already have faced, in addition to watching film, and Cooper knew that Graber would want to assist anyone about to play Paterno's team. "I left a message with his secretary that we are playing his favorite team and I need to talk to him," Cooper said. "He'll be glad to help us. He doesn't think too much of ol' Joe."

Cooper had another small correction to make with his players this week. It was not a serious matter, unlike the defense and the kicking game, by any means. Nike officials had called to lodge a complaint. They were agitated that Ohio State players had been covering up their famed swoosh logo with tape during games, thus robbing the shoe company of advertising. It was just another small headache in being a head coach.

After viewing the Penn State tapes for two days, the coaches went through their self-scouting report, trying to discover tendencies of their own offense — if any existed. "On third and one-to-four (yards), we have 13 runs and 13 passes so far," Hollis said.

"Perfect," Chuck Stobart answered. "Perfect balance."

By 11:15, the coaches had agreed on several plays to successfully attack Penn State. "I am not impressed with their front seven at all," Harris said, adding that out routes would be open against Penn State's defense. "They will give us a lot of room in the secondary."

Hollis yawned again. "Man, these early days of the week are killers," he said. "Well, we could be at Mississippi State today. They've got to be licking their wounds after Northeast Louisiana beat them." Cooper's staff often discussed other college programs, realizing things were always worse somewhere else where the talent wasn't as rich, the facilities weren't as plush and where 96,000 fans didn't show up to watch them work on Saturday. Following a loss, when the week couldn't seem any longer, that was a consolation of the business. Someone, somewhere, was experiencing the same pain. But with a 4-0 record and No. 5 ranking, it was somewhere else than Columbus. Like where Harris and Jacobs came from.

"Just think Walt, you could still be with the Jets," Hollis said, chuckling about Harris' former employer, which was off to a 1-4 start and had lost 47-10 to Oakland two days earlier.

"And Mike's glad to be out of West Virginia," Stobart chimed in, referring to the Mountaineers' shocking loss to East Carolina over the weekend. "Yep," Hollis continued, "they were like rats jumping off a sinking ship."

Everyone laughed, feeling the daily high that came with winning.

Cooper headed out the door for his weekly media luncheon, at which he gave the usual array of radio and television interviews before listening to Paterno's press conference over the intercom. He had to wait until the Penn State coach finished so he could visit with the team's beat writers. Paterno was laying on the usual praise. "Ohio State is the best team we've played in three or four years," he said. Cooper smiled. He had heard the rhetoric before. Heck, he had just gone through it with the professor of Butter-Up-Your-Opponent-101 — Holtz.

The minutes ticked away, and Paterno continued to answer questions about the loss to Wisconsin. With each question, Cooper eyed his watch. At 12:50, he whispered into Sports Information Director Steve Snapp's ear: "I am going back to watch the verdict. Tell the writers to meet me at 1:30." Ten minutes later, he and two secretaries gathered in front of the television as O.J. Simpson entered the courtroom three time zones away in Los Angeles. "Just think," the coach said, "how many television sets around the world are tuned into this." Then came the words that stunned the nation: "Not guilty."

Cooper stared out the window at a steady rain. "Can you believe that?" he asked no one in particular. "Can you believe it?"

He hurried downstairs, and naturally, a reporter asked what he thought of the verdict. "No comment," he said, knowing it wouldn't be wise to get publicly involved one way or the other in such a volatile matter that had divided the nation racially. Cooper was no different than the majority of whites across the nation, according to several polls following the trial. He believed Simpson committed the crime. But whatever the head football coach at Ohio State said publicly would make news and Cooper had learned that lesson the hard way years earlier. Meanwhile, the assistants were holed up in their meeting rooms, oblivious to the news of the verdict.

A few minutes later, when the players headed into the locker room, Mike Vrabel shouted sarcastically, "Yeah, you can't beat the system, coach." Cooper laughed. "I am always telling them they can't beat the system," he said.

As Hollis had joked earlier in the day, others around the Big Ten believed Paterno had done just that. Big Ten coaches had griped privately about supposed concessions made to the Nittany Lions' during their first three years in the conference. The easier schedule had been undeniably obvious, but who was to blame? Having to travel to Happy Valley two years in a row was something that irked Cooper whenever he gave it a second's thought. And he had given it more than that.

"Papa Joe's got a great schedule," he told a few writers after practice. "I don't know how that came about." He often referred to Paterno as "Papa Joe" even though he was known as "Joe Pa." Bruce Hooley of the *Cleveland Plain-Dealer* asked him about it. "Papa Joe, Joe Papa, what is it?" Cooper asked back. "What do you call him?"

During one meeting early in the week, Hollis even asked Cooper, "Coach, I know you have no control over it, but gosh, how is it that we go over there two years in a row? You know this is the first year we've faced them that they aren't coming off an off week."

Apparently, scrutiny of the subject was wearing thin on Paterno, too, since he snapped when a writer brought it up during his weekly luncheon. "I resent it very much," he said. "Why are we playing Ohio State two years in a row here? Don't ask me, ask the Big Ten office. If anybody's got a problem with the schedule, that's their problem — not mine. There are lot of people shooting their mouth off that don't know what they are talking about."

Writers speculated that Paterno likely had been referring to Cooper, who mentioned the subject to the media during the Big Ten's preseason meetings. Thus, the two coaches would have plenty to discuss at their midfield, pregame meeting.

The scheduling controversy wasn't high on Young's list of concerns. He had to stop Penn State's offense, or at least slow it down, whether the game was played at Happy Valley, Columbus or Alaska. By Wednesday, he thought that he had discovered one wrinkle. He had noticed that Wisconsin rushed four defenders on one side of the field — usually the strong side. Not only did it limit the Nittany Lions' running game to 93 yards, it resulted in an effective pass rush on quarterback Wally Richardson. Richardson, who completed a school-record 33 passes against Wisconsin, was a first-year starter who wasn't about to beat a top team by himself. "It's a guessing game, but that's what football is," Young said. "If they adjust to it, we'll try sending four off the weak side. We just hope we guess right."

Young had to try something. The defense was having too much trouble stopping the run. His defensive line and linebackers were small by Big Ten standards. So far, nothing had worked consistently, although the team had faced two excellent offenses in Washington and Notre Dame. "We really aren't that far away," he said. "I don't want it to sound like we are panicking. You've got to remember — Notre Dame was very, very good on offense.

"But I still feel frustrated."

Perhaps the previous year's loss to Penn State was more embarrassing to Young than anyone. After all, it was his defense that gave up 33 first downs, 572 yards and nine touchdowns. Not to mention 63 mind-boggling points. By comparison to the current season, his defense had given up only 66 in the first four games. "All I'll say is that it was a long, long day," he said. "But it hurt me. I really feel I did an awful job. That's one of the great things about Coach Cooper. When we came home, he didn't want anyone to take the blame individually. We got humiliated as a staff and as a team. He just said, 'It's a team loss — let's go back to work and find the problems.'"

Now was the time for Cooper to retrieve some benefit from that loss.

The next night, he pulled out a prop to fire up his team during the usual Thursday night meeting. He held up a T-shirt, on which featured a drawing of a player in an Ohio State uniform giving water to a Penn State player. "This Ohio State player is a waterboy for Penn State," Cooper said. "Now they tell me this is the hottest-selling shirt over there. I am going to put it in the locker room and you look at it — not that you should need anything like that. Talk isn't going to get it done, is it? Let's just go over there, kick their ass and come back home."

12

We're Nobody's Waterboys

The night before the game, at Joe Paterno's weekly home game social, Andy Geiger sipped a glass of white wine and talked of how he felt more at home this season, his second in Columbus. "I really feel like this is more of my team this season," he said. "A year ago, I was feeling my way around. I had just been hired, and I was evaluating things. It was a learning process. Now I feel more involved with this team and with these coaches. And I hope it shows."

Nearby stood Paterno, being asked by a reporter about his blowup earlier in the week over the scheduling issue. "I guess I did get a little hot over it," he said. Now the winningest active coach in college football appeared as relaxed as possible, considering the importance of the next day's game.

Back at the State College Holiday Inn, Bobby Hoying received a message from Wisconsin quarterback Darrell Bevell, who had walked out of Beaver Stadium happy a week earlier. Following the team's dinner, Hoying, who struck up a friendship with Bevell at a Big Ten luncheon, returned the call to Madison — next week's destination. "His wife answered," Hoying said. "I wasn't prepared for that. He wished me good luck and told me to keep the (first-down) chains moving. He's a great guy."

The next morning, an hour before the noon kickoff, Geiger and Archie Griffin sat on the Ohio State bench as players trickled onto the field. Griffin appeared calm and relaxed. Geiger was a nervous wreck, sweating in the mid-70 degree heat and chatting in every direction. He darted from his seat to give a high-five to kicker Josh Jackson, who had wandered over before warming up. "Man," Griffin said of his boss, "Andy gets a little tight for these big ones. I think he's ready to play."

Ten minutes before kickoff, in the visitors' locker room at Beaver Stadium, everybody was bouncing off the walls. The intensity was unmistakable. Cooper paced. Young bellowed. Hollis instructed. Players listened, nodded and glared at the walls. Some linemen pounded their fists.

In one room, in his raspy voice, Young yelled, "We've got to stop that fullback. The first guy makes the tackle — the second guy goes for the football. We want some turnovers today! Don't worry about the last play. If you give up some yards, put it behind you and go on."

In another room, Hollis calmly gave his final words in his thick Alabama accent, "Eliminate pep rallies on defense. Take it to 'em. Wide receivers and tight ends, when you get an opportunity, start peppering the backside (defensive backs). You never know when your block might be the one that springs somebody for a touchdown. Finish blocks, guys. Finish blocks! Let it go. This is the reason why we are here. This is a big ballgame, a big ballgame. Have a little fun."

Strength coach Dave Kennedy, who kept track of the stadium clock before games, bellowed, "Five minutes! Five minutes!"

Cooper then taped the Penn State T-shirt to the chalkboard and called the entire team into the room. The Ohio State player on the shirt still was retrieving water for his Nittany Lion counterpart. "Look at it good!" Cooper screamed. "They think you are a bunch of waterboys! They think Ohio State is Penn State's waterboys!

"I don't know if you'll ever play a more meaningful game. I feel real good about our chances. We are the best football team. Let's give great effort on every play today. That's what it's going to take. Great effort will block a punt. Great effort will get you an interception. There's not a damn football team in the world that can outfight the Buckeyes for 60 minutes! Let's play some wild-eyed but poised football. We lost a ballgame here last year in the first half. That won't happen today. Carry the fight to them. It's time to separate the men from the boys."

The final sentence, coincidence or not, echoed the message on the T-shirt. Cooper stopped and pointed to it, dangling from the chalkboard like the helpless piece of cloth it was. "Doesn't that piss you off?" he asked. "It does me. I wish I was playing today!"

By now, he and that lifeless T-shirt had worked the entire team into a rage. Players pounded shoulder pads, rammed helmets, howled and screamed. As they gathered at the locker room door, with Cooper and captains Hoying, George and Matt Bonhaus at the front, their eyes were glazed as if they were hypnotized soldiers about to capture an enemy territory. "Controlled rage, y'all," George yelled. "Controlled rage." A voice yelled from the back: "F- Happy Valley." Hoying turned around to face the rest of the team and said, "This is our day! Our day!"

George smiled and replied, "You bet it is. Let's go. It's us against the world."

At least it seemed that way as they took the long walk to the field under the stadium. Behind barriers, Penn State fans were lined in unison, hollering obscenities along the way. And Cooper was their favorite target. "You have no chance Cooper! Go home now — save your embarrassment!" Seconds later, they were headed onto the field as most of the 96,655 fans booed.

The fans appeared prophetic as Penn State jumped to a 10-0 lead after George fumbled following a short reception. A taped lion's roar, part of the ambiance of Beaver Stadium, blasted out of the scoreboard and echoed off Buckeye ears. Fans dressed in blue and white celebrated and taunted. Paterno, his pants cuffed as usual, paced his trademark satisfied pace. He had his team ready. Was 1994 about to repeat itself all over again? How did Wisconsin come here and win just seven days earlier? Would the defense be able to slow Penn State's offense at all?

All these questions passed through the players' heads.

Hoying, for the third straight week, threw most of his early passes high. But he and Ohio State had one thing going for them — Terry Glenn's vertical leaping ability. He was catching everything Hoying threw his way. It was just a case of repeating all those highlight catches he had made in practice since the beginning of August camp. As Hoying threw high time and again on out patterns, Glenn made one leaping grab after another, dragging his toes to stay in bounds.

Walt Harris had predicted correctly once again. Penn State was giving the Buckeyes all the out routes, short and underneath routes they wanted.

Glenn's leaping grab on a crucial third down for 13 yards, spectacular diving reception for 33 more and routine catch on a 28-yard post pattern had cut the lead to 10-7. If ever a team had been ignited by one player, this was it. Glenn was running like Deion Sanders, catching like Jerry Rice and jumping like Michael Jordan. And by the time he threw the touchdown pass three minutes into the second quarter, Hoying had settled down as he had against Notre Dame. Later, he threw another beautiful pass over a linebacker's shoulder for a 25-yard score to Ricky Dudley, giving Ohio State a 14-10 halftime lead. It was Hoying's 10th consecutive completion to finish a brilliant half. He had completed 13-of-15 for 175 yards. Glenn had caught five of his passes for 97 yards.

Kennedy greeted the players as they entered the locker room: "Get some water, gentlemen, and change your T-shirts. Get on a dry shirt."

Hollis felt good about the final three possessions. A penalty stopped the offense on the first series and George's fumble stopped the second. What he saw was more than a receiver and quarterback playing their best. He realized now that his offense and its players possessed something he couldn't draw up on the blackboard.

"The protection was good. We are going to mix it up now," he told them. "We figured they would move to stop the running game. That's what they did. Let me tell you guys something — you got out of that hole because you have something we can't coach. You have chemistry. You are together. Everybody is pulling for everybody else. We can't teach that. God, that gives me chills."

Hollis wasn't just preaching inspirational rhetoric, either. The staff had been pleased every day since the previous season had ended at Orlando, Fla. They really believed that every player cared only about winning, not who got the credit for what. The players got along as well as 18- to 22-year-old men who work, eat, sleep, sweat and live together possibly could. Offense and defense. Black and white. Starters and scout team. "This team has great chemistry," Dudley had said before the game. "Everybody is great friends with everybody else. It's a special feeling."

This was one of those days when those intangibles were paying off. They had been behind in a hostile environment, and they had fought back. It wouldn't have happened in every game a year ago, when a few of the players who now played in the NFL had divided the team during the rough times. Later, Hollis would say, "You can't coach chemistry. You can't coach togetherness. You can't coach heart. We've got a few guys on this team who have been through it before, and they have got a few scars. And we've got some coaches who got a few scars."

Cooper wasn't about to let this game provide another one for his scar-riddled body. He walked into the offensive room and added his thoughts when Hollis finished. "They didn't stop us," he said. "We stopped ourselves a few times. But you are in better shape than they are. We are going to own the second half. We are getting the ball, so let's take it and score on the first drive."

Once Young, whose defense had allowed 128 rushing yards, went over his specific adjustments, he made a prediction to his players. "Guys, our offense will be on the field first. They are better than Penn State's defense. They are going to take the ball and score to make it 21-10, and then it's going to be lights out. We will knock their ass out! Thirty minutes! There's 30 minutes between us and a big win. How bad do you want it?"

When the entire team gathered at the locker room door, Cooper repeated what Young had told the defense as if the two had worn headsets into the locker room. "It's our half," he bellowed. "Let's go knock their ass out."

Bonhaus turned around before heading out the door and told his teammates, "Remember our goal. It's thirteen and oh."

Young was proven correct — the offense took the second-half kickoff and drove 80 yards to make it 21-10. Again, Hoying hooked up with Glenn, this time on a 37-yard touchdown in which Glenn beat the defensive back by about five steps. But it didn't happen without a little outside help. On the previous play, George had clearly fumbled. Yet, the side judge ruled he had been down before the fumble.

It was a rare break for a visiting team in Happy Valley. Midway through the third quarter, Shawn Springs limped badly to the sideline after a receiver had rolled up on his left ankle while making a block. On the next play, Ty Howard wobbled off the field with a concussion. In two plays, the two starting cornerbacks were injured. It didn't look promising.

Young hadn't been correct on what happened next. The Nittany Lions answered the touchdown drive with one of their own — capped by a one-yard run by fullback Jon Witman. Then quarterback Wally Richardson followed with an easy two-point conversion pass to cut the lead to 21-18. With 12:50 remaining in the game, on a third-and-11, Richardson scrambled to the right as linebacker Ryan Miller honed in on a blitz. He whirled and threw a high pass to the left sideline. It looked more like a punt. As the football finally fell to the field, All-American receiver Bobby Engram jumped and snatched it away from freshman Antoine Winfield, who had replaced Springs at the one-yard line. Witman scored on the next play, his third touchdown, giving Penn State a 25-21 lead.

Suddenly, Happy Valley was happy again for the home team. Paterno's players had not lost consecutive home games in three years and it didn't appear they would this time, either.

Ohio State's explosive offense had began to stutter. Hoying was sacked on third down to end one series. He then threw toward Glenn into double coverage and was intercepted. After the defense forced a punt, the offense moved to Penn State's 21 where it faced a fourth-and-one with only 5:15 remaining. Surely, George would get the ball. Instead, Hollis gambled. It was a chance he wouldn't have dared take in past years. But now he had a confident quarterback and an amazing receiver. Why not surprise Penn State and take advantage of the combination? He called for a short out route to Glenn. But Hoying threw high as he had early in the game. As Glenn's hands touched the ball, he was hit by cornerback Mark Tate. The football bounced off Glenn's hands and flopped to the ground. The opportunity was wasted.

But for the second straight time, Young's defense forced a punt after three plays. This time, with only 3:10 left, and Ohio State 58 yards from the end zone, it was do-or-die. The tension had peaked. Dudley popped a joke in the huddle, and a few players smiled. "That relaxed us," George would say later. Three plays later, Hoying made the throw of his life. He fired over the middle between two defensive backs and over the left shoulder of a linebacker. And Dudley, the towering tight end turned jokester, made the catch of his life. He cradled the pass, was rocked from both sides and came crashing to the grass with the football in his right hand.

Two great players had combined for one remarkable play and a 32-yard gain.

George ran left to the six and then, following a crushing block by Nicky Sualua on the next play, he galloped into the end zone around left end. Only 1:42 remained. Ohio State had a 28-25 lead.

Young gathered his defense on the sideline. "Listen, they need a touchdown," he screamed. "A field goal and a tie knocks them out of the Big Ten race. They won't even try one. They need a touchdown! They need a touchdown!"

The next two plays gave Penn State fans hope that they would score one. Richardson passed for 18 and then for 12 more. The Nittany Lions had a first down at Ohio State's 48-yard line and plenty of time.

Richardson threw poorly on first down. Freshman running back Curtis Enis — an Ohioan that spurned the Buckeyes' offer a year earlier and was now insulting them further by rushing for 146 yards — gained only three on second down. On third down nose guard Luke Fickell forced Richardson into a fumble. Richardson then picked up the loose ball, scrambled and was sacked by Matt Finkes for a loss of 12 yards. It was the first sack of the season for the All-Big Ten defensive end. On the next play, fourth-and-19, Richardson aimed high toward Engram, but the pass was tipped by Anthony Gwinn before falling harmlessly to the ground. Engram had slipped beyond Winfield on the play, but Richardson had underthrown him which prevented a disaster for Young and secondary coach Lovie Smith.

A minute later, Ohio State was throwing a celebration party right there in the heart of Happy Valley. The band blared "The Buckeye Battle Cry" as Penn State fans angrily scrambled for the parking lot. Cooper, talking to ABC's Lynn Swann, let everyone know how great it felt to beat "Papa Joe at his place."

Young shook his head as he walked off the field. "We lost containment on that last play. Boy were we lucky." Not that he would turn it down. The defense had stopped Penn State when it mattered most — on the final three series of the game. Their resilience not only helped win the most important game of the season so far, it had given Young and his players reason to believe the defense was coming around. "I think we realized it was a crossroads of our season," Mike Vrabel said. "We knew our offense wouldn't fail if we kept getting the ball back for them."

Once the hugging and high-fiving in the locker room wavered, Cooper told his team: "That was a real gut-check right there. That is what you work for all summer. Defense, those last three series — they went three-and-out — I am so proud of you. Let's stay focused and put this game into perspective. We have another big game next week."

Then it hit him. Cooper looked around, searching for his prop. "Hey, where's that T-shirt? Where's that T-shirt?" A player had already grabbed it to wear home.

Just then, the coaches from the press box entered the locker room. "What a throw! What a throw!" Harris screamed at Hoying, referring to the crucial pass to Dudley. Hoying, who completed a career-high 24 passes in 35 attempts for another career-high 354 yards, jumped into his arms and then held his hands about a foot apart. "There was this much of a lane there," he said.

Outside, Hoying's father, Vern, awaited his two sons. "They don't come any sweeter than that," he said.

"It's the best football game I've played in," Bobby said. "Coming off the field, that's the best feeling I've had playing football."

Cooper headed to speak on his post-game radio show, when he addressed the rivalry with Paterno. Two years earlier, following a 24-6 win over Penn State at Ohio Stadium, University President E. Gordon Gee had told reporters that Cooper "out-coached Joe Paterno." This time, Cooper was gracious. "I didn't out-coach Joe Paterno," he said. "Bobby Hoying, Terry Glenn and Eddie George made plays. I didn't beat Joe Paterno. They beat Joe Paterno's players."

Still, Cooper hated the term "hands-off coach," which some people around Ohio State had tagged him. This day, he did his share of coaching. "I don't want to brag, but I can see what they're doing on the field and what they're not doing like this," he said, snapping his fingers. "But I still get called a 'hands-off' coach."

As players and coaches gathered around the busses before heading to the airport, Harris was happy for the entire staff and team naturally, but especially happy for his prized pupil. Hoying had been booed and ridiculed by fans in the past two years, and now he ranked second nationally in passing efficiency. For the first time, he had brought his team from behind in a crucial game facing hostile circumstances. "He's the best quarterback in the league," Cooper said. "I've been saying that all long. It's time people start believing it."

The other usual stars had big days too — George rushed for 105 yards, Glenn had nine catches for 175 yards and Dudley had his best game yet — five catches for 97 yards.

Suddenly, the team heard some shocking news: Northwestern had upset Michigan 19-13 in Ann Arbor. Now only Ohio State, Northwestern and Wisconsin were unbeaten in the Big Ten.

"It's good news," Cooper said. "Anytime Michigan loses, it's a great day for us."

It already had been a great day for the Buckeyes. They had earned revenge from that 63-14 pasting a year ago. They were about to depart Happy Valley happy for the first time. They had won all five games, beaten four ranked teams and had given notice that they were genuine national championship contenders for the first time in 16 years.

And, in some silly way, they had proven that they were nobody's waterboys.

John Cooper once joked that someone should take "before" and "after" photos of him to illustrate the pressures of coaching at Ohio State. Here it is. At left, Cooper in his first season of 1988, and below, before the 1995 season *(OSU Sports Information)*.

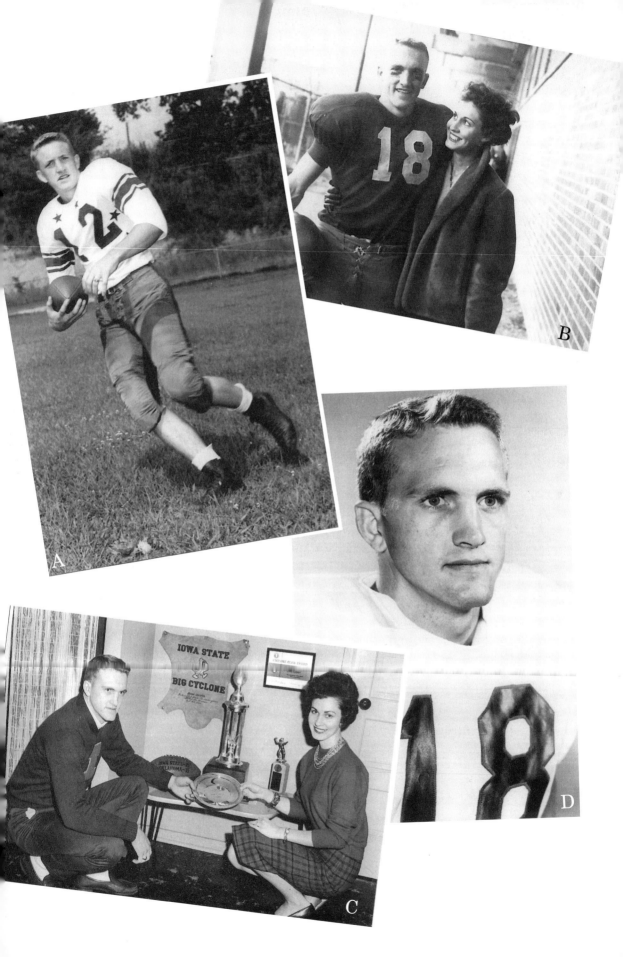

John Harold Cooper through the years. (A) While at Powell (Tenn.) High wearing number 12; (B) Sharing a hug with the love of his life, Helen, while at Iowa State; (C) The Coopers in their Ames, Iowa, apartment; (D) His official photo as a member of the "Dirty Thirty" at Iowa State; (E) His first year at Arizona State (1985); (F) With a pompom stuck in his back pocket during the 22-15 victory over Michigan in the 1987 Rose Bowl; (G) The Cooper family today — John Jr., Helen, John and Cindy *(photos courtesy of Helen Cooper)*.

The offensive meeting room. From top (clockwise), offensive coordinator Joe Hollis, receivers coach Chuck Stobart, quarterbacks coach Walt Harris, tackles/tight ends coach Mike Jacobs (back to camera) and running backs coach Tim Spencer *(Photo by Patrick Wells)*.

The defensive staff hard at work in defensive coordinator Bill Young's office. From left to right, secondary coach Lovie Smith, graduate assistant Dustin Calhoun, defensive ends coach Bill Conley and Young *(photo by Patrick Wells)*. *inset:* linebackers coach Fred Pagac *(OSU Sports Information)*.

From the start, Bobby Hoying's improvement under first-year quarterbacks coach Walt Harris was obvious. He led the nation in passing efficiency until the last week of November *(OSU Sports Information)*.

Cornerback Shawn Springs became one of the best defensive backs in the nation in 1995. He started the season by returning a kickoff 97 yards for a touchdown in the Kickoff Classic. Here, he returns an interception *(OSU Sports Information)*.

left: The surprise of the season was receiver Terry Glenn, who caught almost everything thrown his way, often broke away for a touchdown and became an All-American in the process. Here, Glenn's humble beginnings, wearing a walk-on-like number 55 as a freshman *(OSU Sports Information)*.

below: Quarterback Bobby Hoying scrambles for eight crucial yards for a first down in the second quarter against Notre Dame. Five plays later, Hoying threw 17 yards to Dimitrious Stanley to cut the Irish's lead to 17-14. The Buckeyes would win the much-anticipated game 45-26 *(photo by Patrick Wells)*.

After Notre Dame had scored to cut the lead to 35-26, Eddie George put the Irish away with this 61-yard run and his second touchdown of the day two plays later *(photo by Mark Hall)*.

John Cooper on the sidelines
making a point to an official
(photo by Patrick Wells).

Working the phone from
his office at the Woody
Hayes Athletic Center
(photos by Patrick Wells).

Greg Bellisari, Ohio State's leading tackler, looks to the sideline for a signal during the 28-25 come-from-behind win at Penn State. The defense held the Nittany Lions to only two first downs in their final three possessions *(OSU Sports Information)*.

Left guard Jamie Sumner blocks during a passing play at Penn State. The Buckeyes got revenge for a 63-14 loss a year earlier at Happy Valley *(OSU Sports Information)*.

Terry Glenn avoids a tackle during the 28-0 win over Purdue. Two weeks later, Glenn came crashing down on his right shoulder at Minnesota, an injury that would force him to miss the Illinois game *(OSU Sports Information)*.

Orlando Pace, a man among boys. The Buckeyes' left tackle, only a sophomore, was simply dominating throughout the season. On Dec. 7, he won the prestigious Lombardi Award *(OSU Sports Information)*.

Tight end Ricky Dudley, here looking for extra yards in the rout of Iowa, often proved to be a mismatch for smaller linebackers. His biggest catch of the season came during the winning drive at Penn State *(OSU Sports Information)*.

Record-setting running back Eddie George sees daylight against Iowa. George surpassed 200 yards against Washington and Notre Dame and set a school record with 314 rushing yards in the 41-3 victory over Illinois. For his efforts, OSU fans had him penciled in for the Heisman Trophy. On Dec. 9, it became reality in New York when he joined Archie Griffin, Howard "Hopalong" Cassady, Vic Janowicz and the late Les Horvath as OSU Heisman winners (*OSU Sports Information and Patrick Wells*).

Ohio State's bookend defensive ends. *below:* Mike Vrabel (94) was named to several All-American teams. *left:* Matt Finkes (92) started slowly but played better during the second half of the season (OSU Sports Information).

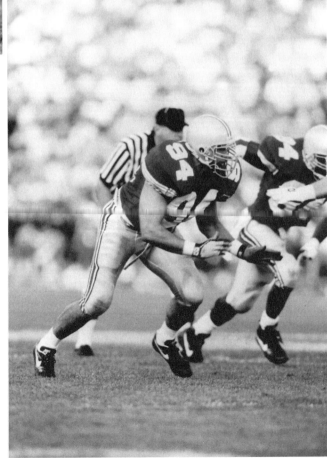

Quarterback Bobby Hoying reaches new heights thanks to tight end Ricky Dudley. Hoying had just scrambled for a touchdown as Ohio State built a 56-0 lead over Iowa *(photo by Patrick Wells)*.

The Buckeyes' recruiting master, Bill Conley. As the season progressed and the Buckeyes continued to roll, it became obvious that Ohio State was headed to one of its best recruiting classes ever *(photo by Patrick Wells)*.

John Cooper watches a fan get away with his hat following the 42-3 win over Indiana that pushed the Buckeyes' record to 11-0 for only the third time in school history. A team manager later chased down the culprit and recovered the hat *(photos by Patrick Wells)*.

Joe Hollis' season mirrored that of the team's. For 11 games his offense had been nearly unstoppable. In the two losses, he was left searching for answers *(photo by Patrick Wells)*.

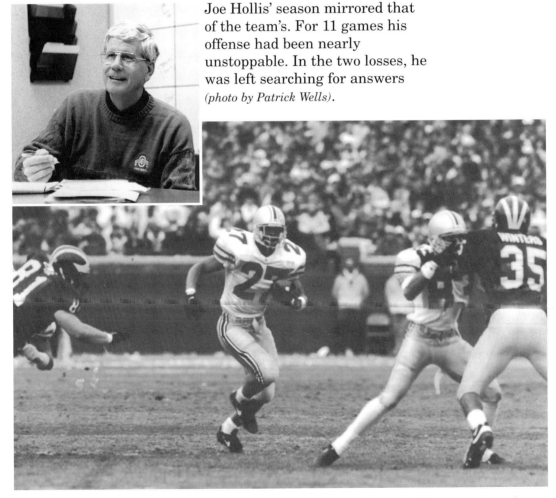

Eddie George finds one of the few holes on the darkest day of the season — the 31-23 loss at Michigan. George would rush for 104 yards but was overshadowed by Tim Biakabutuka *(photo by Patrick Wells)*.

13.

Six Yards and a Turf Burn

Sunday morning, Cooper's secretary, Julie Bonfini, called in his ballot for the coach's top-25 poll as usual. There was one change. He had elevated his team to number one for the first time. When *Columbus Dispatch* beat writer Tim May asked him where he had ranked his team, Cooper answered with a smile, "I can't tell you that. You know I am not going to tell you."

The exchange had become a running joke between the two. Each week, May would ask. Each week, Cooper wouldn't answer. Now that his team had beaten four ranked teams in five games, and had redeemed themselves from the personal hell of a year ago, he felt his Buckeyes were ready for the highest ranking possible. He just wondered why more coaches and writers weren't agreeing with him. They had Florida State ranked No. 1.

Perhaps his team was just that good. One thing was certain — no team had played a tougher schedule so far and survived unscathed. Anyway, for whatever it was worth, they had climbed to No. 4 in the polls and people around the nation were beginning to take them seriously. "We realize we're just getting started in the Big Ten, with the ultimate goal the Rose Bowl," Bobby Hoying said. "But we're pleased with the national attention." There was, however, a downside to too much attention.

Most of the assistant coaches believed it could distract certain players, or at least make them big-headed. Terry Glenn, for one, wasn't ready to handle it, not that he was becoming overconfident. He had almost single-handedly carried the team with one amazing catch after another in the second quarter when they trailed 10-0. Now he was among the nation's leaders with 32 receptions for 752 yards and nine touchdowns after just five games. It was the best start by any receiver in school history and suddenly, it seemed everybody wanted a piece of him.

For a guy who went virtually unnoticed his entire career until September, it resulted in too much media attention too soon. "Terry came to us the other day and said he can't handle the attention," Cooper said. "He wants to get out of all these interviews. You've got to admire that. He's getting bombarded from all sides — the media, agents, pimps. He's an amazing story, he really is. He's a good kid, but he could cross the line and go back to the way he was at any moment. You ought to see where he came from."

Other kids on the team had come from poor backgrounds. Others had come from broken homes. And others had been poor students. But nobody, probably nobody in the history of Ohio State football, had come further than Terrence Tyree Glenn.

His mother had been murdered when he was 13 years old, leaving he and his sister Dorothy, six years younger, virtually homeless. He didn't know his father. "At one time, he didn't even have a place go home to and eat," Cooper said. After bouncing around living with aunts and uncles, Terry and his sister moved in with the family of a high school teammate. Charles "June" Henley's family became his family. "They became great parents to me," Glenn said. "They taught me discipline and loved me like their own." There he stayed until arriving at Ohio State as a walk-on, but not a typical walk-on. "No, we knew Terry could play, could really play," Cooper said. But Glenn's grades had been poor, so Cooper told him he had to earn a scholarship by improving his grades. Meanwhile, he was redshirted, improved his grades and waited two years behind Chris Sanders and Joey Galloway, each on their way to becoming NFL stars.

Entering the season, Glenn had never scored a touchdown and had never started a game. Now he was making catches even Galloway never made. In five games he had become a star and everyone — fans, coaches, media and NFL scouts — watched his every move.

"It's been unbelievable," he said. "Every night I lay awake and wonder — 'Is this really happening or is it a dream?'"

Cooper came jogging to the sideline as the week's practices to prepare for Wisconsin began Tuesday with special team drills. "Coach Conley thinks we can block a punt this week," he said. "We could use one. They've had two blocked already this season. But then they've had a week off to correct their problems and get people healthy. Wish we had a week off."

With the injuries mounting, it would have been a perfect week to ease off during practices, let the injuries heal and recover for what would be another physical game. In years past, it seemed more players visited the whirlpools following the Wisconsin game, win or lose. The Badgers, 2-1-1 with an impressive win at Penn State on their resume, usually were very physical.

Shawn Springs limped around wearing a yellow jersey — the color of the walking wounded. Fellow cornerback Ty Howard also wore yellow, a result of a concussion. So did safety Rob Kelly, who had a sore shoulder. But the injury to Springs, by far the team's best cover cornerback, was the most serious. "I still think he's going to play," Bill Young said. "You know why? Because he's a tough kid. If he can play, I have no doubts he will."

This was one game in which Young badly needed Springs healthy because of his plans. He wanted to blitz the middle often and play man-to-man coverage with the cornerbacks. But with Springs hobbling and Howard counting fingers after the Penn State game, that would be risky. "We got another wrinkle for them," Young said. "I am going to move (Matt) Finkes inside and put him over the right guard. Then we'll put Jeff Wilson at end."

In the scheme the two All-Big Ten ends, Finkes and Vrabel, would line up next to each other. For some reason, the defensive line had not provided the consistent pass rush it had the previous season. Vrabel had set a school record with 12 sacks and Finkes had 11 in 1994. After five games, Vrabel had just two and Finkes had only one, the sack of Richardson in the final minutes at Penn State. "I don't know," Vrabel said. "I can't tell you or explain it, but I'll be the first to tell you that the sacks aren't there this year."

On Tuesday, as Young stared at film of Wisconsin's offense against Penn State, he repeated, "We must stop them on third down, we *must* stop them on third down. Third down is the key. Third down is the key." Wisconsin had the type of offense that rarely struck quickly. The Badgers usually lulled the defense to sleep with a good, methodical running game and short, dink passes on third down. Just as Bevell threw a short pass on third-and-four that turned into a 28-yard gain on his office screen, Young groaned. "Look at that! Look at that!" he shouted. "That's what they love to do. They want to win on third-and-short. They just kicked Penn State's butt on third down. We must stop them on third down."

None of Ohio State's defensive coaches had been impressed with Bevell's skills. Bevell was a great leader and had been somewhere they hadn't — the Rose Bowl — but he wasn't a quarterback who put fear into a defensive coordinator. Young figured a few well-disguised blitzes would bother him, and he would become confused. If the defense could stop the Badgers' running game, or at least slow it down, Bevell wouldn't be able to beat them alone, he figured.

But so far during the season, his hopes and plans weren't working out exactly the way he had wanted, even though the team was undefeated. "You just have to keep searching," he said. "Keep searching and keep working."

———————◆◆◆———————

Wednesday night, Hollis and Young filled in for Cooper and spoke at the bi-weekly booster meeting. The coaches didn't mind the chore, since it was across the hall from their offices. The two coordinators summarized the first five games, the players, Wisconsin and then answered questions. One fan asked Young about the lack of pressure on opposing quarterbacks. "I could give you a bunch of reasons, but they will sound like excuses," he said.

While Hollis and Young held court, Harris watched film of quarterback recruits in his office. "There supposedly are all these great quarterbacks out there," he said. "I am not sure I like any of them that I have seen."

Harris had to think ahead. From the seven months he had been on campus, he didn't figure backups Stanley Jackson, Tommy Hoying and junior-college transfer Joe Germaine would be ready to play consistently by 1996. The coaches had to sign at least one top high school quarterback, perhaps two, and maybe a junior-college transfer, also. Harris' NFL experience had to help lure top quarterback recruits, Cooper figured. But for now, Harris had a star pupil in Bobby Hoying, and he did everything he could to surround him with positive feedback. If anyone criticized an Ohio State quarterback, Harris took it personally. "You have to understand that the guy wasn't treated too well by fans here in the past," he said. "He's had a rough career, and he's a very sensitive young man. That's why I want to protect him. I want the only criticism of him coming from me — in private."

If any coach on the staff was aware of fans, media or outsiders at practice, it was Harris. He may not have been paranoid, but he was close. He constantly noticed who watched practice. And because Cooper liked to keep his practices open to the media and the public, it was a tougher chore than he was used to. "A lot of my coaches want practices closed," Cooper said. "But when they become head coaches, they can do it their way."

But what was to criticize? Hoying had been nearly perfect, completing 66.2 percent of his passes for 1,383 yards and 15 touchdowns — against only four interceptions. He was off to the best passing start of any quarterback in school history.

Harris and Hollis figured that he would be the key again Saturday, since it appeared Wisconsin's defense would try to take away Ohio State's running game. "We've got to loosen them up throwing," Hollis said. "I think their secondary is their weakest link." The question was, would the weather at Madison, Wis., — usually cold and windy by mid-October — allow such a game plan to be executed?

By Thursday, Springs' ankle was improving. At least he wasn't limping as noticeably. Trainer Bill Davis, promoted when longtime trainer Billy Hill died of a heart attack in the off-season, said the treatment was working. "Ice, then heat, then all kinds of other stuff you wouldn't understand," Davis said to a reporter. "It's getting better."

After catching a few passes when practice began, Springs walked over to the sideline to Davis. "Now listen, Shawn," Davis began. "Get in there after practice for more treatment. We'll go with some more ice, and then you need to stay off of it. You got 48 hours, but I think you'll be OK."

Springs grimaced. He planted his left foot and then cut to his left in a demonstration. "It just hurts when I cut like that," he said, jogging away slowly. "He's such a good kid," Davis said. "That turf up there isn't going to help any, but I don't want to say anything to him or he will be thinking about it. No use putting that in his mind right now."

Following practice, Cooper reminded his team what the Badgers had done, and where they had been. It was an accomplishment and a destination that none of his players had experienced. "These guys have been to the Rose Bowl," he said. "You haven't, have you? Not one player in this room has been to the Rose Bowl.

"I don't want to hear any excuses this week — how tough that place is to play, the officiating, the weather, nothing. I want us to play better defense. I want us to play our best defensive game yet. I don't think they are as good offensively. Their offensive line isn't as good. Their running back isn't as good. I respect their quarterback, but we can't let him dink the ball all day. That's what he does. We should go up there and kick their ass."

Moments later, Hollis lectured the offense as he did each Thursday night. He preferred to address the big picture, much the way a head coach would, rather than specifics. After all, he was the head coach of the offense. "They don't score a lot of points," he said. "We want to control the ball by running and throwing. They sure don't score a lot of points when they are over there on the bench. If we are not concerned who gets the credit, good things will happen. Let's have fun, but remember, fun is winning."

One Buckeye wouldn't have any fun Saturday. Mike Malfatt, who handled kickoffs, would not make the trip after he was caught drinking in a campus bar. Since many of the players drank beer, what was the big deal? Malfatt was under 21.

"I am not taking his scholarship away," Cooper said. "But he is suspended for a game."

By Saturday morning, the temperature had dropped into the 40s and the wind was blowing hard, exactly what Wisconsin would have wanted to play havoc with the Buckeyes' vertical passing game. Hollis didn't want to hear any nonsense about the conditions. "We are not going to let any of it affect our play-calling," he said after the team's ritual morning walk on game days.

On the other hand, Bevell preferred to throw short so there was no denying the conditions were to Wisconsin's advantage.

Eddie George must have sensed something unusual from his teammates, because he gave them a short, motivational speech during the pregame meal. "I want us to come out steaming," George said. "Take no prisoners. Last week is over."

In the coffee shop of the Madison Sheraton, Archie Griffin was worried, too. As he devoured eggs and biscuits covered with sausage gravy, he couldn't help but think of OSU's recent history in this town — a 2-4-1 record since 1980. "Wisconsin is ready for us," he said. "They've had a week off to prepare for us, and they got things in their favor. And I've never been here when it wasn't cold and windy. We never seem to get a break up here with the weather."

Team doctor John Lombardo, watching Griffin eat the high-cholesterol breakfast, wasn't as much concerned about the Badgers at the moment. "Arch," he said, "who's your doctor?"

While the conditions would take away the offense's advantage, Young didn't mind. He knew he could play more man-to-man coverage and force Bevell to try to throw long. An hour before the game, when he walked out of the locker room to check the conditions, he said, "We might tighten up on their receivers now knowing that he won't want to go deep. His ball will flutter in that wind."

Cooper walked out of the locker room when someone happened to ask, "Are you ready?"

"Am I ready?" he answered. "Are you kidding? I am always ready. I've never seen a team yet that I didn't think was ready to play. It's a matter of who makes the plays and who doesn't. Ask these guys today if they want to win, and they all are going to jump up and say 'Yes.' But what did they do to prepare to win during the week? That's the key."

Andy Geiger was ready. And tense. In the cold, concrete hallway outside the locker room, he whispered into Fred Pagac's ear, "You guys are going to play a good one today. I can feel it." Of course, that was how he felt before every game.

Minutes later, Hollis gave the offense final instructions: "We are going to mix it up now. All you have to do is execute. We've put ourselves in a great situation. We've got a great plan. We are competing against ourselves, not Wisconsin. If we don't beat ourselves, they are not going to beat us. Let's have some fun."

Cooper's pregame speech made it obvious that he wanted to take a blue-collar approach in this game. Wisconsin, known in Big Ten circles as a physical team each year, would try to run right at the defense. "Let's turn this game into a hitting contest," he started. "Let's dominate the line of scrimmage. Their offensive line isn't as good as a year ago. The team that makes the fewest mistakes wins the game. If they leave the ball on the ground, put it in the end zone. If you get an oskie (interception), put it in the end zone. The kicking game will be a big factor with the wind. Let's win the kicking game. Carry the fight to 'em. Find a way to win. I told (ABC analyst) Dick Vermeil last night that I thought we had an excellent football team. Everybody else is wondering how good you are. Let's go get it done and get out of here!"

What followed was the team's worst display of offensive football since that infamous 63-14 pounding from Penn State a year earlier.

On the first possession, Ricky Dudley held the football away from his body and fumbled after gaining 17 on a short pass.

On the second possession, Hoying was sacked on third down.

On the third, his overthrown pass bounced off a receiver's hands and was intercepted in the end zone.

On the fourth, Hoying scrambled to avoid another sack on third down.

Fortunately for the offense, the Buckeyes' defense was playing its best game yet, stuffing Wisconsin's running game and harassing Bevell. It was a time of the season that Young knew would arrive sooner or later. The offense, explosive every game so far, would stall. And his defense, pushed around so far, would rise to keep the game close until the offense awakened. This was the time. This was the place. But he didn't have his best defensive back at full strength, since Springs would hobble on and off the field the entire game.

Finally, on the fifth possession, OSU put together a 56-yard, eight-play drive that George capped with a one yard run to give the Buckeyes a 7-3 lead. The offense got the ball back immediately, but Hoying threw two incompletions into the wind and then tripped while dropping back on third down. His fall was one of several weird plays for Ohio State. On another, Vrabel had a clear shot to block a punt but missed, aiming at the punter's right foot. He had forgotten the Badgers' punter was left-footed. On yet another, Young made a perfect call to blitz and Greg Bellisari broke free, but pulled Bevell's face mask during the sack.

Suddenly, Bevell got hot, completing six straight passes as the Badgers drove 70 yards to take a 9-7 lead before fullback Nicky Sualua fumbled to end a lethargic first half for Ohio State.

It shouldn't have been surprising, because what had happened wasn't anything new to the Buckeyes. They had played awful in almost every trip to Madison since the 24-21 loss in 1981. Until that game, the Badgers hadn't beaten Ohio State since 1959. But since, the Buckeyes often saved one of their letdowns for the Wisconsin game, especially in Madison where they had lost in 1984, '87, '92 and tied in '93 when

Wisconsin earned a Rose Bowl berth. Cooper, however, had done what Earle Bruce had trouble doing — he had a 5-1-1 record against Wisconsin.

At halftime, Hollis wrote: "2 fumbles, 1 interception, 2 sacks, 2 holding penalties" on the chalkboard. The offense was puzzled and frustrated, the defense satisfied, and Cooper irate. He walked through the offense's room, ranting and raving, throwing his arms through the air. "They are not worth a crap," he said. "This team is not worth crap — and they are beating you. They are beating you! You've got 10 minutes to think about it." Then, he walked out of the room.

The players weren't alone in their funk. While the defense had played its best half yet, the play-calling on offense had been questionable. Hollis had fallen in love with the offense's balance, and he may have been so determined to not let the wind affect his play-calling that he neglected the obvious on this day — Ohio State could pound away at Wisconsin with its power running game. George had gained only 33 yards on 10 carries, so Hollis had drifted away to counters, sweeps and of course, the passing game. "Don't hang your heads," Harris told the offense. "We've got a lot of football to play."

Ten minutes later, Cooper reappeared and picked up where he had left off.

"It's your ballgame to win," he said. "You ought to be up by three touchdowns by now. We're not into it mentally. You should be playing your best football, but none of you did. Did you? This team shouldn't be on the same field with you. Now get out there and win this game!"

After Hollis and the offensive coaches had huddled, they were sure of a way to win.

"We are going to RUN the football at them all half," Hollis said. "We are going to eat them up. I think this — and you should too — but we should score every time we touch the ball. I really believe that. I really do. All summer long when you are working out, there are times when you have to call on your character. Now is one of those times. You have to play your heart out for the next 30 minutes. Our defense is playing their ass off. You are a lot better football team than this team, now let's go show it."

As the defensive players walked by the offense, George told them, "You get the ball back for us 'D.' We'll do the job this half."

George had wanted to take control, emotionally and physically. This was the emotion. The physical part was soon to come.

Thanks to heavy pressure from Finkes, linebacker Ryan Miller picked off one of Bevell's short floaters and rambled to Wisconsin's five-yard line to start the second half. That led to a two-yard flip from Hoying to Glenn, who was being double-teamed all day, to give the Buckeyes a 13-9 lead. Wisconsin used only four plays to take the lead again at 16-13 heading into the fourth quarter, and it now appeared the game would be a fight to the end. Especially after Josh Jackson's 37-yard field goal attempt was knocked down by a gust of wind just a few feet short of the crossbar early in the fourth quarter.

Before the next possession, Mike Jacobs, in the press box, was getting his message through on the headsets. He thought more isolation running plays, more power football would work. "Let's go right at 'em," he suggested. "Let's go right at 'em." Hollis agreed. So did Orlando Pace, Jamie Sumner, Juan Porter, LeShun Daniels and Eric Gohlstin — 1,500 pounds of a pretty good offensive line.

George carried six straight times for 35 yards, the sixth resulting in a touchdown on a pitch to the left on third down from one yard out to give the Buckeyes the lead again.

Bevell then missed badly on second and third down on the next series. After George gained three, he put the game away on his next carry. He busted through a hole opened by Sumner, Daniels and Sualua, then cut left behind a downfield block by Glenn and ran 51 yards to make it 27-16. "Just a simple isolation play," Hollis said later. "You can't get any more basic than that." The call, and the run, symbolized the-back-to-basics second half. Following George's third touchdown of the day, ABC's Brent Musburger told the nation: "That's why the man is a serious Heisman candidate."

With an 11-point lead and only 6:33 remaining, Young knew he could turn his defensive line loose. "We've got 'em right where we want 'em," he screamed at the defense on the sideline. "Don't let 'em off the hook!"

They didn't. Wisconsin never responded. And Young was correct — third-down had been the key. The Badgers converted only three-of-14 and totaled only 271 yards. Bevell, too, had proven Young correct. The Wisconsin quarterback played inconsistently, missing open receivers throughout the second half. He completed 15-of-31 for 158 yards and was intercepted twice. The numbers brightened Young's outlook on his defense, which had shut Penn State down on the final three series a week earlier and now responded with a solid four quarters on the road. "Best day yet," he said as he walked off the field. "I feel a whole lot better now." Vrabel, the All-Big Ten end who had started slowly sack-wise, had two tackles for loss and a 12-yard sack. Finkes had another sack.

On the downside, Wisconsin running back Carl McCullough's 102 yards accounted for the fifth 100-yard game by an opposing back in six games. For some reason, it seemed as if opponent's running backs were having their best games against Ohio State's defense, but none of them had yet to walk away a winner.

Unlike a week earlier, there was no celebration or ecstasy in the locker room. Just pure and simple relief to get out of cold and windy and unfriendly Camp Randall Stadium with a win and an undefeated record. Cooper was as relieved as anyone. This was the type of game that his seven previous teams at Ohio State might not have pulled out. But now, with six of their toughest games and two consecutive come-from-behind wins behind them, he knew this team and these players were different. They were talented, they were resilient, and they had the character it took to come from behind. But he didn't dare let on that he was pleased or satisfied. He had to show them some fire and anger after the game, since he didn't want to go through the agony of a close game every week.

"We didn't play our best football game — you know that," he told the team. "I tell you what — there will be no letdown on this football team. No letdowns! We will not be flat for Purdue. Get your ass ready to play." When he finished and walked out, George stepped in and picked it up. It was, after all, his day and he was still somewhat angry.

"We can't go out flat like that," he said, as every teammate listened. "No way. That first half was bullshit. No more! I won't stand for it. No more!"

George had displayed the leadership the public never saw. He and Hoying resembled coaches in the huddle. Nobody wanted to lose, but George wouldn't stand for it. He had willed his teammates to be better, to work harder, and on this day, he inspired them to a win. "That's what you love about the guy," Sumner said. Later, George said it was as if his teammates didn't hear him at breakfast, but he sensed the first half would be disgusting offensively. "We kept shooting ourselves in the foot," he said. "A lot of guys just didn't take me seriously, I guess. I didn't want to come up here and go through the pain and agony of getting beat by these guys. In the huddle, I didn't yell or scream. That doesn't put points on the board. I just reminded them what was on the line."

When it was all said and done, and the game was won, he made his statement. "He was pretty vocal after the game," said Hoying, who completed 18-of-26 for 206 yards despite the gusty conditions. "It was just one of those games when the odds got us. At least we came back and won it. We could be feeling a lot worse right now."

Hollis knew, too, that he didn't have his best day. He second-guessed himself for not going to George earlier. "I never said it over the (head) phones, but I wondered 'Are we trying to make too many big plays?'" he said. Jacobs' second opinion had helped reinforce what he had wondered. Fortunately for them, they realized their mistake as it was happening, rather than when it became too late to change course.

When Cooper met the media, he said the offense "went back to Ohio State-style football. The tailback went north and south and we went right after them. When the game was on the line, we went to big number 27." And big number 27 delivered again, rushing for 141 yards and three touchdowns — certainly nothing to hurt his Heisman chances. It didn't come without sacrifice. George needed 20 minutes of treatment from the trainers to ease the pain of dozens of rug burns from the artificial turf. As he limped out of the locker room, he looked down at his feet. His skin burned and his muscles ached. "Playing up here," he said, "is a real bitch."

When he slowly glided into the interview room, Hoying, walking out, unofficially introduced him: "Here's the man of the hour."

"It was just go-back-to-the-basics football," George said. "I felt I was getting into a groove. We were just beating ourselves, and we had to settle down." As George spoke, Sports Information Director Steve Snapp smiled. He was relieved with each big game by George, since he had decided to promote the running back — instead of Glenn or Hoying — for the Heisman Trophy. "We had a choice to make, and we made it," he said. "It seems to be working out, but you can't change course in midstream."

George gave his usual modest answers and then limped toward the team busses. A Wisconsin fan did a double-take, saying, "Is that Eddie George? He's so big for a running back."

An hour later, as the charter flight to Columbus was loading, George settled his big body and heart into a first-class seat next to his soul mates — some offensive linemen. The group had earned special treatment for pulling the team out of Madison with a perfect record. He was a team player, yet his teammates didn't mind. The wind was blowing hard on the tarmac. Undoubtedly, if any player could have flown the airplane home that night, it was Eddie George. Why not? He had done everything else on this day.

In coach class, Hollis loosened his tie. "In weather like that, it is easy being an offensive coordinator," he said. "You just give the ball to Eddie George, win the game and go home."

14.

Two Presidents and a Shutout

The next day, when most people were waking to orange juice or coffee, Fred Pagac spit tobacco juice into a cup and continued to run the tape of the Wisconsin game back and forth. It was the type of game Pagac loved — hard-nosed, blue-collar, smash-mouth football. Two running attacks colliding with two solid defenses on a cold, windy, October day. No reverses. No trick plays. No gimmicks. If only the game had been played in the mud, instead of on artificial turf, it would have been perfect. He could watch film like that forever, it seemed, especially since Pagac's linebackers had played one of their best games. Ryan Miller had nine tackles and an interception. Greg Bellisari also had nine tackles.

Any day Ohio State won a football game was a great day in Pagac's life. If anybody on Cooper's staff would live as a Buckeye and ultimately die as a Buckeye, it was Fred Pagac.

A native of Richeyville, Pa., he had played tight end for Woody Hayes from 1971-73 and following four seasons in the NFL, he had returned to campus as a graduate assistant for Hayes' final season in 1978. He hadn't left since, coaching during Earle Bruce's nine years and Cooper's eight years. His office wall was covered with photos of Hayes, his mind was filled with memories and his heart was filled with reverence for his late coach.

Pagac pointed to a photo of the legend, kneeling on one knee at Ohio Stadium, holding a football and peering through those famed, silver-rimmed glasses.

"Other than my dad," he said, "there was no one I respected more."

Hayes, in turn, loved Pagac the player, then a tight end who later played for the Bears and Buccaneers. "He was a nut, a real crazy guy on the football field," former teammate Rick Middleton said. "But I'll tell you one thing — nobody hustled more, worked harder or wanted to win like Pug. Woody loved that."

When Pagac decided to make coaching his profession, Hayes' style became his style. Intense. Driven. Focused. Old-fashioned. At times, loud and abrasive. All the peripheral duties that went with the job — dealing with the media, speaking and catering to people outside the program, were mostly nonsense to Pagac. A waste of time.

He was a coach's coach.

If you would watch an Ohio State practice for the first time and close your eyes, chances are that the screaming that rang off your ears would be coming from Pagac's mouth. Along with a few unprintable words and a steady stream of tobacco juice.

A real throwback.

"That's me," Pagac said. "That's how I played in the NFL, and that's how I coach. I like that style of coaching, but you have to treat everyone differently. Some guys you can't get after that hard."

Whether he was in the midst of chewing them out with a string of four-letter words or telling a raunchy joke, players loved him. Most important, he knew football and he knew how to communicate it to his pupils. "He's got our respect, I know that," Miller said. "He's vocal. He's intense. He's got a lot of fire in him, but that's what you need from a linebackers coach. He's grabbed me by the face mask a couple of times in my career or whacked me on the helmet. Doesn't bother me one bit, because you know he cares about you. You really want to do your best for a guy like that."

Bellisari saw a good example of Pagac's fire when a couple of players joked around on the bus ride following a 28-0 loss to Michigan in 1993. "He got right in their face and let 'em have it," Bellisari said. "He was real hot that day. He loves the tradition of this place, and he brings the past to the present here. You had better not take a game or a practice lightly around him if you wear an Ohio State uniform."

Pagac, naturally, understood the tradition and the pressures of coaching at Ohio State. He loved the tradition and scoffed at the idea of pressure, even to the point of being angered by fellow assistants who moaned about it.

"See, all that talk about pressure on coaches pisses me off," he said. "It's bullshit. We *should* be under pressure to win. I want to win every game, every season. If you can't stand the heat, get the hell out of my kitchen. We've had two offensive assistants who have always moaned about that. One is gone now. That's why I am always busting Joe Hollis. Everybody should have pressure to win. That's just an excuse."

It wasn't beyond Pagac to correct his head coach, either, although Pagac liked and respected Cooper. Cooper often said former receivers coach Mike Stock, who left following the 1994 season to become special teams coach of the Kansas City Chiefs, had not bought a house in Columbus because of the uncertainty surrounding Cooper's status. "Not true," Pagac said. "Mike Stock didn't own a house because his wife worked in Cincinnati, and they wanted to rent."

At times, it had to be difficult for Pagac to watch the countless number of assistant coaches who made their way to Ohio State without a solid grasp of the tradition or history of the program. They would come and go, always looking for a better position. To them, reporting to work at the Woody Hayes Center was another stop on their resume. Some probably wouldn't be able to find Mirror Lake or the Oval, or any spot on campus other than Ohio Stadium, without a map.

"I played here, I have coached here for 17 years...Ohio State has been good to me," Pagac said. "I love this place. When Coach Cooper leaves, I want to be the next head coach here."

With that, Pagac spit a stream of tobacco juice into the cup and turned back to the screen. There was tape of his linebackers to grade, work to do. There was no time for idle chit-chat.

———————◆•◆•◆———————

Six down, six to go. All the talk in Columbus among fans, the radio call-in shows and in the media was that the Buckeyes had survived the toughest part of their schedule.

After all, of their six victories, five had come at the expense of ranked teams. The remaining six were scheduled, played and chalked up as wins. It was exactly the outlook Cooper had to prevent his players from absorbing. In turn, they talked as if they realized what was important and what wasn't. "We're only six games into the season," nose guard Luke Fickell said. "Nobody wants to focus on the Rose Bowl now. It's one game at a time."

Still, local media continued to ask Cooper if he felt his team was "over the hump."

"Over the hump?" Cooper asked Sunday morning. "That's exactly what I don't want to hear. I'll show you the Purdue-Penn State film."

Penn State had barely survived the Boilermakers the previous day, winning 26-23. It was Purdue's third loss by a total of just 11 points, giving the Boilermakers a 2-3-1 record. They would represent only the second non-ranked opponent for Ohio State in seven games.

"The worst thing we can do is say the tough games are over," Cooper said. "You know (Jim) Colletto — it would make their season to come in here and beat us."

Colletto, in his fifth season as Purdue's head coach, had been Cooper's offensive coordinator for six years — three at Arizona State and three from 1988-90 at Ohio State. Although both sides denied it publicly, obvious animosity remained between Colletto and some of Cooper's assistants, if not between the head coaches themselves. Some believe that Cooper angered Colletto when he endorsed Larry Marmie to succeed him at Arizona State once he accepted the job at OSU. Colletto wanted and thought he deserved the endorsement, and even though he soon followed Cooper to Columbus, the subject remained a sore spot, insiders believed.

Colletto also wasn't the easiest guy to get along with. His strong personality and opinions soon wore on several OSU assistants. "The guy was just plain stubborn at times," one assistant said. "He would be bullheaded to the detriment of the team. He acted like the head coach when he wasn't the head coach."

By some accounts, Colletto was about to run out of time in West Lafayette if he didn't turn the program around soon. Entering the game, he had a 15-32-3 record at Purdue and probably needed to string together some wins to save his job.

"I would think he's in trouble," Cooper said. "You know though, Jimmy's a good football coach, a sound football coach. He'll probably wind up as an offensive line coach in the NFL someday."

———————————◆———————————

While Cooper took a break from watching film with the offense Monday, Mike Vrabel stopped by his office to ask, "Where's training table on Thursday?" Cooper still was shaking his head over Vrabel's explanation for failing to block the punt at Wisconsin. He had forgotten the punter was left-footed, and afterwards, he was honest with the media. "Why would you say that?" Cooper wondered. "It makes you look stupid."

Despite an unbeaten record and No. 4 national ranking, the Buckeyes were being pushed out of the Fawcett Center, where they normally ate dinner, Thursday and Friday before the Purdue game. Now this was no common occurrence. Who would be so important to supersede the Buckeyes on their own campus?

The President of the United States, for one.

Bill Clinton and Vice-President Al Gore were scheduled to lead an economic summit meeting at the Fawcett Center Friday morning before Clinton would speak on the Oval that afternoon.

Would he stop by to see the coach of the nation's fourth-ranked team, now riding a crest of popularity unseen in his eight seasons in Columbus?

"If he's smart he will," Cooper said with a laugh. "I'll bet he does. President Bush stopped by here once when he was in town."

Of course, neither Bush nor Clinton knew Cooper's politics, but they probably knew getting a photo-op with him wouldn't hurt. "Actually," Cooper said, "my daddy always voted a straight democratic ticket no matter what. I've been listed as a democrat, but I've always voted for the best candidate no matter what party. Last time, I voted for Bush."

While a nationally syndicated sports show interviewed Eddie George Tuesday afternoon, running backs coach Tim Spencer happened to walk by. "What's going on?" Spencer asked.

"They are going to take a picture of Eddie in front of the Heisman Trophy case," someone answered.

George was only 22 years old, so he wasn't to blame for not knowing superstition. But there's a theory that Heisman candidates who usually get their pictures taken with the trophy never win the award.

"Hey Eddie, come here," Spencer shouted down the hallway. "Are you superstitious?"

"Why?" George asked.

"Because you shouldn't let them film you with the Heismans," Spencer said. "It's bad luck. Tell them to forget it."

"Can I do that?" George asked.

"Eddie," Spencer shot back. "You're the man. You can do whatever you want. Now go tell them."

George moped down the hallway like a bashful puppy and broke the news to a disappointed cameraman. Instead, they filmed him in front of the wall of pictures of OSU All-Americans. No superstition there. It would be the most grueling part of George's day, since the coaches held him out of practice for the first time all season. When they wanted George well-rested, they had to take action themselves, since the running back never slacked off on his own.

"We just need to rest him," Cooper said. "He can get tired legs if we practice him too hard, because he goes 100 percent every time he's out there. He runs out every play 30 yards while some backs stop at 10."

When practice started, Cooper stood on the sidelines talking to a few reporters as he often did. A big change was taking place in the Cooper household, which presented a dilemma for the future. His only daughter, Cindy, had planned to move out to get her own place. "And you know how close she and Helen are," he said. "Now when she moves out and Helen is all alone in that big house for a while, what am I going to do? Helen is going to be miserable. Do I want to coach 10 more years or just two or three more? I got a big decision to make."

The 6-0 start had invigorated Cooper's desire to stay in coaching longer than he originally had planned. He had beaten Michigan the year before. Finally, it appeared he was winning over most of the fans for the first time since he had arrived at Ohio State. The ensuing recruiting class already shaped up to be a great one. Maybe he and his program were on the verge of taking control of the Big Ten for the upcoming years, climbing past Penn State and Michigan. Who would want to walk away from that situation and the spoils that would come with it?

"That's just the thing," he said. "We should be able to kick ass in recruiting this year. We can get the program to where it is the best in the Big Ten every year. Penn State isn't getting any better. Depending on what happens at Michigan (coaching-wise), they may fall off some."

He stared out at his team, in the midst of practice, and started to count heads. "Look at who we got coming back defensively — everybody but (Matt) Bonhaus," he said. "Offensively, we lose all our stars. But Pepe (Pearson) will be a good running back. The offensive line will be fine. We just need to get the right man under center."

Cooper saw the program improving in all phases, yet he scoffed at the idea that he had improved himself. He was coaching the same as he always had, he said. Still, others believed he didn't delegate as much responsibility as he did when he first arrived in Columbus. Even Geiger had said he noticed a new intensity that was missing until the final three games of the 1994 season. "I am doing nothing different than I always have," Cooper said. "Maybe I am spending more time recruiting because I have such a good staff to coach. I recruit much more than people realize."

The next day, he interrupted practice when the president stopped by — OSU President E. Gordon Gee not President Clinton. Gee had made the appearance since it was homecoming week. The team circled around Gee, wearing his trademark bow tie, as television cameras rolled.

"You're undefeated, and I am proud of you," said Gee, nationally renowned as one the movers and shakers among NCAA presidents. "The only thing I can say is that you're making me too nervous. How about an easy game for a change? Let's put Purdue away early and make it easier on me this week. I like the way you handle yourselves. It's obvious you all get along. You like each other, and I like that. I love the way you represent this university. Anyway, I just wanted to come talk to you. Good luck Saturday."

During the offense's weekly scouting report, Hollis knew he couldn't bluff his players by pumping up Purdue's defense. The Boilermakers were allowing 29 points and 456 yards per game. He knew his players watched film and read the newspapers, too, and saw for themselves how poor Purdue's defense was playing. There was no sense lying to them, or he would lose credibility for when he really needed to scare them.

"Let's put ourselves in their shoes and anticipate what they are going to do," Hollis said. "They aren't a good defense by any stretch of the imagination. So they probably will come in here and gamble and blitz a little bit, right? Hey, these are guys you like to play. They are searching and they haven't found it yet. The whole key to putting 50 points on the board and having a fun day is execution. It's us — not them. We just have to worry about us."

Nevertheless, Cooper decided he had to chew out his players during Thursday night's meeting with the team. It was part contrived, part genuine, but exactly the right time, he thought.

"I am very concerned about this ballgame," he said, pacing in front of room. "This football team is a hell of a lot better than you think they are. They led West Virginia 17-0 at the half and had a chance to beat Notre Dame and Penn State. They are 12 points from being undefeated. Are we better than they are? Yes. We should kick their butt. But you can't go out there and screw around. Let's get focused and put them away early. Now it's homecoming and there's a lot of people around...your parents...the president's in town. But nothing is more important than getting ready for this game."

Outside in the hallway, administrative assistant Larry Petroff mulled over a letter that Cooper ordered to send Clinton on behalf of the program — along with a Buckeyes' jersey. "Hey, Coach Petroff, what time do I get to meet Bill tomorrow?" Hoying joked.

"You mean 'Mr. Bill' don't you?" Vrabel shot back.

Hollis, sensing a lack of concentration during the week's practices, had changed his tune a little when he called Hoying and the offense into the usual Thursday night meeting. Like his boss minutes earlier, he realized it was time to send a message. "Purdue probably gained on us today," he said. "We probably weren't concentrating today. Guys, don't let a golden opportunity slip by. The best team doesn't always win the game. We might beat them eight out of ten, but that doesn't count. If we don't beat them Saturday at 12:30, it doesn't matter, does it?

"Guys, we got a chance to do something really special. Let's not screw it up. I don't want to be negative, but I want to be truthful. We haven't played consistent offense since we hung 45 on Notre Dame, have we? Not at Penn State and certainly not at Wisconsin. The physical part is there, but the mental part is not. We were all disturbed at the way we practiced today. Defensively, (the Boilermakers) are very average but they are pretty good on offense. If we have to score every time we touch the ball to beat them, let's do it. We really should go out there and score a lot of points, have some fun and let it be a great day. Shouldn't we Eddie? Bobby?"

The players nodded.

Friday morning, Oct. 20, Cooper, donning sweat clothes soaked in sweat, had just finished his daily two-mile run before a cold front moved in. Now it was raining and the temperature was dropping into the 50s. He admitted the previous day's outburst was mostly a ploy to prevent any letdown for Saturday. "We just said that to prevent them from taking Purdue lightly," he said. "Joe didn't feel the offense practiced all that well, but I was with the defense all week and they had a good week."

Cooper then paced around the building the entire day, bouncing in one room and then another. He walked up to his upstairs office, collected his messages, and headed to his downstairs office near the locker room. His secretary, Julie Bonfini, admitted he was anxious over whether Clinton would appear.

"You can tell that's what's on his mind," she said. "It's always a thrill to meet a president, and he loves meeting guys like that...politicians or celebrities."

Minutes later, Cooper climbed the steps again.

"Hey, guess what?" he asked. "Bobby was named as a National Football Foundation scholar. That's worth about $18,000."

A few minutes later, Hoying walked into the building searching for Harris. "Bobby, got a minute?" Cooper asked, calling the quarterback into his office. "Walt's speaking at the Agonis Club luncheon so he won't be back until 2 o'clock." Then Cooper broke the good news and Hoying walked out smiling a moment later.

"Man, I was hoping to get that one," he said of the scholarship. "Yes! Guess I have to go to graduate school someday, huh?"

"It's a prestigious deal," Cooper said. "You should be proud of yourself."

Finally, somebody from the Secret Service called to say that if Cooper and a few players walked to the roadside of Olentangy River Road in a few minutes, Clinton and Gore would be driving by.

Cooper grabbed two scarlet jerseys, numbered one and two, that Petroff had ordered. Above No. 1 was Clinton's name. He gathered whatever players he could find and walked out to the road. Most of the players were walk-ons since it was Friday, when the special teams usually met. Vrabel was about the only starter present.

The motorcade stopped and Clinton jumped out to shake hands.

"I've seen you on TV a few times, you've got a real fine team," he said. "Good luck."

The President walked down the line of players shaking hands. "No autographs," a secret service agent instructed.

Scout team quarterback Joe Germaine had carried a new football. "You want me to sign that for you?" Clinton asked. Germaine, being redshirted, had made his one big play for the season.

"Joe was smarter than all of us," Cooper said later. "(Clinton) told me he helped us beat Notre Dame by occupying the pope that day."

For Cooper, the meeting was typical of his year. He was an honored speaker at his high school class reunion, he had been to the Super Bowl and Kentucky Derby, thrown out the first pitch at Yankee Stadium, and now he had greeted the President of the United States. And his team had won all six games.

What would be next?

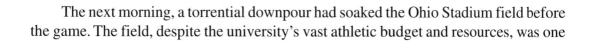

The next morning, a torrential downpour had soaked the Ohio Stadium field before the game. The field, despite the university's vast athletic budget and resources, was one of the worst in the Big Ten. Since the artificial turf had been removed in the late '80s, the natural grass field never drained well and usually tore up when it became wet.

"Guys, it's going to be very slippery out there," Young told his defense. "So be aware of it. Keep your feet under you and get your footing."

Young had been confident about this game, despite Purdue's average of 30 points and 436 yards per game. "We've got some strong tendencies on them," he said. "When they have those two fullbacks in there at once, they are going to run. That's when we'll bring the safeties up inside." Once he realized that Purdue had to start backup quarterback John Reeves because starter Rick Trefzger had not recovered from a concussion, he knew the game would be easier. He would blitz Reeves silly.

Purdue punter Rob Deignan suffered through what would be a long day when Vrabel busted through to block his first punt. Vrabel had no problems this time — Deignan was right-footed. Central McClellion recovered at the Boilermakers' 24-yard line. George then carried four consecutive times, the final carry a one-yard touchdown.

Three plays later, Deignan didn't have time again and was tackled for a 15-yard loss by McClellion at the Purdue 17. However, Hoying made one of the worst throws of his season, missing Glenn near the goal line. The pass was intercepted.

Later in the first quarter, the Buckeyes put together their second-longest drive of the season. It lasted 7:02 and totaled 95 yards, with Hoying completing 6-of-7 for 83 yards. But it resulted in zero points because George slipped on the wet field before taking the handoff on fourth-and-goal at the one-yard line.

Near the end of the half, Hoying hooked up with Dudley, who caught the pass at the 11 and cut down the sideline before diving into the end zone to make it 14-0.

As Reeves struggled, the Boilermakers hadn't even sniffed the end zone in the half, totaling just 128 yards. Their farthest penetration was to the OSU 21, where Finkes came up with a sack before Miller intercepted a pass for the second straight week.

Cooper, growing increasingly dissatisfied with the offense, took his frustrations out on Hollis' group at halftime. "We should be up by four touchdowns," he barked. "The defense is playing great. We need to get the ball and start putting it in the end zone. Quit screwing around out there."

Nothing changed in the second half. The offense scored two more touchdowns and left another potential touchdown on the field, just as it had in the first half. Glenn scored each second-half touchdown — catching a seven-yard pass and then a 12-yard pass from Hoying — to give him a school-record 12 for the season. "When I saw the ball coming to me," Glenn said later, "I thought, 'Here it comes. Here comes the record.'" George fumbled at the one-yard line after gaining eight on a screen pass, leaving the Buckeyes with just 28 points. By the end of the day, it could have been 49 if not for their own mistakes.

The defense, however, had its best day yet, shutting out the Boilermakers. Since Colletto was an offensive coach, the day was very sweet for Young, who often referred to Purdue as 'Pur-don't'. His defense had shut out Colletto's offense, giving up only 259 yards even though Springs did not play because of his sore ankle. Young was feeling better by the day. His defense had allowed only two touchdowns in the last eight and one-half quarters, dating back to midway through the final quarter at Happy Valley.

"You go into every game hoping for a shutout," he said. It was only the team's second shutout in three seasons.

For some reason, a reason Cooper said he didn't have, Colletto was ungracious following the game. He had coached for Cooper for six years, including three at Ohio State, but when asked if he thought the Buckeyes should be ranked No. 1, he replied, "They're pretty good, but I don't think they're the No. 1 team."

Cooper, his assistants and Gee took turns addressing a roomful of recruits in the corner of Ohio Stadium following the game. "If you come to Ohio State," Gee said, "I can assure you that you will get a great Ohio State education and play for coaches who care about you."

When the president left, Cooper told them, "I was real disappointed that we turned the ball over today and didn't score more points. But I've been in coaching long enough to realize that you be happy with any victory. You take it and don't complain."

Accordingly, that was seven victories, and no complaints.

15.

To Run Up the Score, or Not to Run Up the Score — That is the Question

USC, ranked right behind Ohio State at fifth, had lost 38-10 at Notre Dame, guaranteeing that the Buckeyes would not face an unbeaten and highly ranked team should they make it to Pasadena. The politics surrounding the new bowl alliance, which would match the No. 1 and No. 2 teams in the Fiesta Bowl, targeted the Big Ten and Pac-10 as public enemies numbers one and one-A.

Now one of them had fallen and coaches, athletic directors and bowl officials across the country were celebrating.

Everybody, that is, but those in the Big Ten, Pac-10 and Rose Bowl.

"USC, USC, USC, what happened?" Chuck Stobart wondered aloud during Monday morning's offensive meeting. "We needed you."

"I could care less about that stuff — it's so far down the line," Hollis said.

"I'll tell you, Joe, it carries a lot of weight to beat an unbeaten team on New Year's Day," Stobart said, "especially if those other top teams are slopping around."

Cooper, too, who told the media that it didn't bother him that USC had lost, had altered his thinking somewhat. "Yeah, I guess," he said. "I see where it would have helped us to have them go unbeaten, too. But they didn't, so we just have to hold up our end and get there. We've got to get back to the Rose Bowl."

Monday afternoon, senior guard Jamie Sumner sat in dark silence watching film of Iowa's defensive line. "They look OK, not great...big and slow," he said. Sumner had been upset with Hollis after the coach had berated him for committing a personal foul in the first quarter against Purdue.

"Jamie, the guy's just doing his job," someone told him. "He doesn't want you to cost the team 15 yards later on during a big game like Michigan."

"Yeah, but the guy is lying there twisting Eddie's head," Sumner said. "Nobody else would do anything so I jumped on him. I mean, Eddie's our meal ticket. What am I supposed to do, let him twist his head off?"

His point was well-taken, but when Sumner came out of the game, Cooper let him have it. During the team's Sunday film session, Hollis reiterated Cooper. "Jamie, I thought you were a heady player," said Hollis, who also coached the centers and guards in addition to being the offensive coordinator. "I thought you were smarter than that."

Committing a personal foul, a needless penalty, was a sign of weakness to most of the coaches. They saw it as a selfish act even though, ironically, Sumner was coming to George's defense. The criticism hit Sumner, who was as sensitive as a guy could be for a 6-foot-4, 295-pounder, hard. When he dropped off the tape in Hollis' office, Hollis tried to make amends. "Jamie, how ya doing?" he asked. "Jamie, everything OK?"

Sumner mumbled something and walked out. "I am still mad about it," he said.

"He wears his emotions half way down his sleeve," Hollis whispered.

It was just a minor disagreement in a five-month-long season. If these problems were Cooper's largest, he could deal with it. While other teams around the nation were having the usual off-the-field troubles, Ohio State had kept its collective nose clean so far during the season, except for Malfatt's indiscretion. That was a minor problem, anyway.

"That's what I like about this team," Cooper said. "We talk to them about not beating the system all the time...doing the right thing. So far, these players know what is important." Cooper, somewhat superstitious, knocked his knuckles on his desk top.

His biggest problem throughout his years at Ohio State, aside from the Robert Smith-Elliott Uzelac feud in 1991, had been keeping agents away from his players. Joey Galloway and Vince Workman were two that had either signed early or accepted money from agents with eligibility remaining. To Cooper, only thieves and murderers ranked below unscrupulous agents. "I tell all those agents that if they stay away from them until their eligibility is through, I will recommend them to the players," he said. "If they don't, I will go out of my way to recommend the players look elsewhere."

Meeting with the media at his Tuesday luncheon, Cooper pulled out his lucky silver dollar and began flipping it. Naturally, it led to a series of questions about the coin. "Always carry it and my lucky buckeye," he said, pulling the tiny nut out of his pocket

He subscribed to the theory that it was better to be good than lucky. So far, his team had been both. "Great players make you feel lucky," he said.

A few minutes later, back at the Woody Hayes Center, Cooper pulled out his buckeye again. "You know, you might not believe this, but we had a buckeye tree on my property when I grew up," he said. "You think buckeye trees only grow in Ohio? Come on. They're all over the place."

Cooper gave them to recruits and it looked as if he was about to give out another nut to perhaps the most important recruit in the state — Westerville South linebacker Andy Katzenmoyer, a 6-foot-4, 250-pound blue-chipper whom every top program wanted. Recruiting coordinator Bill Conley, anxious to tell Cooper, had busted into an offensive meeting with the good news.

"Coach, coach, just got a call from Katzenmoyer's father," bubbled Conley, so excited he was jiggling his coffee. "He's scheduled a press conference for Thursday. It's got to be us. It's got to be us."

"Why else would he call us?" Hollis asked.

"Great," Cooper said. "Great."

If it was true, it would be the Buckeyes' 10th oral commitment out of a possible class of 25 but the most crucial catch yet.

"With all those commitments, we'll be through recruiting in December," Stobart said.

"That's the way Notre Dame does it every year," Hollis said. "We're on our way."

Stobart, in charge of recruiting Florida, laughed. "We can go to Florida and play golf," he said.

The scenario, of course, was pure fantasy for the coaches. Even if they had a full class of 25 recruits committed, they would have to spend January preventing them from changing their minds. It would be constant work, one way or the other. "That's why I like recruiting so much," Hollis said sarcastically.

Once he returned from the media luncheon, Cooper stuck his head in Hollis' office to play a little joke on his offensive coordinator. He walked out chuckling like a grade-school kid who successfully placed a tack on the teacher's chair. "You know how nervous Joe gets," he said. "I just told him I guaranteed a huge victory. Fifty-some points. He said 'Oh, no, you didn't! No, you didn't.'"

Hollis didn't believe Cooper. "He's always trying to get me to bite on that one," he said. "I know better. He's learned his lesson about predictions." Hollis may have been referring to the 1993 Holiday Bowl, in which Cooper guaranteed a win over Brigham Young. The Buckeyes had won 28-21, but not without a dropped pass in the end zone by a BYU receiver during the final minutes.

* * *

When film of Iowa and Michigan State rolled, Harris, who coached in East Lansing in 1978, said, "Michigan State, on the banks of the Grand River..."

"You know what's funny?" Mike Jacobs, chomping on a huge cigar, interjected. "There isn't one team we see on film where Walt or Chuck hasn't coached before."

The staff broke into laughter.

Winning and having top recruits commit early did wonders for the staff's morale. And it seemed Cooper's staff couldn't have been giddier. Another factor was confidence. Despite a 5-1 record and No. 23 ranking, the Iowa Hawkeyes weren't about to throw much fear into the coaches. Iowa's defense, at least on film, appeared very vulnerable. It had been shredded for 41 points by Penn State the previous week — Iowa's first and only loss.

"Why would they be doing this?" Cooper asked while watching one particular pass coverage.

The Hawkeyes had played mostly bump-and-run, tight coverage with their cornerbacks on opposing receivers, leaving only one safety deep. Hollis, Harris and

Stobart knew that if they tried it against Terry Glenn and Buster Tillman, there would no reason not to score 50 points this week.

"Joe, they are so simple to read — where they are going and what they are doing," Stobart said. "We should have a field day in front of us."

"We'll be able to get downfield and stretch the safeties," Harris said.

"I don't know," Hollis interjected. "I don't see them playing us this way."

"How do you see them playing us?" Harris asked.

"Look at the teams they have been playing, other than Penn State," Hollis said. "They haven't played any good teams."

"Come on, you guys, we'll score early and often," Jacobs predicted.

"We've just got to get better each week," Harris said. "We didn't do that last week. A couple of years ago, when you guys were undefeated, didn't you get better each week?"

Hollis, not one to forget OSU's 8-0 start in 1993 but 1-1-1 finish following a 28-0 loss at Michigan, said, "No, I didn't think we did."

"Is this the toughest team we'll play until Michigan?" Harris asked.

"Hell no," Hollis answered. "I think Minnesota up in that dome will be tough."

"Illinois," Jacobs said.

"Hey Joe, how about some trick plays (against Iowa)?" Harris asked.

"Yeah, it's Halloween," Jacobs said. "We need some tricks."

What did concern the staff was somehow finding a way to motivate fullback Nicky Sualua. It had become an old problem. Sualua still weighed more than 255 pounds and had played only 25 plays against Purdue. It seemed his mind usually was elsewhere, even though he was talented enough to have a future in the NFL if he ever became motivated enough to take the game seriously.

"We need to make Nicky the best he can be," Harris said. "For us to be our best, we need him. He's one of our special players."

"I know, I am not that naive," Hollis said. "I agree. But he's a classic underachiever. He could be the best fullback in the country if he weighed 235."

"I'll bet our opponents think he is now," Harris said.

Prompting the defensive scout team to practice harder had become another priority. It had become a common problem in college football since scholarship limits had been cut to 85. There never seemed to be enough good players to imitate the upcoming opponent.

"I am going to talk to the scout team tomorrow myself," Hollis said. "We got too many walk-ons who aren't trying worth a shit." Hollis and running backs coach Tim Spencer also decided to give backup tailback Pepe Pearson, a quick and shifty sophomore, more playing time against Iowa. "I would like to see him play more," Spencer said. "He works hard in practice, and he can do anything we are doing."

"It's a nice change-up, and he deserves to play," Hollis said. "Plus, it helps Eddie out. We'll give Eddie some rest this week."

After studying Iowa's offense with Young, Cooper joined his offensive assistants by Tuesday afternoon. "They're not bad on offense," he told them. "They killed Penn State on those wheel routes, but their left tackle is just awful. He gave up about six sacks."

If there was any coach Cooper had grown fond of since coming to the Big Ten, it was Iowa's Hayden Fry. "We have a lot in common," Cooper said. "We used to have the same shoe company, and would get together during those conventions. Just us and our wives would have dinner. We always played golf together. He calls me about once a month."

By Tuesday's practice, Cooper had decided to take a friend up on his invitation to see a World Series game in Cleveland Thursday night. He had it all planned. He would hustle out of practice by 5:30 p.m., with son John Jr. at the wheel and be at Jacobs Field to see the first pitch between the Indians and Braves at 8:20. No problem. When the assistants found out his plans, a few raised their eyebrows. What if they would lose to Iowa? Wouldn't word of Cooper's trip find its way to the media and fans? Even if he never missed a minute of preparation, it would look bad, they figured. The headlines would read: "OSU Coach Traveled to World Series Two Days Before Shocking Loss."

"That's why we aren't going to lose," Cooper joked. "What's the big deal? I am not missing practice."

Following Wednesday's practice, he hustled into his office to take a prearranged call from Katzenmoyer. He just wanted to hear the news in person a day before the player's press conference. While the defense was showering and the offense studying in the usual scouting report meeting, Cooper walked out of his office beaming. He heard what he wanted to hear.

Katzenmoyer, some said, could be the next Chris Spielman. "He's big and he can run," Cooper said. "What more do you need to know?"

Cooper's chore for Thursday was to find a kickoff man. Still in the dog house looking out, Malfatt was out of the question. Josh Jackson's kickoffs, deep enough against Wisconsin, had rarely grazed the 15-yard line against Purdue.

"I got a call from Malfatt's mother the other day," Conley told Cooper. "I don't think she's mad. She just wanted to talk."

"Let her be mad," Cooper said. "She might have to save her money to pay for his way to school next year."

Cooper wasn't serious. He never would take away a player's scholarship without just cause. "I am not going to let Josh kick off this week," Cooper decided midway through practice, watching walk-on Andy Stamp's kickoffs repeatedly land near the five-yard line. "I think I'll let that kid try. I forget his name."

Following practice, Cooper ran into his office, showered and changed. He walked back into the conference room for the usual Thursday night meeting. It was 5:30 p.m. and he had less than three hours until the first pitch more than 130 miles away.

"Listen up, guys," he said. "I want to put it together Saturday, offensively and defensively. We haven't done it yet, have we? I want you to go out and kick Hayden's ass. Hayden Fox. He acts like they don't have a chance. He's right. Now root for the Indians tonight and get off your feet."

With that, he was headed for his car. Whether he intentionally referred to Hayden Fry as Hayden Fox or not, nobody knew. Perhaps he was just a huge fan of "Coach."

Hollis' message to his offense in the ensuing meeting was more philosophical.

"We are there, we are there," he said. "If you don't believe me, turn on ESPN tonight at 7:30 and see if they aren't talking about Ohio State. You don't have one game left. You don't have two left. You have five left. People aren't satisfied with us winning by just 28 points, are they? Iowa is a good team, but not as good as we are. If you want to know what people are thinking of you, just check at 7:30 on ESPN. They'll tell you how good you are. But you all know it's a bunch of bull.

"If you look at the whole season, we are entering the third quarter. We need to make a big push into the fourth. We've got to play smart. We don't miss blitzes. We don't miss stunts. That's for the Minnesotas and the Rutgers. We are not going to be making those mistakes."

A few minutes later, Cooper called from his cellular phone to WBNS' studios for his radio show. He was speeding up I-71 to catch a World Series game, talking football over the radio in Columbus.

He wasn't missing a beat.

The Indians won 5-4, cutting Atlanta's lead to three-to-two in the series. Cooper left the stadium in the eighth inning to beat traffic, crawled into the back of his car and went to sleep as John Jr. drove home.

Saturday at 12:15 p.m. in the locker room at Ohio Stadium, he summoned his players to produce a "great" performance. "Today is the day we can put it all together — offense and defense — for four quarters," he said. "Let's show Iowa and Hayden how good we are."

Since that first Ohio State victory in 1890, a 20-14 squeaker over Ohio Wesleyan, the Buckeyes had never put on such an impressive offensive display as they were about to show Fry's team. Sure, there had been 80-0 wins over Marietta and Miami of Ohio, a 74-0 pasting of Wooster and who could forget the 128-0 embarrassment of Oberlin? But those games were played before helmets, before the forward pass and even before Ohio Stadium had been built.

Oct. 28, 1995 would be even more impressive.

By the end of the first half, the 93,314 fans, the ESPN audience (what was left of it), Fry, and even Cooper had gone through their individual stages of disbelief.

The halftime score was Ohio State 56, Iowa 7, and the game wasn't that close.

The offense had scored touchdowns on its first six possessions and on one of Iowa's when Springs returned a tipped pass 60 yards for another.

Hoying, who had entered the game as the nation's leader in passing efficiency, threw bombs of 55, 38, and 56 yards to Glenn, who turned the last two into touchdowns. The Hawkeyes had tried to play man coverage, as the coaches had seen in film, and it was no match for Glenn. Hoying's eight completions totaled 273 yards, and his first touchdown pass — his 20th of the season — broke Jim Karsatos' school record. George had rushed for 110 yards and four touchdowns. But what was amazing was how quickly the offense struck, scoring in two, four, six and three plays to make it 28-0 after one quarter. In the second, which started with Springs' interception, the offense scored in one, six and six plays. When George crossed the goal line on a three-yard run with 2:14 remaining in the second quarter, it was 56-0.

Iowa running back Sedrick Shaw recovered quarterback Matt Sherman's fumble in the end zone on the final play of the half to cut the lead to 56-7. Jogging off the field, Cooper already had formed his strategy for the second half. "I am taking Eddie, Bobby, Ricky and Terry out of the game for the second half," he said. "I don't want those guys to get hurt in a game like this. Am I surprised? I thought we would play well, but who would have guessed this? You think I thought we might be up 56-0?"

Cooper didn't even address his team at the half. No sense wasting any type of speech. Harris pulled Stanley Jackson into the bathroom to tell him that Tommy Hoying, not he, would start the second half at quarterback.

Once the starters took off their shoulder pads, the offense turned lethargic. Tommy Hoying missed badly on his first two passes and then took a sack for a 16-yard loss, as the offense failed to gain a first down on the first two series. Jackson then replaced Hoying, but couldn't do any better. Each backup quarterback appeared tentative and unsure, as the offense gained only five first downs and 52 yards in seven second-half possessions.

"Pathetic," Hollis said later. "Just pathetic."

As bad as they were, the defense may have been worse because Young shuttled in second- and third-teamers. They missed tackles, lined up in the wrong position and at times, didn't have a clue.

When it was all over, Ohio State had a 56-35 win and coaches were shaking their heads over what they had just seen. They had been so good in the first half, and so bad in the second. Did it mean anything?

"It means there's a heck of a drop-off between our first- and second-teamers," Young said.

Fry called Ohio State "one of the greatest teams ever to play in the Big Ten," but then pointed out that his "second-team is better than their second team."

The mood in the locker room after the game resembled a loss. There was little laughter, few smiles and some disgust. Players showered, dressed and left in a huff.

"It almost feels like we didn't win," Bellisari said. "It's weird, real weird." Luke Fickell called the locker room a "morgue."

Giving up 35 points probably wouldn't look good to the pollsters, many of the players admitted. The players, perhaps more than some of the coaches, realized how running up the score affected the polls. "When you are fighting for a national championship, 56-7 looks a lot better than 56-35," Finkes said.

The game proved something about Cooper, however. Right or wrong, he wasn't about to play the rankings game and embarrass an opponent, especially a friend like Fry, as other coaches of ranked teams had done earlier in the season. If he had left George or Hoying in the game, and one of them was injured, fans would have ripped his heart out, he figured. And he would have watched a great team turn into a good one. At the same time, he never imagined his backup players would look so awful.

Cooper told the media after the game that he didn't want to run up the score, but admitted his fear of injuries was the primary reason for his decision.

"It is very important for us to stay healthy," he told the media after the game. "You have to count your blessings when you come away from another game without any major injuries. Plus, we wanted to play as many players as possible. That doesn't mean we told those guys to go in there and play bad."

Then he walked out of the room and headed down the steps to the locker room. "Guess my old buddy Hayden owes me one, doesn't he?" he said. "I think we could have scored 80 if we wanted to."

Cooper always joked that before he went to bed, he took one Tylenol after a win and two after a loss. How many would he take tonight? How about one for the first half, and two for the second?

"Winning," he said, "is winning, no matter the score."

16.

A Walk in the Clouds

Bill Young turned on the lights to his office at 9:15 the next morning, poured some coffee and hit the switch to his film projector. It was broken. "I've got a splitting headache, too," he said, standing on a chair fidgeting with the wiring of the mechanism.

Since halftime of the Iowa game less than 24 hours earlier, things hadn't gone his way. His defense had given up a touchdown on the final play of the first half and then four more in the second half, although he had used every defensive player in uniform. "I am still mad about that first touchdown," he said. "The replays showed the ball was down on the one-yard line. For the rest of the game, we looked like the Keystone Cops out there. Even our experienced guys looked like they didn't have a clue. I think we have too many guys screwing around not giving a shit in practice, and then they don't know what to do when they get into the games."

When he finished grading the film two hours later, Young shook his head and headed for the water fountain. "I need some damn aspirin after that," he said. "My head is just throbbing."

Young had counted 20 missed tackles when he added up the big plays and big hits, as he did every week in order to pass out Buckeye leaves for the players' helmets. "Some of these guys ought to take them with their hands out backwards this week," he joked. "Oh well. We sit in here and bitch and moan, and then when the kids get in here later, we have to be positive."

Not that the coaches dwelled on statistics, but Young did take pride in his defense's ranking in the Big Ten. The defense had entered the game allowing 15 points per game after the shutout of Purdue, but left it giving up an average of 17.8. Fred Pagac mentioned it when the film was completed. "You know," he said, "this knocks us out of the Big Ten scoring championship." Young moaned, "Yep, I know, I know. I just got back into keeping track of our statistics, and now I can forget it again."

Cooper stuck his head in the door, telling secondary coach Lovie Smith, "We need to get some tackling drills for those safeties." Smith, a quiet, soft-spoken coach who played for Cooper at Tulsa, looked up at Cooper. "It's a catch-22, coach," he said. "Rob (Kelly) had a sore shoulder and couldn't practice all week. If we tackle in practice, they wouldn't be able to play on Saturday."

As he had gone through with Springs two weeks earlier, Young had another injury to worry about. Linebacker Ryan Miller sustained a sprained knee, and it initially appeared to be serious enough to force him to miss a game or two. That was all Young needed with Minnesota's pass-happy attack awaiting in six days in Minneapolis. "This headache will go away when Doctor Lombardo gets in here and tells me that Ryan will be OK," he said.

Instead, Larry Petroff walked in. Comedian Richard Lewis, an Ohio State graduate and avid Buckeye fan, had sent a fax to the coaches at halftime of the Iowa game. It read: "I know it's supposed to be one game at a time, but take no prisoners in the second half. When I go on all of these talks shows, the whole country will know about your (difficult) schedule. Bring on Florida State!"

The part about taking no prisoners in the second half was ironic, as the coaches sat there disgustingly watching film of the second half. Instead, the Buckeyes had become prisoners of their own large lead. Debate waged around Columbus. Should Cooper have kept the starters in the game longer, or should he have done just what he did? He was getting worn out answering the question. Imagine, he thought, getting second-guessed following a three-touchdown win.

Later in the day, a graduate assistant slipped copies of the coaches' and writers' polls to Cooper. Nebraska had jumped Florida State to No. 1 while the Buckeyes had edged within a few points of No. 3 Florida. "It's encouraging," Cooper said. "Let me put it this way, I've got Nebraska up there pretty high, too." But he still had his team No. 1 and eight other coaches agreed with him — the Buckeyes now were receiving nine first-place votes in the coaches' poll, six in the writers' poll. If he had wondered before, it was obvious that voters had watched the first half of Saturday's game on ESPN, and didn't put much stock in the second.

However, the Cornhuskers' 44-21 win at Colorado was bad news. Colorado had been one of the few remaining obstacles remaining for Nebraska. The way things were heading, the winner of the Nov. 25 game between Florida State and Florida would play Nebraska in the Fiesta Bowl for the national championship. Cooper feared that politics would enter into the polls, if they hadn't already. On one side, the bowl alliance (the Big East, Big Eight, ACC, SWC, SEC and Notre Dame) rooted against Big Ten and Pac-10 teams.

"You know what we ought to do?" Cooper asked Sports Information Director Steve Snapp. "All us coaches in the Pac-10 and Big Ten ought to get together and not vote those alliance teams so high. Because you know they may be holding it against us when they vote since we are not part of the alliance." Of course, he wasn't completely serious. Snapp knew, and he knew, that such a conspiracy would backfire.

At 6 p.m., the staff and players headed outside to run wind sprints. It was already dark, since the clocks had been turned back one hour that day. The temperature had dipped into the 40s for the first time, as players groaned when they felt the air. "I'll never forgive Dick Vermeil on nights like this," Young said. "He's convinced John that it's not good to do anything on artificial turf."

The Buckeyes stretched on the cold grass, as the warm field inside the $11-million Woody Hayes Athletic Center sat empty. "They think I am crazy," Cooper said, bundled in sweat clothes. "We got this beautiful practice facility, and I got them running outside." He then turned toward his players, who were barely noticeable in the darkness, and bellowed, "You don't need to see to run. Just run!"

When they came inside, Cooper addressed them for the second-half collapse of the day before. He had saved the speech until he watched the film of the game — just to make sure it was as bad as it looked from the sideline. It was. "In the second half," he said, "you just weren't mentally sharp. You backups — you weren't ready to play. It wasn't just the quarterbacks. None of you were ready, were you?"

Young started viewing tapes of Minnesota's offense the next morning at 7:10. The coaches watched film all day on Mondays since it was the players' only day off. His projector still hadn't been repaired, so he was forced to use a portable unit. The Golden Gophers had won three out of seven games, but had committed three turnovers inside Syracuse's 20 in one loss and dropped a sure game-winning touchdown pass in another against Michigan State. Thus, they could have easily had a 5-2 record. In two hours, Young and Pagac had a good idea how to defense the Golden Gophers' run-and-shoot offense. Minnesota was easily readable, according to formations. Young and Pagac also noticed that Minnesota's tailback would line up seven yards deep on running plays and five on passing plays. If the linebackers saw that, they could make the proper call before the play began.

Pagac had another idea, too. They would drop a lineman now and then in passing situations. "One lineman will get (an interception) this week," Pagac said. "Who do you want to get it?"

"We had better get more than one," Young replied. "They'll throw it 80 times this week."

Cooper had planned to play a practical joke on Young this week, as he had on Hollis the past week. During the Iowa game, Young had lost his temper for a brief moment on the sideline. He had screamed at Petroff when Petroff told him he was about to be penalized for standing too far onto the field. Cooper thought the episode was funny, so he told Petroff to send Young a fake memo concerning sideline behavior. The memo would be addressed from Andy Geiger's office. "We'll get Bill on that one," Cooper told Pagac.

Young didn't get to where he was for being a dummy, however. He knew immediately that the fake memo was Cooper's doing. "Freddie, they aren't going to get me," Young said. "I know better than that. Sideline behavior? Right."

At 4 p.m., Lombardo popped into Young's office. "Well," Young said. "What do you think about Ryan Miller?" Lombardo answered, "I think he will be OK. John may be scared about him because the game's on artificial turf, but you know how tough Ryan is." Young knew. If anybody would play through an injury, it would be Miller, who hadn't missed a practice in his four-year career.

Monday also was a good day to watch film of high-school recruits. So Young, Pagac, Conley, Smith and Cooper, already possessing 12 oral commitments from recruits, gathered around the television set to watch tape of a lineman from Phoenix, Ariz. "What do you think of him?" Cooper asked Young. "I like his effort and he's very smart, has a 3.5 GPA," Young said. "Lovie, what do you think of him?" Smith, after watching the film, said. "I think he's a defensive tackle." Cooper asked, "We want him then, right?"

Later, Conley told Young, "The offensive guys said they would take him if we don't want him on defense." Since Young had recruited him, he said he would break the good news to the player that night.

At 6:40 p.m., Young turned off his projector and hit the lights. "Let's go home," he said, "and start over again tomorrow."

The next morning at 7, Cooper asked Young, "What'd Joe Brown say?" Young laughed. "He loves us," he said. "We set up a visit for Dec. 8. He said his dream was to play football at Ohio State."

In Tuesday morning's weekly staff meeting, in which the coaches discussed schedules, became updated on injuries from team trainers and debated to which recruits to offer scholarships, the decision on Brown was finalized when Cooper asked Hollis, "Joe, Bill wants Joe Brown on defense, is that OK?" Hollis had no problems with it, since Brown looked quick and agile.

Brown would be accepted as a Buckeye, the 13th player to commit to the program. Although the class wouldn't become official until February, the work of Conley and the staff already had paid off. In his second year as recruiting coordinator, Conley admitted the process was better-organized now, since the staff had evaluated high school players sooner than in past years. Plus, competing recruiters no longer told top prospects that Cooper would be fired soon. Thus — the better results.

The staff also decided to offer tight end Bobby Houser's brother, Kevin, also a tight end, a scholarship. "If we don't," Conley said. "He'll commit to Michigan." That thought, if the player turned out to be productive, always terrified the coaches.

Later, Young admitted it was easy to make mistakes recruiting. He had just hoped Brown was the real thing. "It's tougher these days with the rules," he said. "You are supposed to offer recruits a scholarship worth $55,000 and you get to see him only once in person. It's not a fun job."

Before the staff meeting ended, Petroff informed Cooper that Columbus Mayor Greg Lashutka, a former OSU quarterback, planned to bring some dignitaries by to watch practice. Also, a few Pop Warner teams were coming by. It would be a normal day at practice on the Buckeyes' sidelines, where sometimes more than a hundred onlookers gathered. Cooper told Petroff, "Gosh, maybe we ought to cut down on that. We are getting so many people out there at practice some days." Before the words were out of his mouth, Harris said, "Yeah, close practice." Cooper, almost as if he had been teasing his assistants, who would have voted to close practice every day, added, "Oh well, as long as we are winning..."

As he headed out of his office to his weekly media luncheon, Cooper wondered aloud, "Should I be politicking for number one?" An hour later, the answer was obvious. A writer asked him where he had voted the Buckeyes. For the first time, he cracked and told everyone he had his team ranked No. 1.

Also, Cooper again had addressed the issue of pulling his starters at the half; explained some of the defense's problems; and gone over the problems of the second and third-teamers from the Iowa game, especially the quarterbacks. Then he said, "You guys know my two theme songs don't you? — 'One Day at a Time, Sweet Jesus' and 'Help Me Make it Through the Night.'" A few writers laughed as Cooper left humming a few bars from the latter.

The next day, sports pages and wire services everywhere focused on where Cooper had voted his team. So why had he finally given in, especially after all those times he had declined to answer?

"I figured if I told one guy, I had to tell them all," he said. "Was it all over the newspapers? All over the country?"

Told yes on both counts, he said, "Well, I figured I had better start politicking."

———————————————◆•◆———————————————

Thursday afternoon, academic advisor John Macko waited for Terry Glenn to come out of a receivers' meeting. Glenn's class load was a heavy 20 hours and he was running out of time to drop a class if he wanted to remain eligible. "He's overloaded," Macko said. Finally, Glenn emerged and promised he would drop the class the next day — the last day to drop classes for the fall quarter. "Don't forget, Terry," Macko warned. "Don't forget."

When Cooper headed out to practice, he razzed Houser, whose brother still had not accepted the scholarship offer. "Tell your brother he'd better take it," Cooper said. "He'd better take it now, or it won't be there for long."

Cooper turned to Eddie George, who had been walking alongside the two. "Eddie, you committed to us on your visit, didn't you?" he asked.

George nodded and smiled. "Loved it from the first day I got here, coach," he said.

Houser, however, was stuck behind Ricky Dudley and John Lumpkin and was unhappy with his lack of playing time. After eight games, he had caught only three passes. That surely wouldn't help land his brother.

During practice, trainer Bill Davis had other concerns. Specifically, whether Miller would be ready to play. "It doesn't look good," he said. "He's sore. I would rather keep him out a week, but we won't decide until right before game time." Miller hobbled over to Davis and smiled, pointing to his knee which was wrapped in a heavy brace. "Feels great," he said. "I can move fine. No problems." He jogged away and soon made an interception against the scout team.

"You know, you try not to have favorites," Davis said. "But he's one of mine. That kid would run through glass for you."

After the practice, Cooper gave his team a bit of a history lesson. "You got a chance to go 9-0 for the first time since....when? Does anybody know when Ohio State went 9-0 the last time?" he asked. "That's right — 1979. (Minnesota) has got all those excuses, don't they? They got ankle sprains, hang nails and hemorrhoids. It doesn't matter to us, does it? Let's just go do our job and beat them and come home."

Hollis then took the offense down the hall for his weekly lecture. "Now guys, we had a brawl with them three years ago here," he said. "Let's not get a costly personal foul this time. A one-for-one tradeoff is not good for us. We want to win the national championship, and you have to look at the big picture. That's the big picture. Northwestern is talking about going somewhere warm and playing in a bowl. We want more than that, don't we?"

Young sure did. He was one coach who wasn't satisfied with the week. "Let's quit the joking and screwing around and get focused to play," he lectured the defense. "You guys aren't serious enough for me." He walked back to his office, his neck still red, while his defensive players moped out of the meeting room. Everyone had their heads down.

"They needed that," Young said. "We're too loosey-goosey. We've got coaches too loose, too. I am concerned we are losing our focus. It's a fine line you cross over, if you are not careful. I don't want to turn around during practice and ask what defense we're in and nobody knows the answer."

Cooper headed out the door, anxious to watch Florida State play Virginia on ESPN. For his team to win the national championship, he needed losses by Nebraska, Florida State and Florida. So rooting for Virginia would be easy. "They want me to give an interview on ESPN during the game," he said. A few hours hour later, while Cooper sat in his easy chair at home, the second-ranked Seminoles trailed 30-21. "I am more nervous now than I am during our games," he told ESPN.

Virginia held on for the shocking 33-28 upset, as a Florida State running back was stopped at the one-yard line on the final play of the game. Ohio State now was sure to move up at least one spot in the polls.

"Neither team played much defense," Cooper said, "but it was an exciting game. I really thought Florida State would pull it out. It's a lesson we can learn though — anything can happen."

An hour before the game against Minnesota, the snow was falling and it was 25 degrees in downtown Minneapolis. Good thing some guy had invented domes, the coaches thought. It was a comfortable 72 degrees inside the Metrodome. The coaches repeatedly glanced up at the scoreboard, which displayed scores of the day. Finally, they saw the bad news: "NW 21, PSU 10."

It was a final. The Nittany Lions had not done the Buckeyes any favors as Northwestern stretched its perfect Big Ten record to 6-0. The Wildcats continued to put pressure on Ohio State, but as long as the Buckeyes won their remaining games, everything would be fine. They would go to the Rose Bowl because of Northwestern's non-conference loss to Miami of Ohio. Also, Michigan was in the midst of a struggle at Michigan State.

"Guys, Florida State got beat Thursday," Cooper said, starting his pregame speech. "Florida was not all that impressive today. Nebraska ran up the score. Northwestern beat Penn State, but that is fine. Let's just take care of ourselves. In my conversation on the field with (Minnesota Coach) Jim Wacker, he just told me we had a great team. Don't disappoint him. Show him just how great the Buckeyes are!"

Five minutes before kickoff, Cooper wandered over to the locker room exit. "What's the Michigan score?" he asked. Told the Wolverines had gone ahead of Michigan State, 25-21, he cringed. Just as he turned around, Petroff walked in and whispered into Cooper's ear as the players were beginning to file out for the start of the game. "Guys, I just got a final score," Cooper announced. "Michigan State 28, Michigan 25."

Not one player acted as if they had heard Cooper. There was no hooting or hollering. It was too close to game time to celebrate a Wolverines' loss now. "That don't mean nothing," George said, turning around to face his teammates. "Let's take care of business. Our business!"

The defense took care of some goal-line business on Minnesota's first possession, stopping the Gophers on eight plays inside the seven-yard line, including four straight plays from the one-yard line.

Later, the offense responded from 7-0 and 14-7 deficits, when Glenn caught a 39-yard pass from Hoying and then made a spectacular diving catch of a bomb that gained 45 more. On the play, however, Glenn came crashing to the artificial turf on his right shoulder. By the time the team trainers helped him to the bench, tears streamed down his face. He thought then that his season, as glorious and perfect as it had been, had come to a sudden, shocking end. He had never felt physical pain like this. He thought his shoulder had been dislocated. What would happen to the remainder of his season? Would his NFL status be tainted if he didn't finish it? A dozen questions raced through his mind.

As Ohio State pulled even on Hoying's nine-yard scramble to make it 14-14, Glenn laid on an X-ray table grimacing inside the Metrodome. Team doctor Chris Kaeding walked out of the room, leaving the player to the X-ray attendant. "I think he's got a separated shoulder," Kaeding said. "He's real upset. Sometimes they think it's worse than it really is because of the pain."

Once the pictures were taken, Glenn lifted himself off the table and walked slowly into the waiting room where a television showed the game. He sat back and stared into the tube. The technician called Kaeding when the X-rays had been developed. Glenn had a slight separation.

"Terry," he said, "the X-rays look good. Let me see you move a little bit."

Kaeding straddled Glenn's right side and slowly worked his arm and shoulder into motion. Glenn winced with every move. "Does this hurt?" the doctor asked.

"Yes!" Glenn said, his face contorted with pain.

Kaeding then took Glenn into the viewing room to show him the X-rays. "Terry, it doesn't look that bad," he said. "(Former defensive back) Marlon Kerner had the same thing last year. It didn't take him long to get over it."

Just before halftime, after George scored on an 11-yard run, Pepe Pearson scored on a tackle-breaking 18-yard run and Hoying threw nine yards to Dudley, the Buckeyes had taken a 35-14 lead. Vikings' star Cris Carter, once an Ohio State star receiver like Glenn, made his way to the X-ray room. It was the past meeting the present. Glenn was lying back on a sofa watching the game on television. What was amazingly ironic was the fact that Glenn's catch had given him the single-season school record with 1,141 receiving yards. Guess whose record he had broken?

Carter's, although neither had realized it at the time, or probably cared for that matter.

"The sun will come up tomorrow — you'll see," Carter told him. "Trust me. You are so close to where you want to be. Just work hard. Enjoy yourself, too. OK? If you need to talk sometime, call me."

With that, Carter took his young son and headed down the Metrodome hallway as Glenn walked slowly back to the locker room. A few minutes later, his teammates filed in at the half, leading by three touchdowns. The receiver headed into the training room to find a comfortable seat where his shoulder wouldn't be bumped. Mike Malfatt sat next to him dumbfounded. Malfatt, knocked silly on a kickoff, didn't recognize Glenn.

The 35-14 lead served as a warning to some players. "Remember what happened last week," Vrabel said. "Let's blow somebody out for a change."

As Glenn sat on a table in the trainer's room, several teammates shuffled in to check on him while Malfatt wondered what the heck was going on. Cooper was happy on two counts — that Glenn wasn't finished for the season and that his team had overcome the 14-7 deficit. "You guys looked like shit out there to start the game," he said. "Now let's show them what Buckeye football is all about."

Center Juan Porter asked Glenn what happened on the play that caused the injury. He answered, "I lost it in the lights. I didn't see it until the last second." By then, he had to dive to make the catch.

Nevertheless, the players were very loose and boisterous at halftime. Even Cooper joked around. He gave a soft lecture to Josh Jackson, who kicked one kickoff out of bounds after Malfatt left the game. "Josh, I don't give a shit where you kick it, just kick it inbounds," he said. "Otherwise, I'll get 500 call-ins about it on my radio show."

Hollis lectured his offense before the third quarter. "Let's put them away on the first drive of the second half," he said. "Then we can have some real fun."

It took only one play.

George started left, saw a hole, cut right and ran 87 yards untouched to make it 42-14. He later scored the final touchdown, too, following Vrabel's interception on a pass that Fickell had batted into the air. As Pagac and Young had planned on Monday, a defensive lineman had made an interception. Cooper noticed on the scoreboard that George had more than 160 yards rushing. "We tried to get Eddie his 200 yards," he said. "But I wasn't going to take any chances," He finished with 178 yards and three touchdowns.

With Glenn's status for next week already in jeopardy, it was a wise move by Cooper. He removed the first-team offense midway through the third quarter with a 49-14 lead.

Once again, the second-team offense couldn't get anything going. And once again, the Buckeyes went scoreless in the fourth quarter, leaving another opposing coach thankful. "Anytime you come up here and win by this margin," Cooper said of the 49-21 thrashing, "I'll be happy with it. And I am happy anytime Michigan loses. But that's the second week in a row that we put in our young people and they couldn't get any points."

Young wasn't satisfied. His first-team defense had held Minnesota to 14 points, but the backups had given up 111 yards in the fourth quarter and a 54-yard touchdown pass with only 13 seconds remaining. "Gosh, I hate to give up a cheap one like that," he said. "Thirteen dang seconds were on the clock." Davis' favorite, Miller, toughed out the pain to play on his bad knee, until Young brought him to sidelines once the team had a big lead. "Still sore," the linebacker said. "No big deal."

When the America West charter headed down the runway of the Minneapolis airport 90 minutes later, Glenn, his arm in a sling, tried to get comfortable in his coach-class seat. "He's nervous in the front of the plane," Petroff said, "or he would be in first class with more room."

None of the players realized it or probably even heard of Fred Crow, but the Buckeyes did sustain a loss on this day. Crow was the former player who blocked a kick with his left arm in the 1935 Notre Dame-Ohio State game and later wrote into his will ordering the limb be cremated and the ashes be spread over the south end zone should he not live to see the rematch.

Five weeks to the day after watching the Buckeyes get revenge on the Irish, he died at the OSU Medical Center just hours before the kickoff at Minnesota. He lived to see the team's 8-0 start.

As the team's charter flight leveled off, the movie "A Walk in the Clouds" began.

Through nine games, it described the season perfectly.

17.

"Whose house is this?"

Monday afternoon, Nov. 6, Cooper munched on a sandwich and sipped a Coke in his office, scanning *USA Today's* sports section. His team had jumped over not only Florida State, but Florida, also. The Buckeyes now were the second-ranked team in the nation, behind Nebraska. Suddenly, he dropped the paper and looked up in amazement. "I can't believe we are a 20-point favorite," he said.

The point spread, which the team had covered in each of its nine games, baffled him for one simple reason — Illinois, in addition to Michigan of course, had been his personal nemesis since he arrived at Ohio State. The Illini, 4-4 during the season, had beaten his teams in six-of-seven games, including 24-10 in 1994. It was Illinois' fourth consecutive win at Ohio Stadium and what had made it worse was that Illini linebacker Dana Howard had guaranteed it. Once it happened, Illinois players danced and pranced off the field as if they owned the place. In fact, they contended they did, labeling Ohio Stadium "our house."

Revenge.

It would be the subject of the week, although coaches and players publicly repeated it wouldn't be a factor.

After the Minnesota game, Hollis dreaded listening or reading what would be repeated in the media. "You know, how Illinois owns us and they can't lose to us and all that other garbage," he said.

The offensive coaches — minus Hollis — had other worries anyway while watching film of Illinois' defense, which ranked second in the Big Ten. Hollis was downtown at the courthouse, finalizing the adoption of a two-year-old boy.

For some reason, the Illini had played a four-deep zone at times in the 26-7 win at Iowa the previous Saturday — the first they had showed that defense and it had the coaches baffled. If Glenn had not recovered by Saturday, moving the ball on Illinois would be tougher than usual, they figured. They needed him to stretch their defense.

"We've got to get Terry jacked up to play," Stobart said. "We need to get him four treatments a day if needed."

When Cooper walked into the film session, Stobart asked him, "John, we need you to call Hayden and ask him a few questions — like, 'Why does he think they played that coverage against him?'"

"I need to call him anyway," Cooper said.

Cooper had expected Fry to call him following the 56-35 win over the Hawkeyes a week earlier — if not to chat then at least to thank him for not running up the score.

But Fry never called. Cooper headed across the hall to his office and picked up the telephone.

"Hayden, I appreciate all those nice things you said about us after our game," Cooper said. "How good is Illinois?"

After several questions about the Illini, Cooper tried to encourage Fry, whose team had to play at Northwestern. This was one week Cooper and the Buckeyes could have used his help. "Don't get down. You can go over there and beat Northwestern," Cooper instructed. "They are due. You guys can beat anybody. Don't get down now."

Cooper hung up and headed back to the meeting.

"Hayden's really down," he told his assistants. "The Illinois game shocked him. He said he doesn't know why they changed coverages. He said we ought to run right at them, then fake the isolation and throw deep all day."

Suddenly, Hollis busted into the room and lit it up like the Fourth of July with his mood. The adoption was final — the Hollis family had expanded. "It's official," he said. "And I've got chocolate cigars to prove it. Now, have you guys figured out how to beat these guys yet?"

Everyone chuckled.

A few minutes later when Hoying dropped off some film, Cooper said, "Bobby, if I was quarterbacking this team this week, I would want to get number 83 some treatment. We need him healthy."

That reminded Hollis, who asked, "Anybody seen Terry today?"

Told by a graduate assistant that the receiver was in the trainer's room, Cooper jumped from his seat. "Just now?" he asked. "I'll go see him. I told them to come and get me when he got here." Two minutes later, he walked back in disappointed. Like dozens of defensive backs during the season, he had missed Glenn.

"They say it's his worst day," Cooper said. "I guess it's supposed to be very sore 48 hours after the injury."

"Terry, Terry...we're smelling the roses, man," Harris mumbled, writing something on his note pad. "Where are you?"

Stobart realized how Glenn felt. He had experienced so much emotional pain in his young life, that whenever something bad happened, he had been conditioned to expect the worst. "He's scared," Stobart said. "Look what's happened to him. The kid has gone through hell in his life and now when he gets hurt, he automatically thinks things are crashing down around him."

The next morning, Hollis still was chipper. It was a feeling that wouldn't wear off soon, realizing how happy he and his wife were every time he looked into the tiny babyface of the youngest of his three sons. "How'd I celebrate?" he said. "Just had a vodka and tonic. That's it. Life is good, right?"

It had been great for Cooper, too, until he was bombarded with questions at his weekly media luncheon about Illinois' domination of his team. Had Lou Tepper and former Illinois Coach John Mackovic out-coached him? Did they recruit better? Was it a jinx? What about Howard's guarantee a year earlier?

"The years they beat us, they were just better than us," he said. "They always play good defense. They made plays and we didn't. We would miss a field goal, get a field goal blocked, fumble going in (for a touchdown). We've always moved the ball on them, we've just had trouble capitalizing. I am not making alibis. We just haven't got it done. I really don't think about it. I really don't — unless you guys bring it up."

This was one of those times Cooper liked to say that talent won or lost games, not coaching. This season, his team had a perfect 9-0 record. There had to be a reason, several reasons. "It's called talent," he said. "I don't know of a quarterback that is playing better than Bobby, a running back running better than Eddie, an offensive lineman blocking better than Orlando, a receiver as good as Terry or a defensive player playing as well as Vrabel."

Illinois' teams had made plays; his didn't. That was his story and he was sticking to it. But this year, oh yes, this year would be different, he thought.

Revenge.

"We don't owe anybody," Hoying said. "We just owe it to ourselves to go out and play our best. We don't get too caught up in what happened last year. We're a different team with different players. Heck, I am one-and-one against them anyway. You can't get too caught up in paying somebody back."

While the television cameras rolled, guard Jamie Sumner said, "It's no big deal really. It's only a hump if you let it be. We are playing for this year only."

Once he walked into the locker room, leaving the glare of the media spotlight, Sumner got serious. Weren't the Buckeyes bothered just a little by Illinois' recent domination of them? Privately, the answer was obvious. "Hell yes," he said. "We just say what we are supposed to say out there. Dana Howard predicted a victory over us — and went out and backed it up. I've never seen that before. You don't think that doesn't bother us? Man, believe me, it's fresh in everyone's minds. It was embarrassing. If Terry plays or doesn't play, it won't matter. We *will* kick their butts."

Before practice, Cooper milled around his office, waiting for 4 o'clock to arrive so he could head out to the field and get started on Illinois. He twirled his whistle around his finger, and considered the big picture. The Rose Bowl picture. "It seems like we never get a break around here," he said. "In any other year, Northwestern would have six losses by now. I don't think they'll lose now, but you never know. Guess we'll just have to win 'em all. You know Michigan will be fired up, if they know they can keep us from the Rose Bowl by beating us. If Northwestern would lose, they wouldn't have that incentive."

———— •◆•◆•————

Wednesday afternoon, Cooper couldn't help but think about Glenn and his injury. Next to the coach's phone was a sheet of paper with "Terry Glenn" written at the top.

"Look at this," he said. "I got every phone number where I can find him at any time. We've got to take care of him. You know what he told me? He said he didn't want to come out (to the NFL) early. He said he wants to stay here another year. I just told him I would do anything I could to help him find out his (draft) status. If I thought it was in his best interests to go, I would encourage him. But I am not sure it is."

Naturally, Cooper knew agents would be knocking on Glenn's door often, telling him every reason why he should turn pro early. "It's going to be tough to keep them away," he said. "Terry comes from a poor background. He doesn't have much. They'll be like vultures."

There were reasons why Glenn would want to leave. One was a dollar sign in front of seven figures. Another was the possibility of injury, which had become a reality four days earlier. A third was Ohio State's unsettled quarterback situation for 1996, so it was natural for Glenn to wonder how he possibly could match his current statistics. "I already talked to him about that," Cooper said. "I told him if he stayed, we would have a quarterback here who would get the ball to him."

While the Buckeyes were recruiting most of the top high school quarterbacks in the nation, Harris had an ace up his sleeve. If only he could get the ace to commit to OSU, things would be fine. His name was Mark Garcia, a 6-foot-2, 210-pounder at Modesto (Calif.) Junior College. Harris didn't want the media to get wind of his pursuit of Garcia, who would be visiting campus as soon as his junior-college season was finished. "What if we don't get the guy?" Harris asked rhetorically. "Plus, I haven't told our (quarterbacks) yet.

"Anyway, the guy sounds like the real deal. His team is 8-0. A guy I trust tells me he reminds him of Trent Dilfer. I saw him in person in the spring and four games on film. He's big-time."

Glenn's injury wasn't the only one for the Buckeyes, who had escaped the first eight games with only Jerry Rudzinski (foot), Shawn Springs (ankle) and Ryan Miller (knee) being hurt. Only Rudzinski had missed more than one game. But this week, when the wounded walked into Bill Davis' training room for treatment, they had to take a number. Sumner hobbled around with "turf toe," a painful bruise under the arch of the big toe. Defensive tackle Matt Bonhaus had a sprained wrist. Backup tight end John Lumpkin had re-fractured his foot and would miss the remainder of the season. Defensive back Central McClellion had a concussion. So did Malfatt, whose melon bumped into a kick returner's knee at Minnesota. "It's that time of year," Davis said. "Everybody's got something. But I can't complain. This has been one of the best years we've ever had. Knock on wood. One year we had six ACLs."

An ACL, a torn knee ligament, symbolized the worst nightmare for any football player. Those three harmless letters made any 300-pounder cringe like a kid getting vaccinated. "This team's been real good about pain," Davis said. "Nobody wants to miss practice, but sometimes it's unavoidable. You watch — during Michigan week everybody will practice unless they are clinically dead."

Fortunately for Glenn, his injury wasn't that serious, although he still wasn't ready to practice. "He's much better today," Davis said while watching practice Wednesday. "He ran this morning and he's supposed to run again pretty soon."

Sure enough, as Davis spoke, Glenn walked out of the locker room in sweat pants. The two were joined by strength coach Dave Kennedy. Noticing the throng of onlookers at practice, they headed outside into 20-degree temperatures. It was the first day it had snowed in Columbus and while his teammates sweated through practice inside, Glenn jogged outside as flurries whistled by his shivering face. Kennedy and Davis watched his every move.

"I want you to get up to 90 percent and get your arms pumping," Kennedy said.

"I can't raise my arm that much," Glenn said, cringing. Suddenly, he slipped and fell hard to the slick turf. "Shit!" he screamed. "That hurt, that hurt."

Kennedy and Davis tried their best not to look concerned, but inside they had to be petrified. At their feet laid the best receiver in college football, moaning in pain on the snow and ice of the lacrosse field. A cameraman from a local television station hopped out of a truck and walked toward the field. Kennedy noticed.

"What are you doing?" Kennedy asked.

"I wanted to get a few shots," he answered.

"No, you don't," Kennedy shot back. "Take off."

The cameraman turned around and headed away with no response. Glenn climbed to his feet, and was brought inside to run behind a curtain. Why all the secrecy?

"Shoot, if we had him run in here, practice would have stopped," Kennedy said. "The guy's a proud athlete. He doesn't want everybody to see him hurting. You saw that cameraman outside."

Cooper wandered over to talk to Glenn. "I told him his legs aren't hurt," the coach said. "He'll play. At the very least, we'll put him out there and let him run deep a few times."

San Diego Chargers' General Manager Bobby Beathard showed up at practice, watching every move Hoying and George made. Afterwards, he stopped George for a quick chat. "I didn't even know who it was at first," George said. "I didn't recognize him."

Following practice, Hollis gave his offense a scouting report of the Illini. "First of all, (linebacker Kevin) Hardy is more productive than Simeon Rice," he said. "Rice is very good in passing situations. He doesn't play the run that well. We can run right at him."

The offensive coaches didn't think much of Rice, despite the linebacker's mountain of preseason publicity. On film, he appeared to be a finesse player, only looking to rush the passer. They figured they could run right at him, and Orlando Pace would knock him into next week, perhaps even into December. A year ago, Howard was better than Rice. This season, Hardy was.

Hollis had made it clear that this would be a game in which Hoying would check off often from run-to-pass and pass-to-run at the line of scrimmage. "Hey," Hollis said, "the media was just asking me about all this Illinois bullshit. Guys, this is a whole new football team. We don't worry about last year. We are entering the fourth quarter of the season, so get ready for it."

The question was: Would it live up to the first three?

Although he wore shoulder pads for the first time and jogged lightly again, the outlook for Glenn wasn't much brighter Thursday afternoon. As his teammates practiced outdoors in 35-degree weather, he shivered and watched for a while and then headed inside.

"It's still sore," he said. "It feels much worse than what they tell me it is. When I go to bed at night, I can't even toss and turn. I just lie on my back." Glenn admitted that when the injury occurred, he figured that was it. His season, and perhaps his career, was finished. "I did," he said. "The pain was something, man. I've watched it three or four times, and I don't want to see it again. It hurts to even look at it on film."

In his address to the team following practice, Cooper began to hint at Illinois' recent domination of his team. He never admitted it to the media, but he wanted revenge on Illinois more than anybody. It angered him not only to lose to the Illini, but to have his face rubbed into the misery as he thought it had been.

"Now, if I have to get up here and fire you up for this game, then you are playing at the wrong school," he said. "They've beaten you four out of five years, and they brag about it. They rub it in. I don't care what the weather's going to be like. Wind or rain or in the 50s — I don't care. Nothing keeps you from winning this game."

Hollis echoed those sentiments to his offense.

"Coach Cooper couldn't have said it better," he said. "If there's an ounce of pride in us... We're nine and oh. We're not looking for the Big Ten championship. That will fall into place. We want more. You've gone from 15th (actually 12th) in the nation to two in the polls. We're a better football team than Illinois. Now there's no school tomorrow (Veterans' Day), so discipline yourself. Get your butt in tonight. You've got a chance to play for something big. Our whole key Saturday is our capability to run the football. We've *got* to run the football."

Hollis then pulled a letter out of his pocket. It had been sent by a Buckeye fan who lived in Chicago and was surrounded by Illini alumni: "Now the guy writes, 'Those who forget history are condemned to live it again.'" It was old, worn out and overused, but it served its purpose for the moment. "Now we don't dwell on the past," Hollis said, "but we won't forget it, either, right?"

Before they headed home for the night, Hollis and Mike Jacobs viewed film on an offensive tackle prospect from Nashville, Tenn. "Six-foot-eight," Hollis read from a lineup card. "Wow."

Jacobs laughed, saying, "Look at that, he blocks with his belly. I guess we can teach him to use his shoulder pads, can't we?" Both snickered and headed for the door. Someone asked Hollis if he thought Glenn would play Saturday. "Hell no," he said. "We're planning on going without him. What else can we do?"

The next day, Cooper didn't seem that worried about Glenn's status.

"Hey, if he doesn't play, somebody else will," he said. "We'll treat him until game time. He'll warm-up and then he'll either say, 'Coach, I feel fine' or 'Coach, I can't play.' You know what fans don't understand: Doctors make those decisions; coaches don't. In the old days, we used to put an aspirin on it and go play. But now, I got no control over it."

George also kept a close eye on Glenn's status. He figured if the receiver couldn't play, a larger burden would fall on his shoulders. There wouldn't have been a better game for it, either. He would never forget his first collegiate game when he fumbled twice against Illinois. It humiliated him, drove him to focus even more intently on this game, as had the previous season's loss.

"We'll just have to pick up the slack," he said. "All I can do is prepare myself to play the best game I can play."

Which already had Illinois Coach Lou Tepper frightened. During his weekly conference call, Tepper was asked if George "was pulling away" in the Heisman race. He said, "I hope he just doesn't pull away from us."

If Glenn didn't play, and with the weather forecast calling for a cold and windy day, Cooper knew this would be one game in which the team with the best running attack would win. It would be bruising. Even if it took talking Hollis into running more and passing less. He sensed that his offensive coordinator had fallen in love with Harris' passing scheme and Hoying's ability to execute it.

"I've got to be careful that we don't get away from what's going good," Cooper said. "Last year we pound it and pound it and get down there and get too cute and throw an interception. We're getting cute at times now, but it's been working."

The Buckeyes awakened Saturday morning at the downtown Hyatt to the worst game-day weather in years. The wind was gusting up to 50 miles per hour. It was 40 degrees and dropping fast. The rain, which appeared to be falling sideways at times, was supposed to change to snow by kickoff.

"Fine with me," Hollis said. "We'll just run it down their throats." That was the attitude Cooper wanted to hear.

Besides, Glenn wasn't feeling much better.

"I asked him how he was doing and he just did this," Harris said, wobbling his hand back and forth. "It doesn't look good — especially with the weather."

An hour before kickoff, team doctors Chris Kaeding and John Lombardo pulled Glenn into the trainer's room at Ohio Stadium. While his teammates milled around getting taped and putting on their shoulder pads, Glenn wore gold slacks and a shirt. The three looked as if they were attending a funeral. "He isn't going to play," Kaeding said. "We told him it would be nice if he was on the sidelines to encourage Buster and the other guys. It was pretty much his call. But you know, I probably agree with him considering the weather."

When assistant strength coach Dave Langworthy walked into the room, Dudley and Sumner turned and smiled. They reached into the bag Langworthy had carried. "Gummy Bears," Langworthy said. "I used to give them to (former OSU All-American basketball player) Jimmy Jackson before every game. Now these guys can't play without them. Did you see them looking around when I walked in? They couldn't wait to get their Gummy Bears."

Josh Jackson trotted off the soggy field shaking his head 30 minutes before kickoff. Snow flurries were flying now. "Man, anything beyond 30 yards and I won't even be aiming down the middle," the kicker said. "The wind is worse than it's ever been here."

Just before kickoff, equipment managers watching the Iowa-Northwestern game solemnly gave everyone the final score: Northwestern 31, Iowa 20. So much for Hayden Fry's chance to help the Buckeyes clinch the Rose Bowl berth before the Michigan game.

Hollis gathered his offense to tell his players they were about to play a blue-collar game. There would be no Terry Glenn, little passing, and lots of power blocking. "Now guys, there will be no gimmes up front today," he said. "Let's blow off the ball. We're a better football team than Illinois. We all know that, but we've got to prove it from 3:30 until 7 o'clock."

Hollis stopped talking, then walked over in front of receiver Dimitrious Stanley, who would start in place of Glenn.

"Dimitrious," he said. "You've been wanting an opportunity and now you've got it. Do something with it!"

Cooper was in another room barking at the second- and third-team players. "You guys on the sideline — get involved in the game," he said. "I don't want to see you sitting over there on the bench freezing."

When Hollis finished, Cooper entered the offensive room and wrote on the blackboard: "The team that won't be beaten can't be beaten!"

"You know every year that one of our goals is to win every game in the horseshoe," he said. "We're in the 'shoe today. The 'shoe belongs to the Buckeyes. It's our house!" It was a rare sign that Illinois' recent domination of the Buckeyes had bothered him, especially those four straight losses at home.

At the start of what was the 1,000th football game in Ohio State history, it appeared the Illinois jinx would continue when Hoying's second pass was intercepted. The defense stopped Illinois in three plays, and OSU took over on its one-yard line. After an offsides penalty, George let everyone in the stadium know this would be his day. He carried five consecutive times for 90 yards to set up Pepe Pearson's four-yard touchdown run.

The next time the Buckeyes touched the ball, George rushed for 38 more yards. On third-and-10 from Illinois' 14, Hoying squeezed a pass over the middle into Stanley's arms. Following Hollis' advice before the game, Stanley made the most of it, fighting his way into the end zone.

Jackson added a 20-yard field goal to give Ohio State a 17-0 halftime lead. George had already gained 180 yards on 23 carries.

The defense had dominated Illinois' one-dimensional offense, allowing only four first downs and 85 yards. Still, Cooper appeared angry at the half. "Let's kick the crap out of this team," he shouted. "They aren't worth a crap. You should be way ahead by now!"

Cooper, huddling with the coaches to determine second-half strategy, decided to take the wind in the third quarter — instead of the fourth as usual. Why? "I don't want them to get back in the game in the third quarter," he told his staff. "I want to put them away in this quarter. If we let them get back into it, we are going to have ourselves a game."

He then gathered his players, and reminded them one last time of what Illinois had put them through in recent seasons. "They've embarrassed you enough," he told them. "This is our house! Now let's go out there and put them away."

George must have been thinking the same thing. On his first carry, after Illinois kicked a field goal to make it 17-3, he darted left and broke a tackle in the backfield. He then cut upfield and ran 64 yards for a touchdown. Afterwards, he walked behind the bench and faced the crowd, his hands on his hips, as if to say "Did you like my run?"

They reciprocated, chanting "Eddie! Eddie!"

Now he had 244 yards — just 30 from Keith Byars' school record which also came against Illinois (1984). Word filtered down to running backs coach Tim Spencer and then to Cooper, who would make sure George would own the record by the end of the day.

Seven carries later, he did, taking the handoff on a simple draw on his way to three yards. On the next play, he broke a tackle and slid into the end zone on a 13-yard run to make it 31-3.

The scoreboard informed 92,639 fans of the school's new single-game rushing record-holder. In turn, the crowd altered their chant to: "Heisman! Heisman!" George wasn't finished yet. Cooper now wanted him to get 300 yards. He did it easily, running for 24 yards around left end early in the fourth quarter. He had 314 yards and three touchdowns after his 36th and final carry. The Heisman Trophy wouldn't be delivered until Dec. 9, but if George would win it, he would win it on this cold and windy day. What made his day even more incredible was the fact that the Illinois defense knew he was getting the ball. Tepper had ordered eight and sometimes nine defenders to the line of scrimmage, but they still couldn't stop him. "I've been coaching 32 years," Illinois defensive coordinator Denny Marcin said later, "and I've never seen a back do that."

As he trotted off the field to another chant calling his name, George saluted the crowd and hugged Cooper and then Hollis. He then stood on the bench, raised his arms and asked, "Whose house is this now? Whose house?"

The answer was simple — Eddie George owned Ohio Stadium on this day.

In the locker room following the 41-3 victory, Cooper was as exultant as a victorious general returning from war.

"The number one defense in the Big Ten just got their butts kicked!" he shouted to his team. "Now, whose house is this?" His players screamed and shouted the obvious answer. "Keep this in perspective. That team had lost four games. We've got Indiana next, don't we? Indiana, right?"

On his radio show minutes later, Cooper vented some frustration again — this time over Illinois' comments from 1994. "I tell our players that when you go on the road, you keep your mouths shut," he said. "We were sick and tired of hearing that this was their house and all that stuff."

George had walked into the recruiting room and began to tell prospects why Ohio State was a great place to play while Cooper lauded him to the media. "That was the finest individual effort I've ever seen by a running back," he said.

Hoying, meanwhile, limited to only 13 throws because of the weather, told the media how enjoyable it had been to hand off and watch the back of number 27 head the other way. "You almost wanted to sit there and enjoy the moment," he said. "But there was a referee there to blow the whistle to get started again."

Young had said he "probably would get another job" if he had to face a running back like George every week.

When Steve Snapp requested George to appear in media room, George insisted that Orlando Pace come with him. Then he proceeded to credit the offensive line for each of his 314 yards. What was it like to have more than 92,000 fans chanting his name in unison? "It gives you goose bumps," he said. He finished, then headed downstairs to talk live on ESPN radio. The big running back, dressed immaculately, sat back on a trainer's table, placed the telephone to his ear and was put on hold of all things. Once he was on the air, he said, "We had to get into the running game and show them who's boss. My first experience with Illinois wasn't a good one." When the host asked about the Heisman Trophy, he said, "If it's meant to be, I will win it. I've had two successful seasons here, and it would be great to win it, but I can't focus on that right now."

He walked out, headed down the steps and bumped into Helen and Cindy Cooper. After hugging her husband's star running back, Helen told him, "Eddie, I am so happy for you. Real happy."

At 7:42 p.m., George walked out of the players' exit to Ohio Stadium and was met by dozens of fans holding pens in one hand and something to sign in the other.

"Hey Eddie, how about a Heisman pose?" one guy in his 40s asked, mocking the trophy with a poor stiff arm.

"Can't do it," George said. "I can't do that."

He stayed until everyone was gone, well past 8 o'clock, and headed out into the night air. It was snowing harder now. The cold, dark, old horseshoe was empty, but the chants still had to be ringing in his ears.

"Eddie! Eddie!"

18.

Eleven and Zero

Three-hundred and 14 reasons.

That's what Eddie George had in earning his third Big Ten Player of the Week Award of the season. The greatest performance of any running back in Ohio State history still was the talk of the town the next day. It naturally was the main topic for the coaches during Sunday morning meetings.

"The thing that I have noticed is that he is so much faster," said Cooper, who earlier in the season had remarked that his senior running back wasn't a "home run hitter." Now he was hitting grand slams. "Usually, running backs get worn down this time of year," he said, "but he seems to be getting stronger."

Running backs coach Tim Spencer, who was about to be passed as Ohio State's second all-time leading rusher by his star pupil, admitted he watched the game in awe. "I never saw Archie Griffin, but that's the best I've ever seen a running back run on this level," he said. "He was in what we call 'The Zone.'"

Bill Young had his own reasons to smile Sunday. His defense had held Illinois to only 160 yards — 99 less than their previous best effort for the season — and a measly field goal. Illinois had rushed 28 times for 59 yards, or in relative numbers, 255 less than George. "It really looked even better on film than it did in person," he said. "We just shut them down. Luke Fickell played tremendous. He was all over the place."

That night, when the team ran wind sprints, George finished first in every one, as if the three dozen carries less than 24 hours earlier never happened.

"What's new?" Cooper asked rhetorically. "He always wins the sprints. That's how hard he works. That's just Eddie George."

Everybody, by now, knew the name.

Illinois was all but forgotten when Hollis and Cooper picked up the Monday morning newspaper. "Guess how much we are favored by this week?" Hollis asked during the morning offensive meeting.

"Twenty-eight?" Jacobs answered.

"Twenty-eight?" Harris echoed.

"Thirty-five?" Stobart guessed.

"Nope," Hollis said. "Thirty-three points. Can you believe that. Hey, this is the time of year that those guys know about all the teams. They are pretty accurate. It's the first thing I look at on Mondays."

"Yeah, you and Coach Cooper," Harris shot back.

It was true. Cooper usually knew the point spread of the college and NFL games on Monday mornings and liked to sucker the other coaches into one-dollar bets. For instance, when the team finished its short practice a day earlier, he had heard the 49ers were shocking Dallas 24-0 in the second quarter. So he wandered into Harris' office and dropped the bait. "Walt, I want to make sure now, didn't you give me San Francisco today?" he asked.

Harris fell for it, jumping on the bet since everyone had expected an easy Cowboys' victory. Cooper laughed and told him the score. "I am taking these guys all the time," Cooper said, chuckling. "Walt's lucky I am a nice guy."

The serious matter of the week, part II, however, would be Glenn's continued recovery. His shoulder obviously was healing, the trainers said, but would he play against Indiana or take another week off and wait until Michigan? "Dave Kennedy doesn't think Terry will play this week," Hollis said.

"I agree with him," Stobart said.

"I think he's waiting for Michigan," Hollis answered.

"Well, that's the first thing he said when he was in the trainer's room after the injury," Stobart remembered. "He said, 'Coach, I won't be ready until Michigan.'"

When Cooper joined the meeting, a trainer told him that Glenn had been in the training room getting treatment. "You owe me another dollar, Joe," he said, walking out to check on his star receiver.

"I admit I am surprised," Hollis said. "I am a little down on him."

"Hold on, Joe," Harris said. "He's done a lot for us, and we need him next week."

Cooper had been thrilled that his own offspring, daughter Cindy, had toughed out the Columbus Marathon in four hours and 15 minutes in 30-degree temperatures a day earlier. "I am so proud of her," he told the other coaches. "If she sets her mind to something, she does it. She finished. She walked a mile between 24 and 25, but she finished. Then she said that's her one and only marathon. It was too cold."

Suddenly, Cooper darted out into the hallway, looking for Fred Pagac. It was tradition for the Ohio State-Illinois winner to receive something called the Illibuck — a glob of a trophy that is supposed to resemble a turtle. Whatever, the Illibuck wasn't a common sight around Columbus in recent years. "Where's the Illibuck?" Cooper asked. "They win, and that's all you hear about. Now we win, and you don't hear anything about the thing.

"Hey Freddie," he shouted down the hall. "Where's the Illibuck?"

The other coaches, watching Cooper scoot down the hall to find Pagac, broke into laughter.

A few minutes later, Cooper walked back into the room no closer to finding the trophy than when he had left, but he did have some news. "It looks like they are going to give Lloyd Carr the job up there," he said. "They've got a 10 a.m. press conference."

Up there, of course, was Michigan, which ironically was appearing on Hollis' screen at the moment against Indiana. Michigan would take 'interim coach' away from

Carr's title. Cooper got on the phone to his secretary. "Julie," he said, "send him a telegram from us congratulating him."

Michigan had stumbled around against Indiana earlier in the season, missing blocks and assignments, although the Wolverines had won 34-17. The coaches were supposed to be watching Indiana's defense, but it was impossible for them not to think ahead one week.

"This is about as bad as I've seen Michigan," Jacobs said.

That made Hollis nervous.

"Oh no, don't say that," he said. "Don't even say that."

"I am just saying that they don't look good in this game," Jacobs said.

Hollis informed a visitor that they were not looking at Michigan film this week, unless the Wolverines appeared against Indiana. Neither had Young and the defensive staff. "I promise you," Hollis said. "We don't do that around here. We won't look at Michigan film until next week. Indiana's got the second-ranked defense in the Big Ten."

Although working on Michigan a week early had been one of Woody Hayes' favorite tricks, it was virtually impossible to look ahead with the state of college football nowadays. Scholarship limits had evened the playing field somewhat, drawing the worst team in the Big Ten closer to the best. Cooper, or any head coach for that matter, could not afford to overlook any team anymore — even 2-7 Indiana. "I never coached anywhere when you work on a team ahead of another team," Cooper said.

"And I am not going to start now."

The way the ensuing weekend shaped up, if Purdue upset Northwestern at home, and Ohio State beat Indiana, the Buckeyes would clinch the Rose Bowl berth. If Northwestern won, they would have to wait and beat Michigan.

Cooper wasn't giving the Boilermakers much of a chance to help his team. "They could do it, but I don't know if they will," he said. "I've been in this game 33 years — anything can happen."

Which is the way he felt when he and Helen met for lunch. If his team beat Indiana as expected and got by Michigan, he could ride a crest of popularity — no matter what happened in the Rose Bowl — into next season. After all, no team in the 106-year history of Ohio State football had won 12 games. The ensuing recruiting class shaped up to be one of his finest, and 17 starters would return next season. The program clearly was nearing the top of the Big Ten again and life in Columbus would have been almost perfect. Finally.

"Believe me, Helen and I have talked about it," he said. "That's exactly the way I want it to go. The administration hasn't always supported me here, but now I think they are. And we are winning. You're always happy when you're winning."

Glenn's outlook improved somewhat Monday afternoon when he lifted light weights under Kennedy's supervision. There was some pain, but much less than during the previous week. He finished, showered and stuck his head into Hollis' office where the coaches were viewing film.

"Terry," Hollis joked, smiling, "are we going to have you back for the bowl game?"

"Terry, get your girlfriend over there to rub down your shoulder," Jacobs suggested.

Glenn just smiled and took the lighthearted barbs as he would single coverage before walking away. He carried his shoulder as if it held an anvil, leaning to the right as he walked.

Just then, Conley walked in with some post-season plans. "Hey you guys, if things go well for Big Ed on December the ninth, we are going to have a Heisman party at Saturday's," he said. "How does that sound?"

"You mean we can't go to New York?" Harris asked.

That decision would be made later by Andy Geiger.

Half-joking anyway, Harris probably wouldn't have time for a side trip to New York during recruiting season. As the regular season was wrapping up, he was using almost every minute recruiting Mark Garcia, the junior-college quarterback from California, and a few of the top high-school quarterbacks. He planned to travel to Kentucky the night before the Indiana game to see the quarterback every collegiate program wanted, Tim Couch.

At his media luncheon Tuesday, Cooper was asked if the attention given to George had taken away from Hoying's season. The school's sports information office had determined following the second game of the season to push George for the Heisman instead of Hoying or Glenn. "Maybe at times," Cooper said, "Bobby is slighted, but I think Bobby understands. He's had a great season. But I've had no problems with pushing Eddie."

For the first time, George began to speak more openly concerning the Heisman Trophy. As he sat in the corner of a hallway, giving a television interview, he reflected back a few years when he was an unknown backup running back. "It was frustrating to me at times," he said. "I tried to be patient and wait for my time, but it was hard. I just had to have faith in my abilities.

"Now here I am and everybody is mentioning my name for the Heisman Trophy. It was a childhood dream of mine to be up for it."

Hoying and George, along with Dudley, Sumner and defensive tackle Matt Bonhaus were the only starters that would be playing their final game at Ohio Stadium. That is, unless a junior such as Glenn decided to turn pro early. They each had their individual memories of the famed horseshoe — the win over Michigan in 1994 and a few nightmares, too. Hoying had been booed off the field against Illinois a year earlier. George had fumbled twice there in his first collegiate game, and now he couldn't set his cleats in the place without fans chanting his name.

"It makes me happy and sad," George said. "I am sure it will be very emotional for me. I have a lot of great memories in that stadium, but I haven't had time to reflect on it all yet. I will just go out there and have fun."

Down the hall, Hoying was telling the media something similar. "It sure goes fast," he said. "It really does. I definitely will take a moment Saturday to stop and soak everything in. It's my last time in the horseshoe. It's funny to look back and see how I've matured, and see how everybody else has matured."

Tuesday night, Ohio State lost one of its first football legends and one of its biggest fans when Les Horvath, 74, died of heart failure in Glendale, Calif. He had been the school's first Heisman Trophy winner, receiving the award in 1944.

The next afternoon, the school's most recent Heisman winner, Archie Griffin, sat in his tiny office inside St. John Arena and signed a few footballs sitting on his desk. The room was cluttered with papers and memorabilia. "Sorry, haven't had a chance to clean this place up in a while," he told a visitor. "I haven't been in here that much lately."

The diamonds from Griffin's second Heisman Trophy ring gleamed off his finger. He not only owned two Heisman Trophies and four Rose Bowl rings, but on this day he owned a heavy heart. Horvath had become a good friend. "We had him back last year to honor him, you know," Griffin said. "I am so glad we did that." The associate athletic director also owned 11 years worth of frustration — the period which had come and gone between trips to Pasadena. "It's a different time than when I played, I realize that," he said. He pointed to a picture of his legendary coach. The two had loved each other as much as a player and coach could. "I realize Woody Hayes was his own man," he said. "I also realize there won't be another Woody Hayes. Still, it's certainly time to get back to the Rose Bowl. I can tell you that the administration expects to get back to the Rose Bowl."

Griffin thought back two years earlier, when the team traveled to Ann Arbor with a 9-0-1 record. A Rose Bowl berth was on the line that day, too, but Ohio State lost 28-0. Those heartbreaking days had to end sometime, he figured.

"Now I wasn't in this position then, but let me tell you it was frustrating," he said. "We got our tails kicked. Didn't score a point. I personally don't think Coach Cooper realized the magnitude of his job when he got here. Maybe he does now, I don't know. But I see a team on a mission this season."

Thursday night, Cooper wanted to make that perfectly clear to his players. The mission wasn't yet accomplished.

"We are playing a lot better football team than most people realize. If you go out there and screw around, you will have a ballgame on your hands. You need to get focused on Indiana and come out and put them away."

Hollis followed by making sure his offense wasn't thinking ahead. "We're not focused on Michigan, are we?" he said. "We are focused on Indiana. If you pay too much attention to their record and to what you see on film, you will stumble into a trap. Approach this game business-like. We've got a job to do. Let's focus and do it. Nobody in this room has ever had a chance to be national champions. That's what we are shooting for. I really believe that. We are three games away from a national championship. Nobody can take that away for the rest of your life. Nobody!"

Friday morning, following an interview with ESPN which would be used during the game telecast, Cooper awaited a teleconference call for the finalists for the Paul "Bear" Bryant Award — the coach of the year award named by football writers. He wasn't in much suspense.

"Gary Barnett's going to win the thing," he said of the Northwestern coach. "I don't doubt that."

Later, Harris hurried out of the office to make his flight to Kentucky to see Couch play in a high school playoff game. Ohio State had entered the recruiting race for Couch late, leaving Harris pessimistic about his chances.

"We are one of six teams he is interested in and he has five visits," Harris said. "It's fun for me, just to see if he is the best like everyone says he is. That gives me something to go by in the future. You've got to remember, for the last three years, I wasn't in the evaluation business. I think we got people's attention this year and changed the perception by throwing the ball."

It was one reason Harris felt good about signing Garcia. Plus, he developed a relationship with the junior-college player long before the season started, when most college recruiters had barely heard of him. He had talked to Garcia once each week since August camp started.

The next morning, on Nov. 18, exactly 17 years to the day that Woody Hayes won his 205th and final game as head coach of the Buckeyes by beating Indiana 21-18, current coaches and players were getting dressed in the Ohio Stadium locker room. Harris still couldn't believe what he had seen the night before. Couch, he said, was everything the quarterback had been built up to be, and more. "He's as good as I've ever seen at that stage," he said. "I saw four throws and that was all I needed to see. The kid can do it all. Right now, we just hope to get one of his five visits."

At 11:15 a.m., one hour and 15 minutes before kickoff, Hollis walked up to Jacobs and asked if he noticed anything different about the team. "Mike, do they seem unusually loose to you?" he said. "I mean, looser than normal?"

"I don't know," Jacobs answered. "I think this is the way they've been all along. They're a loose bunch of guys."

As kickoff neared, for the fourth consecutive game at the horseshoe, the weather had turned miserable. It was cold and overcast, a typical day in November in the Big Ten.

"The effects of the field won't bother us," Hollis told the offense. "We will run it and throw it, whatever we want to do. We will put points on the board, and we won't care who gets the credit. We all get the credit when we win, you know that."

Cooper pulled the seniors to the front of the locker room when he began his pregame speech.

"I want to thank all of you seniors for what you've done for this program," he said. "Enjoy your last game in the horseshoe. Good luck to you all. Those fans will be behind you. Now we all know we are much better than Indiana. They know that. You know that. They expect you to kick their butts, so don't disappoint them."

When he finished, George, Hoying and Sumner gathered behind the other seniors after the rest of the team ran onto the field. The three took turns hugging each other near the exit to the locker room. "I think I am welling up right now," Sumner said, his eyes filling with tears behind his face mask. "Look out! Eddie's going to cry, too," he said. There he was, 230 pounds of a Heisman Trophy candidate with tears in his eyes. Hoying walked outside and looked around the stadium, as the crowd of 92,352 exploded in a roar when the seniors appeared. "I plan to enjoy every moment of this," the quarterback said. "I don't think I'll ever forget this."

In a moment, they were introduced individually, with George and then Hoying bringing thunderous standing ovations as they ran from the south end zone to midfield. "That was one of the greatest moments of my life," Hoying said later.

It was a wonder Hoying remembered it, considering what happened with less than nine minutes remaining in the third quarter. When he dropped back to pass, an Indiana defender had twisted his neck around one way before his helmet collided with another pass rusher's chest. As he laid prone on the grass, the crowd went silent. Cooper, Hollis and Harris were horrified, not only for their quarterback's health, but at the prospect of facing Michigan without him. Hoying's father said a quick prayer from his seat. His mother, underneath the stands buying food, noticed her son lying unconscious on the television monitor. "He was knocked out cold," trainer Bill Davis said. Moments later, Hoying wobbled to the sideline, sat down to count fingers , and everyone started breathing normally again.

At that point, the Buckeyes held a 21-3 lead, and nothing offensively had pleased the coaches except for Glenn's return.

On the second play of the game, Hoying had thrown short to Glenn, who turned the play into a 24-yard gain. The play allowed Hoying to break Art Schlichter's single-season passing yardage record of 2,551 yards. More importantly, it showed everyone that Glenn was back. One play later, he caught a 12-yard touchdown pass. Later in the first quarter, he caught a four-yard touchdown pass. Before halftime, he darted down the right sideline on a 36-yard reception and took a hard hit at the one-yard line. The play not only set up George's touchdown that made it 21-3, it left Glenn hurting again. It would be his final play of the game, although his five receptions amounted to 105 yards.

At the half, the team had 99 yards rushing, including only 66 from George.

"That's embarrassing," Hollis screamed at the offensive line. "We should be able to run the ball a lot more on this defense than we are."

Once Hoying was hurt, everyone had feared the same lethargic, sloppy offense they had seen in the second half of the Iowa game. But Stanley Jackson surprised them by completing all four of his passes, including a two-yard score to Ricky Dudley. He also ran for 39 more yards. When Pepe Pearson scored on an eight-yard run with 5:08 remaining, the Buckeyes were on their way to a 42-3 victory and an 11-0 record, joining the 1975 and '79 teams as the only in school history to achieve that record.

The team laughed a little and smiled a lot, but didn't celebrate much in the locker room.

There had been some bad — Josh Jackson missed field goal attempts of 34 and 39 yards, Hoying had thrown two interceptions in his first 13 attempts before the injury and the Buckeyes had committed nine penalties. And some fan had stole Cooper's hat as he walked across the field to shake Indiana Coach Bill Mallory's hand.

"If there's any area that needs work," Cooper said, "it's our kicking game."

Not to mention the work of his two campus cops doubling as bodyguards, who missed the block on the hat-stealing culprit.

But there had been plenty of good, too. For starters, a student manager, Jason Vag, had chased the thief, made the recovery and later presented his bounty to Cooper. For his effort, he received the Big Hit Award of the week and a Buckeye leaf. George finished with 130 yards, not hurting his Heisman chances any. Stanley Jackson had shown signs that he could produce with the first-team offense. And the defense had been simply stifling since the first quarter at Minnesota. In the past 11 quarters, the defense had allowed only two field goals. Indiana managed only 168 yards and 11 first downs. The Hoosiers rushed for 48 yards, giving Young plenty of reason to believe he had fixed his run defense. The Buckeyes had held their last three opponents to a combined 180 rushing yards on 93 carries, an amazingly low 1.9 per carry average.

Of all the numbers, only two meant anything — the 11 in the win column and the big, fat zero in the loss column.

"Congratulations!" Cooper told his team. "Particularly to you seniors. Say nice things about these guys. We know we kicked their asses like we should have. Now get out there a little earlier tomorrow, because some of you have interviews to do. Get them over with and get in there on time. I don't even want to talk about this game. You know how important next week is. Now Michigan got beat today (at Penn State). The only thing they can do to make their season is beat you guys. And as far as I am concerned, we haven't done nothing yet!"

Cooper headed into the recruiting room where several high school prospects had gathered with their families.

"I want to tell you that there's not a whole of celebrating down there," he told them, pointing to the locker room. "Even though we are 11-0, we have a big game ahead of us."

The coach then headed into the interview room to meet the media. It didn't take long before the M-word was brought up. "The biggest game of our season is next week," he said. "The only thing Michigan can salvage is to keep us from the Big Ten championship, from going to the Rose Bowl and from winning a national championship."

A reporter asked, "That's a lot, isn't it?"

"Yes," Cooper said, "that's a lot."

To be precise, it was *everything*.

"We are right where we thought we would be," Cooper said. "I am probably the only guy in here who thought we'd be 11-0."

As he walked out of the interview room, Geiger tapped him on the shoulder. "I thought we'd be 11-0, too, John," he said.

So there were two, and perhaps a few players. Boston College. Washington. Pittsburgh. Notre Dame. Penn State. Wisconsin. Purdue. Iowa. Minnesota. Illinois and now Indiana. One by one, they were lined up and knocked down. By the time the players and coaches heard of Northwestern's 23-8 victory at Purdue three hours after they left the stadium, they realized then that those 11 wins did not guarantee them anything.

Except the most important game of their lives, one week away in Ann Arbor, Mich.

19.

Preparing for *'The Game'*

Sunday morning, as the coaches gathered to hurriedly grade the Indiana film and get to more important matters, John Cooper leaned back in a chair in Bill Young's office and shook his head. "Here we are 11-0," he said, "and we still don't have the bowl game we want. It seems like we can't get a break around here. When will Northwestern ever win all eight games in the Big Ten again?"

"Screw 'em," Fred Pagac replied. "We'll just have to go up there and win it ourselves."

"Yep, we don't have a choice now," Cooper said. "It's the Citrus or the Rose. Do we want to play Tennessee or USC?"

His question, of course, had been rhetorical and laughable. The thought of losing to Michigan, having all their goals and dreams vanish in one day at the hands of their hated rival, and returning to the Citrus where they had been twice in three years, was nothing less than sickening.

"I'll vote for USC," Pagac said.

He, Cooper and Young chuckled as film of their 11th victory started to roll. What was sure to be a longer week than usual had begun.

Later, as they finished the usual ribs-and-chicken lunch they devoured each Sunday, the head coach wiped barbecue sauce from his fingers and made a prediction. "Now you watch this week," he said. "Before it was, 'John Cooper can't beat Michigan.' Now we beat Michigan last year, right? Now count the number of times that writers will write what my record is *at* Michigan. All week long it will be 'How we've never won up there.'"

To say that Cooper had his problems with "the school up north" as Woody Hayes had referred to Michigan, would have been understating the obvious. He now had a 2-6 record against Illinois and he had won only one bowl game in six trips while at Ohio State, but those were secondary statistics for Cooper's critics. It was that 0-5-1 record against the hated Wolverines, until the breakthrough 22-6 victory in Columbus in 1994, that they pointed to most often. Ironically, it was his victory over Michigan in the 1987 Rose Bowl while at Arizona State that helped earn him the Ohio State job in the first place.

In his first season in Columbus, while entering the game with a 4-5-1 team, the Buckeyes lost a 34-31 heartbreaker to the Wolverines.

"The first year I am here they are beating us 20-0 and it should have been 50-0," he explained to Stobart in one meeting. "Then we come back and go ahead and they can't stop us. Then this quarterback, who couldn't throw it to the wall there, throws one up and their guy out-jumps our guy for a touchdown."

From that point on, nothing improved as far as the Michigan series went until the 1994 victory, of course. "You get sick and tired of hearing people say you can't beat Michigan," he said. The win the previous year had been so important and became such a happy memory, that Cooper had the blackboard which he smashed at halftime posted in the staff meeting room. The 22-6 score was written in chalk.

In 1990, Cooper's third season, the Buckeyes could have earned a Rose Bowl trip with a win but faced a 13-13 tie while deep in their own territory. The Wolverines had nothing on the line but pride. To his credit, Cooper gambled and decided to go for the first down on fourth-and-one late in the game. Quarterback Greg Frey, however, was tackled for a loss on an option play. Films showed that if Frey had pitched the ball, tailback Butler By'not'e may have scored. It was a perfect call at the perfect time. It just wasn't executed properly, Cooper contended. The Wolverines took possession, then kicked a last-second field goal to send Iowa to the Rose Bowl.

Frey, now a radio analyst in Columbus, still gets asked about the play. "I never had a chance to pitch it," he said. "One of our lineman got pushed back into me before I got the chance."

The aftermath of that game had been ugly. Ohio State went to the Liberty Bowl, losing three assistant coaches to other jobs before the game. The players didn't want to spend Christmas in Memphis, Tenn., and played uninspired in a 23-10 loss to undermanned Air Force. It was embarrassing for the program and for Cooper and turned many fans against him.

The next year, Cooper received a contract extension before the Buckeyes lost 31-3 in Ann Arbor. In 1992, in a game that may have saved his job, a late touchdown pass saved a 13-13 tie in Columbus. Then came the heartbreak of 1993, when the Buckeyes were 9-0-1 and could have earned a Rose Bowl berth again. They were whipped 28-0 in Ann Arbor. "I remember seeing the seniors and how they reacted," Mike Vrabel said, "after how hard they had worked to get to that point and to have it all dashed in one afternoon."

The record against Michigan issue illustrated Cooper's misunderstanding of the media, even though he treated reporters better than most any other coach in the country. He was always accessible, sometimes even leaving meetings to grant an interview. But if the media publicized his record against Wisconsin (6-1-1), Purdue (5-1), Minnesota (6-0), Northwestern (6-0) and Iowa (4-1-1), it surely would expound on it against the school's rival.

By comparison, Hayes had a 16-11-1 record against the Wolverines and Bruce was 5-4. Cooper was now 1-5-1 with a one-game winning streak. "I'll tell you how quickly you learn what Ohio State-Michigan is all about," said Larry Petroff, the coaching staff's administrative assistant. "We had been here just three months when I sent one of my boys up to his room for fighting with his brother. He was four years old then. I walked into his room and he was really, really mad at me. He just looked at me and gritted his teeth and said, "Go Michigan!"

And as usual, there are always the Ohio State-Michigan recruiting war stories. Several players on each team were offered scholarships to their chief rival. Ohio State lost Ohioans to Michigan and Michigan lost natives to Ohio State. "I called up Gary Moeller and told him I was coming to Michigan," said Shawn Springs, whose father Ron was a running back for Hayes from 1976-77. "Then we came to town, I changed my mind. I became a Buckeye and never looked back." Safety Rob Kelly, a native of Newark, Ohio, about three Tom Skladany punts from Ohio Stadium, was another defensive back who would have been headed to Ann Arbor. "Then one day I read in the paper where some guy said Ohio players should stay in Ohio and help beat Michigan," he said. "I guess it sank in."

Ryan Miller, of Allen Park, Mich., said the Wolverines committed the worst sin as far as he was concerned — they didn't want him. "They told me I was too small," he said. Miller grew up wearing Michigan's colors and his parents had season-tickets at Michigan Stadium. "Now," he said, "they are bigger Ohio State fans than they ever were Michigan fans.

"I am glad I came here. We're 11-0 and Michigan has lost three games. Now it's an all-or-nothing game for us."

⎯⎯⎯◆⎯◆⎯◆⎯⎯⎯

Bobby Hoying awakened to a massive headache, a leftover from the concussion, Sunday morning in his apartment. The apartment, which he shared with brother Tommy and Matt Finkes, was located on Michigan Avenue of all places. "I took two Motrin and it went away," he said. Doctors assured the coaches he would be fine, as long as he didn't take a hit any time soon. When the coaches examined the film, Cooper said, "When you looked at it, you wonder how he got the concussion."

Other than that, there were no other injuries from the Indiana game. Glenn was sore from a hit on his final catch, but his injury was mostly healed.

That afternoon, when Young began to study the Wolverines, 8-3 and ranked 18th after a 27-17 loss at Penn State, he already realized what the key to the game would be for his defense without watching one minute of tape. "When they get down there," he told Pagac, "we have to hold them to field goals. You know they are going to move the ball with their running backs, we just can't let them score touchdowns."

His assessment was somewhat surprising, considering that his defense had shut down three teams in a row and appeared to be coming together. Since Minnesota scored 14 points in the first quarter three weeks earlier, the defense had allowed only two field goals and a 1.9-yard per carry average. But Young must have realized his defense's limitations, as well as the plain fact that Minnesota's, Illinois' and Indiana's offenses were mediocre at best. His defensive line was small but quick, his linebackers were small and his safeties were limited. Stopping a power running game behind a good offensive line would be difficult. He hadn't forgotten that six running backs in the season's first seven games had rushed for more than 100 yards against his defense.

"Ah, we'll kick the shit out of them," Young joked to the offensive coaches later that day. "I am not worried about that. I am worried about what kind of bowl ring I am getting."

He smiled and walked out.

When the coaches and players gathered to go over the Indiana tapes, Cooper started by saying, "You will play the best defensive team you've seen yet on Saturday. Now talking doesn't beat Michigan. Hard work does. Let's get focused, beginning today. Let's get ready to go up there and kick their ass. You are a better football team than they are. You know that."

———— •◆•—◆—•◆• ————

The first thing the coaches did on Monday at 7 a.m., was canvass Michigan's personnel — getting the names and numbers straight. Spencer recounted seeing Michigan freshman outside linebacker David Bowens, who was now starting, playing basketball in high school.

"I am telling you, he turned around and dunked ten straight times," he said.

"Spence," Jacobs said, "good thing we're playing football Saturday and not basketball."

Immediately, while watching film, it became apparent how preparing for Michigan would be different. Instead of viewing an opponent's play two or three times which was the norm for other games, coaches watched it five or six times. The offensive coaches, for example, spent two hours on the Michigan-Michigan State tape — a 28-25 Wolverines' loss — on their first time through it.

It was one of three losses for Michigan, the first being a 19-13 loss to Northwestern at home. Looking back, the outcome of that game had to be ironic for the Buckeyes. The players and coaches spent that Oct. 7th rallying to beat Penn State and then reveling in the news of Michigan's loss as they boarded the busses for a trip to the State College airport. If only Michigan had won the game, instead, the Buckeyes now would have the Rose Bowl berth secured. "Any time Michigan loses is a great day for us," Cooper had said then. If only he had known.

The Wolverines' loss the previous Saturday had given Ohio State's offensive coaches so much optimism. The Nittany Lions could have scored two more touchdowns, but lost two fumbles inside Michigan's 15-yard line.

"Penn State could have easily scored more than 40 points," Cooper said. "And don't forget, Virginia could have beaten them in the first game." In that August game, the day before the Buckeyes were about to whip Boston College, the Wolverines scored on the final play to win 17-16. So how good could they possibly be, Cooper wondered.

As usual, as he always did on Monday of Michigan Week, Pagac wanted to make them out to be the point-a-minute team of old. He walked into the offensive staff meeting with a noose hanging around his neck. He tied it atop the door, cocked his head and said, "Talk about being able to run the football — man can they do it!"

The offensive coaches, a little more serious as a group than the defensive staff, acted as if they hardly noticed. Hollis and Spencer had seen it all before. Harris was too focused to laugh, while Stobart and Jacobs chuckled a little. Pagac untied the noose and got serious for a moment. "Damn, nine and a half point favorites," he said. "Wow!"

The point spread had stunned all of the coaches when they grabbed Monday morning's newspaper. Although no records were kept of such statistics, it had to be 26 years since Ohio State had been such a large favorite in Ann Arbor — dating to the great upset of the Buckeyes' top-ranked team in 1969.

Stobart was Bo Schembechler's offensive coordinator then.

"I remember it like it was yesterday," Stobart said. "After we beat Iowa, Jim Mandich stood up on a table and fired everybody up. He said, 'Now we are going to kick Ohio State's butt real good.' I firmly believe that game was won right there and then."

When Glenn walked in to pick up some film, the coaches tried their best to get him fired up for the game. "Terry, look at this," Harris said pointing at the screen. "Look at the middle of the defense here. Think you can run the post on that?" Glenn gazed at the open field, lacking a safety and just sighed, "Oh man." Then he left.

"Is he better this week, Chuck?" Hollis asked.

"He'll be ready," Stobart answered. "He's already been over here getting treatment, and we've already talked about what the Michigan game means."

"I liked what he said in the paper," Harris interjected. "Those were some nice comments."

Glenn had said all the right things following the Indiana game, like not wanting to let his teammates down. "I wanted to come back this week, so I definitely would be ready for next week," he said. "I've been hearing a lot of those guys up there talking smack, like I am overrated. So I want to prove something to them."

That night, a local television station aired an interview of Michigan defensive back Chuck Winters, who predicted freshman cornerback Charles Woodson, a Freemont, Ohio, native who spurned the Buckeyes, would shut down Glenn.

It also was a week Cooper used any motivational technique he could get his hands on, though realizing he probably didn't need anything extra for this game. When Pepe Pearson and George walked in, he said, "Pepe, I would be pissed off if Michigan never offered me (a scholarship)."

Pearson said that Michigan did offer him, prompting Cooper to laugh.

"Come on, Pepe, it was just us and Toledo," he said laughing. "You know that."

Whatever, the Buckeyes' running attack appeared to be in good hands next season. In the Indiana game, Pearson had his best day in relief of George, slicing his way for 79 yards and a touchdown on 14 carries against Indiana. George had gained 1,773 yards in 11 games, but Pearson had averaged 4.7 yards per carry in his relief, mostly in the fourth quarters throughout the season.

A few minutes later, Cooper left and reentered the room with Pagac's noose around his neck, not realizing the gag had been used up for the day. "Freddie's already done that, coach," Jacobs said. One thing about Cooper — even during Michigan Week — he was never uptight. Not until gameday, anyway.

When guard Jamie Sumner, who played his freshman and sophomore seasons at Coffeyville (Kansas) Junior College, walked in to get some film, Cooper shouted, "From Coffeyville JC to the Rose Bowl...Jamie, you ready?"

"I can't wait," Sumner shot back.

Just then, Cooper's secretary called down to tell him a local television station was waiting for its usual Monday interview. "Yeah, I guess," he said. "I guess I've got nothing better to do on Michigan week. Channel Six, the Quarterback Club, my press luncheon, my talk show — good thing I got good coaches, isn't it?"

Cooper threw on a jacket from a shoe company and headed out for his interview. "How do I look?" he asked. "Might as well promote Nike whenever I can."

Later, Snapp walked in to give Cooper the run-down of his national television interviews for the week. He had one after the other, it seemed.

"Hey, did you hear anything about (ESPN's) Todd Christiansen ripping Eddie on the broadcast (of the Indiana game)?" Cooper asked Snapp. "Somebody told me he said Eddie was the third-best back in the Big Ten. Shoot, (Michigan's Tim) Biakabutuka takes himself out every other play. (Northwestern's Darnell) Autry is a good back, but he's not as good as Eddie. The guy is busting his ass to win the Heisman Trophy — why would he say anything like that?"

Just then, Young walked in and joked again, "If you guys can guarantee you won't throw an interception for a touchdown, we can order our (championship) rings now." The whole room broke into laughter. "I guess we can all joke around because it's only Monday," Young said. "By Friday, we'll all be like dogs shitting peanuts." The jocularity served its purpose during a week such as this — it relieved pressure. There was no sense getting too tight when a little comedy could relieve some stress. But inside, each coach was going through his own anxiety. Some showed it, some didn't.

As he did before big games, Cooper wanted to check with another head coach who had played Michigan, so he called Colletto, whose Purdue team was beaten 5-0 by the Wolverines in snow and heavy wind two weeks earlier. Two days earlier, Colletto's team couldn't beat Northwestern to guarantee Ohio State the title a week earlier. "Jimmy, how ya doing? You know we got the big one this week," he said. "I was hoping you could knock (Northwestern) off, but they are pretty good, aren't they?"

Cooper returned to the offensive coaches with Colletto's report: "He said they are bigger than you think. The secondary is physical. He kept saying that we need to be blitz-protection sound."

Like the assistants had already noticed, Colletto had mentioned a special blitz Michigan had been using. It made it appear that four linebackers were rushing the quarterback. However, two inside linebackers would stop at the line of scrimmage — hogging the attention of the two running backs. That would leave two outside blitzers to come free.

"And you've got nobody to throw to because your backs are in to block," Harris told him. "This will be a real challenge."

Hollis laughed. "I'll tell you it will be a challenge," he said. "We need to protect like hell and call the draw when in doubt." He may have been joking. Then again, he may not have been.

By the end of the day, the offensive coaches already had a few ideas how to attack Michigan's various defensive schemes. Hoying would be effective on naked bootlegs, they thought. Dudley would be open on short tight-end delays and Glenn on post patterns when the Wolverines were not in two-deep coverage. That was a good start. But they knew the key, as Colletto had said, was to protect Hoying from all of Michigan's various blitzes.

"They will come after us, because they know their chances go way up if they knock Bobby out of the game," Jacobs said.

"If we can handle their blitzes," Hollis said, "their hearts will jump into their throats trying to deal with us." Cooper walked outside to talk with a reporter, who asked "how is

Michigan Week different?" He smiled and threw up his hands, saying, "You can't practice any longer or work any harder than we have every week. You just don't get as many hours of sleep and the phone rings a lot more. It can't get bigger than this, obviously. I mean, how many times do you have a chance to get to the Rose Bowl and win a national championship?"

"Do you have an extra spring in your step this week?" the reporter asked.

"Now how I am supposed to answer that?" Cooper replied. "If I say 'no,' then all of Columbus will say 'Cooper doesn't think this is a big game.'"

A year ago Cooper had discovered, at least after the fact, that he needed to beat Michigan to keep his job. So if he didn't learn what this rivalry was about when he first arrived in Columbus, he knew now. Or at least, he should have known. To stay in the coaching business, winning the rivalry games didn't hurt, although he owned only one win in 10 years over first Arizona and now Michigan.

Rumors were beginning to become reality around the country when it came to coaches being fired. And as usual at this time of the season, top assistants like Hollis, Young and Harris were paying close attention to the jobs that were open or expected to come open soon. Especially now, since they were coaching an 11-0 team that was ranked second nationally.

Georgia's Ray Goff had announced he was resigning under pressure a few days earlier and now it appeared to be Kentucky Coach Bill Curry's turn. "Curry has scheduled a press conference at noon," Cooper announced to his staff in the morning. "It's a great game," Hollis said, "but a shitty business."

"That's for sure," said Stobart, who ought to know, having been unjustly fired at Memphis less than a year earlier — following three straight winning seasons.

Before the staff broke up for the day, however, they were told Curry would stay at Kentucky. It was one less chance for Hollis. By 8 p.m., another coach had been fired — Cal's Keith Gilbertson. Given his background in California, Harris's name naturally surfaced as a possible candidate immediately on the West Coast. But Harris, always among the most serious on the Buckeyes' staff, wasn't about to let that become a distraction during the biggest week of the season.

Tim May of the *Columbus Dispatch* discovered that fact when he called him at home when the news on Gilbertson broke. "Tim, it's Michigan week," Harris said. "I have talked to no official from the University of California. I am totally concentrating on preparing for Michigan."

The next day, Harris' telephone rang off the hook with calls from California. "Media guys," Harris said. "I don't know if I would take that job if it's offered. That's a tough conference to win in with a middle-of-the-pack program." He then cupped his hands around his mouth and whispered, "but anybody can be bought — even me." Harris was happy for another reason — he was the first to tell his quarterbacks of his efforts to land junior-college quarterback Mark Garcia. He had worried they would hear it through the media, but none had.

During his weekly media luncheon, which attracted the largest crowd of the season, Cooper was asked if he "now realized the importance of Ohio State-Michigan compared to your past rivalries."

"You think the fans at UCLA didn't want to beat USC?" he asked. "You think the fans at Arizona State didn't want to beat Arizona? Do Ohio State fans enjoy a rivalry game more than them? No." The question clearly had irritated him, but it wasn't the answer much of Columbus probably wanted to hear. Buckeye fans didn't care much for UCLA-USC or Arizona State-Arizona.

Following lunch, Cooper received the phone call he had been waiting for. It was from his good friend Terry Donahue, who had finished his season by upsetting his rival, Rose Bowl-bound USC, 24-20. "Congratulations, you deserve it," Cooper told Donahue. "Five in a row over USC and the winningest coach ever in the Pac-Ten."

"We're 11-0, ranked second in the country, going to Michigan and scared to death. Hey, it's snowing here and we have to practice inside. How's the weather out there — 75 I'll bet."

Cooper and Donahue were such good friends, it once got him in trouble with Big Ten Commissioner Jim Delaney. Homer Smith, UCLA's offensive coordinator, had visited the Buckeyes' staff while preparing to play Wisconsin in the 1994 Rose Bowl. It was the year Ohio State had lost to Michigan 28-0, opening the door for the Badgers. Smith's visit made Cooper appear to be not exactly a Big Ten supporter.

"Yeah, I got a letter from the commissioner on that one," he said. "But you can bet if we get to the Rose Bowl, I'll check with Terry (on ways to beat USC)."

After Glenn had said all the right things on Saturday, he blurted out something he shouldn't have when reporters and cameramen gathered at the Woody Hayes Center Tuesday afternoon. Asked if he was predicting a victory, Glenn said, "No." When another reporter started to ask a question, he interrupted, "but I am predicting we will go to the Rose Bowl."

When word got back to Cooper, he shook his head and said, "They peck away and peck away until somebody says something," not realizing Glenn offered his comments without prompting.

Glenn also had said, among other things, that "...Michigan is nobody." He had been explaining how he and his teammates no longer feared the Wolverines or expected to lose to them. However, the local ABC television station caught the words on tape. They soon found their way to Detroit's ABC affiliate and the receiver became the most hated man in Michigan. His words were played over and over again. *"Michigan is nobody. Michigan is nobody. Michigan is nobody."*

Other players were saying all the right things. George, as usual, was being his humble self when the topic came to All-American teams and the Heisman Trophy. Like Glenn's, his life certainly had changed in one season. "I had to change my phone number about three times already this season," he said. "A few agents, long-lost friends and new family members. It rang off the hook."

Hoying spoke of handling pressure during a week such as Michigan Week and anticipating a game with such importance. "I've been through a lot of games here and the pressure is just something I've learned to deal with," he said.

During such a week at Ohio State, the football facility resembled a communications headquarters. Satellite dishes were scattered everywhere outside. CNN's cameras were set up in the hallway. ESPN was on the artificial turf. ABC had taken over the room where NFL scouts viewed film. The local stations had planted themselves, too. Cooper and the star players made the rounds while Sports Information Director Steve Snapp orchestrated who went where. "There's just so much damn hype for this game," Cooper said, sitting down for the ESPN interview. "If there's nothing on the line, this would still be a big ballgame. I just hope the players don't get too caught up in it all and forget what got them here in the first place."

Practice, the first of the season officially closed to the media and public as it would be all week although several fans wandered in to watch anyway, started with field goals as it did every Tuesday, but for the first time Cooper ordered Mike Malfatt to take Josh Jackson's place. It was either a message to Jackson, or Cooper actually was making a change.

As Jackson and Malfatt walked off the field, Malfatt said, "Don't worry, you know he's not going to put me in there."

A few minutes later, Jackson, still stinging from his two missed field goals against Indiana, meandered off to the side to practice a few kicks. "They're playing mind games with me now," he said. "I wish they would just tell me how it stands. I guess he's just trying to get me mad at him so I'll do the job. I know I can do the job." Jackson, one of the nicest kids on a team with few — if any — bad characters, was trying his best not to beat himself up over his poor day against Indiana. He just wanted another chance.

Midway through practice, Dublin Scioto's High School team marched into the facility wearing their uniforms. The team had advanced to the state semifinals and with snow falling and temperatures dropping into the 20s, OSU officials agreed to let the team practice on the artificial turf. So while the Buckeyes practiced, one of the high school running backs they wanted badly watched from the sidelines with his teammates. "I already know where I am going, pretty much," Nick Goings said, watching George run out a play. Goings had told Ohio State's coaches he would become a Buckeye, but he still wanted to take the maximum-allowed five visits.

Goings was a running back the Buckeyes couldn't afford to let get away. From all indications, he was the real deal — like Ki-Jana Carter four years earlier. Except Carter, from nearby Westerville, had headed for Penn State and had helped inflict that horrible Ohio State loss in 1994. "I really think he can be as good as Carter was," said Goings' coach Bryan Deal. "He's got it all — speed, power, vision, instincts...."

Spencer agreed. "He's very quick and he'll get bigger," he said. "He's only 205 (pounds) now and I think he'll get to 220. The way I look at it — what would stop him from coming here?"

Following practice, former Buckeye guard Ken Fritz spoke to the team. Fritz was the player whose photo, while trying to restrain Hayes following the punch that changed the course of Ohio State football, appeared nationally following the 1978 Gator Bowl. "It still gives me chills to walk in here during Michigan week," Fritz said. "You are the better team. You just have to go up there and kick their butts."

When Fritz finished, Cooper walked toward the locker room and was approached by autograph-seekers carrying a football. They held out a blue felt pen. "Blue ink?" Cooper asked. It wasn't a good week to use blue, he joked. He then got word of the first All-America team released — by the *Football News*. It included George, Glenn and

Vrabel. "Mike," Cooper said, grabbing Vrabel by the collar in the hallway. "You're an All-American. Congratulations. I just got the *Football News*' team."

Cooper was concerned, however, about Hoying's omission from the All-American team. Was this just a first of things to come? Would Nebraska's Tommie Frazier be named to every team? "I hope not," Cooper said. "Gosh I hope Bobby gets on at least one of them. He deserves it. They can't leave him off all of them, can they?"

A few minutes later, Vrabel emerged from an interview with ABC. If he was ecstatic, he didn't show it. "Sure, it feels good, but I can't think about it right now," he said. "I've got bigger things on my mind — a lot to take care of on Saturday. I'll go home and call my mom. She'll be thrilled. This is the biggest game of our lives. I remember how the seniors had everything dashed two years ago. I'll never forget the look on their faces. In one afternoon, they went from Big Ten champs to the third-place bowl game."

He headed outside into the cold air, throwing his bag over his shoulder.

Geiger wandered through the hallways of the Woody Hayes Center wishing everyone a Happy Thanksgiving Wednesday before practice. Andy Katzenmoyer, the highly touted linebacker from nearby Westerville who already had committed to the Buckeyes, happened to be visiting Pagac.

When Cooper spotted him, he said, "Andy, meet Andy." The 6-foot-4 player smiled politely and extended his hand. He appeared much less than his listed weight of 250 pounds.

"Yeah," Cooper said. "You know how those high schools list them. They add two inches and 15 pounds, but he's still a big kid."

"He's solid," Geiger said. "Did you grab his arms?"

Cooper asked Geiger for the latest forecast for Michigan on gameday. "Snow flurries, 43 to 24 degrees," he answered. "Well, yeah it's got to be somewhere in between," Cooper said, laughing. "I mean that's the high and the low," Geiger said.

The weather on this day, however, was almost perfect for the Buckeyes to practice outside for the first time in two weeks. It was 35 degrees and sunny. "We've got to get outside just to throw and kick," Cooper said. "That's what I think suffers when you are indoors. You can't throw it deep and get a good feel inside."

As Houser walked outside, he was asked if his younger brother had decided yet to accept Ohio State's scholarship offer. He cringed and said, "Yeah, he's coming here. I just hope it's for all the right reasons. His girlfriend is coming here and that is probably why." His brother, however, had not told the coaches yet.

Before practice, the team had two visitors. The first was an administrator from the school's cancer hospital, where Cooper and a few players visited every Friday afternoon. "I'll tell you," Cooper said, "it breaks your heart sometimes. I usually give away lucky buckeyes over there and the other day this one guy gives it back and said 'Oh no, you keep it. I want you to have good luck.' A few weeks ago, this one guy had tears running down his cheek when we said good-bye to him. He knew it was the last time he probably would see us."

The administrator had carried a six-foot card, signed by patients, to the practice field. It read: "Beat Michigan."

"You guys have given so much inspiration to them," he said. "Some of them are no longer with us, but what they learned from you was to keep on fighting no matter the odds. I came here to thank you for coming over each Friday. Good luck on Saturday."

The second visitor took the team from a state of melancholy to enthusiasm. It was Ken Kuhn, captain of OSU's 1975 team that finished 11-0 but lost to UCLA in the Rose Bowl. Next to him stood three small boys. "I want to commend you guys because you played your butts off this year," Kuhn said, "but the biggest game of the year is Saturday. I have three pair of gold pants here. I guess one of my old girlfriends got away with the fourth. I played in four Rose Bowls."

Kuhn held out his Rose Bowl ring.

"Listen," he said, placing his left arm around one of his sons. "This ring means almost as much to me as these little guys right here. Twenty years ago, I stood right here where you are. We went up to Michigan and kicked their butts. We went to the Rose Bowl as the number one-ranked team and lost to UCLA. That game sits in my gut to this day. I never played on a national championship team. You guys have that chance. I wish you good luck and I want you to go kick some f- ass on Saturday."

Kuhn had referred to the "gold pants" — a tradition coach Francis Schmidt started in 1934 when he told his players that "Michigan puts their pants on the same way we do — one leg at a time." From that point, each Buckeye had been given a tiny ornament of gold pants following a victory over the Wolverines. Problem was, that since 1987, only the 1994 players had owned a pair.

Chris Carr, the school's sports psychologist, talked with Jackson during the last portion of practice. Unlike the day before, Jackson kicked field goals as practice started — even though Malfatt later practiced three longer field goals. He missed them all. "Josh will be fine," Carr said. "He knows what he needs to do. Problem is, you go tell Greg Bellisari that he's going to be in on one play, and he has to make the tackle. If he misses that tackle, he's got 20 plays before he gets back on the field again. That's what is tough about being a kicker."

Following practice, Jimmy Moore, who played tight end in the 1970s, spoke to the team. His message was similar to Kuhn's. "My teammates and I can't help but reflect on what we didn't do," he said. "You've got it all right here for the taking. You've got to realize it's been since 1968 since we won a national championship. That's 26 or so years of players always asking 'What if?' We all let it go. Don't let it go!"

There was no shortage of motivators during Michigan Week. Former players filed into and out of practice and Cooper asked them all to address the team. By Friday, they had heard every speech possible. Whether it helped, or even hurt by adding more pressure to what would be a pressure-filled game, who knew?

Still, coaches realized that motivation should have taken care of itself against Michigan. Preparation and putting the players in position to make plays was more important. Young had his gameplan by Wednesday: Defend Michigan's running game first, even if it meant sometimes putting eight players near the line of scrimmage. Coaches didn't think much of Michigan quarterback Brian Griese, who became the starter when Scott Dreisbach was injured earlier in the season. "We just can't give up the big play," Young said. "We've got smarter kids now, not like two years ago. We had some kids who weren't too sharp then."

The 28-0 loss at Michigan in 1993 still stuck in the coaches' craw, especially Young's. The night before the game, Young uncharacteristically told a Columbus television station "that folks will be celebrating in Columbus tomorrow night." The night of the game, the team took what he called "the longest bus ride ever" home to Columbus.

"It probably was the worst defeat we've ever had since we've been here," Young said. "I don't know why I ever said something like that before a game."

***

It didn't matter that Thanksgiving came the next morning. It was just another Thursday. There was more work to be done, so coaches began arriving at 6:45 a.m. "Hey guys, I made a fresh pot," Cooper said, ducking his head into the offensive meeting. "Who wants a refill?" Harris chuckled as Cooper walked out. "Now let me ask you," Harris said. "How many head coaches in America would be making coffee?"

When Cooper reentered the room, Harris had a suggestion. "Coach, we ought to talk to somebody about making a video of when the busses pull back into campus Saturday night," he said.

"I mean, if things go well."

Cooper smiled and admitted he liked the idea.

Unlike the three other new coaches on the staff, Stobart had been through all the Ohio State-Michigan ramifications before — but from the other side as Schembechler's offensive coordinator. "You've never been more depressed in your life until after you lose an Ohio State-Michigan game," he said.

Cooper interrupted, "Tell me about it, Chuck."

The coaches took a break while Hollis, a former Georgia assistant, took a call from the school's pregame radio host. Georgia was playing Georgia Tech in a few hours in what would be Goff's final game. "People still perceive we're 'three yards and a cloud of dust' but we aren't," Hollis said into the telephone. The host asked Hollis the difference between the SEC and the Big Ten. "The biggest difference is that it could 15 degrees and blowing when you play in November," he said. "So you had better be able to run the football."

When the coaches resumed their meeting, Hollis' phone rang again. "Hey Joe, it's Vince," Jacobs joked. "He heard your interview and he wants you" — referring to Georgia Athletic Director Vince Dooley who would be selecting a new coach soon.

The other coaches started laughing. "Oh, that's cold," Harris said. "That's cold, Mike."

ABC staffers had arranged Cooper's office for a live interview during halftime of the Georgia-Georgia Tech game. As the backdrop, they laid a Wolverine pelt behind his chair. "Get that thing out of here," Cooper said. "If they saw that behind me, it would fire people up."

As Georgia Tech led 14-0 at the half, Cooper answered Keith Jackson's questions. "Keith, by looking at their film, I don't know how Michigan has lost three games," he said. It was his most-used line of the week.

The next afternoon, as the team loaded into busses for one last trip to Ohio Stadium for the senior tackle ceremony, it had dropped into the low 30s and the players shivered in their sweat clothes. But inside the stadium, there was plenty of warmth coming from 6,000 or so appreciative fans. The senior tackle tradition started in 1913 and ever since, a Buckeye about to play his final game would take one last whack at a cushioned dummy. The drill had become a bit more mundane in recent years, with players going through the motions as if they were tackling their mothers. In Hayes' days, seniors used to get a running start and whack the dummy as if it was a free shot at Michigan's quarterback.

Cooper grabbed the microphone to address the crowd: "On behalf of the coaching staff, I want to thank the greatest football fans in the world. We will be playing this game for the players and for the coaches, but most importantly, we will be playing it for you." Now somehow, that probably wasn't the case entirely, but the fans roared their approval. Each senior then accepted an ovation, jogged up and bumped the dummy. Cooper thanked the fans before the players fought their way through the crowd to the busses, signing autographs along the way.

While they changed to coats and ties for dinner and the flight to Detroit, several gathered around the big screen television in the players' lounge. Number one-ranked Nebraska was beating Oklahoma 30-0.

"If you could coach any of the top three undefeated teams," ABC's Brent Musburger asked analyst Dick Vermeil on the air, "which one would it be?" Vermeil answered, "I would say Ohio State because of their style. They can run and throw. Great balance." Young laughed. "He's trying to make up with us now," he said. Vermeil earlier had said no team came close to matching Nebraska.

When the team filed to their seats on the airplane at Port Columbus, three Michigan helmets were placed in an above compartment. "They were stolen before last year's game," said one of the campus police officers who protected Cooper on gamedays. "We're just returning them."

After the airplane landed and the busses were headed to the hotel near the airport, Geiger stared out the window. "Tomorrow night at this time, I think we will be ecstatic," he whispered. His eight-year-old son looked up at him. "Daddy," he asked. "What does 'eckstack' mean?" Geiger laughed. "It's ec-stat-tic," he said. "It means joy beyond belief. We're trying for a perfect season, a championship season. If we win, we'll be playing in the Rose Bowl." The boy nodded and mumbled, "The Rose Bowl?"

Although the players had to be in their rooms by 10:30, Glenn strolled into the hotel lobby 15 minutes later carrying his bag over his shoulder. He had been afraid to fly, so a team manager had driven him to Penn State and now Michigan. Glenn signed a few autographs, gave his number to an attractive girl and headed upstairs to his room. He had made a bold prediction and statement, each of which had been posted in

Michigan's locker room and shown over the airwaves over and over again. Now, could he do his part to back it up?

20.

The Dream Dies

When the wake-up call came to all the coaches Saturday at 6:30 a.m., they got up and peeked outside and smiled. They had received the first break of the day — sunny skies, no wind and the temperature was already over 40 degrees. Michigan's defense would receive no help from poor weather today.

"We got a break," Cooper said. "It looks great to me."

Fifteen minutes before kickoff, Archie Griffin made the rounds in the locker room. He always made a point to seek out George.

"This is it, baby, this is it," he told George.

The big running back just smiled and looked determined. He said nothing.

That job was left to the coaches. And as usual, Hollis tried to put it all into perspective for the offense. "Look guys, all we have to do is execute," he said.

Cooper was wandering in and out, ping-ponging between Hollis' talk and Young's address to the defense. He popped into the offense's room and said, "Maintain all your blocks today." Then he walked back over to the defense and said loudly, "Wrap up. Make the tackle. No broken tackles today!" His nervous energy was obvious, and his voice carried across the room, since the locker room was quieter than normal.

Hollis continued, "Guys, make sure you secure the football. Protection will be the big key for us. For 12 straight weeks we've said this, but we *are* a better football team than Michigan. Ninety-nine percent of all the college football players in the country would trade places with you today. Good luck to everybody."

Cooper walked back in and rambled from thought to thought. "This is the greatest offense in Ohio State history," he said. "Number 96 will jump offsides today more than anybody you've seen this year. Let him. Let's do a good job on the snap count." He wandered back over to the defense. "Big games are won by defense," he said.

He then called for the team to gather near the exit of the locker room. It was almost noon.

"We aren't changing anything today," he said. "It's the same game plan as all year. I think you will find out when you get out there, that they aren't that good of a football team. Just play your game. I am really proud of you. Go way back to August camp and you have really worked your butts off. Now here we are today, and all eyes of the world are on the Buckeyes. How good are they? We are ranked second in the country, but are we better than that? They've outscored their opponents 75-3 in the first quarter, so let's play hard to start the game."

Cooper then turned it up a notch. He now was feeling the emotion, and there would never be a better time to let it all out.

"We've had a good year, but now let's make it a great year and go out and beat their ass!" he said. "Remember, we've dedicated this season to Billy Hill. Remember Billy today. Remember Jason. He would have been 22 years old today. Remember them every play and play your butts off. Let's go!"

Billy Hill, the long-time trainer at OSU had died of a heart attack in the off-season and since the postgame speech following the Kickoff Classic, Cooper hadn't mentioned him to the team. Jason Gwinn, a linebacker and brother of free safety Anthony Gwinn, had died in a car accident two years earlier. Their memories had symbolized a melancholy finish to his most important pregame speech of the season.

As the team filed out one-by-one through the skinny doorway, someone yelled, "Let's get a ring today, fellas, let's get a ring." Other than that, there wasn't much talk. It was quieter than normal, with little hooting and no hollering. They jogged down the ramp and onto the field. The Wolverines already stood on the far sideline, waiting.

On the very first play from scrimmage, reality began to tug on Young's worst fear. Michigan tailback Tshimanga Biakabutuka gained 22 yards by cutting back over right tackle. On the next play, he gained 19 more. The defense held Michigan to a 49-yard field goal attempt, which Remy Hamilton missed, but Biakabutuka's 45 yards on three carries wasn't a good sign for the defense.

On the Buckeyes' first possession, they moved down the field to Michigan's four, but Hoying was tripped on a naked rollout before Jackson's 37-yard attempt hit the right upright and slipped barely over the crossbar. Ohio State 3, Michigan 0.

It was the first time they had posted a lead in Ann Arbor since 1987, and it would be the last time for the day.

Biakabutuka, known simply as "Tim," was about to put on a show. The 6-foot-1, 205-pound junior had gained a whopping three yards in relief of Tyrone Wheatley against Ohio State a year earlier. He would better that by 192 on this day — in the first half alone. His 44-yard run set up a four-yard touchdown pass from Griese to Clarence Williams to make it 7-3 with 5:34 remaining in the first quarter. When his beleaguered defense came to the bench, Young walked back to greet his players and pulled his headset down to his neck. "The big thing is you guys are not getting off their blocks," he said. "Be aggressive! You are playing tentative!"

Once again, Ohio State moved inside Michigan's five-yard line but couldn't score a touchdown. This time, George had come out of the game after gains of eight, eight and seven yards to get his shoe re-taped. With a first-and-goal at the four, backup tailback Pepe Pearson was thrown for a six-yard loss on a pitch to the left. The sweep wasn't a wise call, since they had been gaining yards heading straight into the teeth of Michigan's defense. Two plays later, Jackson's 21-yard field goal made it 7-6.

The Wolverines and Biakabutuka came right back, moving to OSU's 21 where they settled for Hamilton's 38-yard field goal. Biakabutuka gained 44 more yards on the drive. As he had feared, Young was not seeing the same defense that held Illinois and Indiana to three points each in the past two weeks. In those games, the run defense had been superb. Now it was awful.

Pagac took his turn to lecture when the defense came off the field. "We are playing tentative out there guys," he said. "Let's play loose. Let's have some fun out there!" His point was well-taken, but it was difficult for them to have fun when offensive linemen were knocking them around like blocking dummies and number 21 was running by them time and time again.

The defense wasn't alone in its funk. When the offense came off the field after one three-and-out series in which Hoying was sacked, Orlando Pace screamed at other offensive linemen. "That's bullshit," he said. "You guys have forgot how hard we worked to get here!" George, too, screamed at his teammates, pleading to change this horrible course now before it became too late.

It was obvious — for the first time since the come-from-behind win at Wisconsin, they were facing real adversity. Since that day, six weeks earlier, almost everything had gone their way. Everything had been so easy in wins over Purdue, Iowa, Minnesota, Illinois and Indiana. Perhaps they just figured it would be as easy against Michigan, too.

One thing the coaches had right — Griese was not going to beat them alone. He threw a second consecutive interception, one that safety Rob Kelly returned to set up Jackson's 37-yard field goal on the final play of the half. That cut Michigan's lead to 10-9. Thirty minutes to the Rose Bowl, Ohio State trailed by one measly point.

Biakabutuka had rushed for 195 of Michigan's 274 first-half yards. He had been unstoppable, while George had 69 yards.

In the locker room, Hollis went over his adjustments for the offensive line while Cooper ranted at the defense: "This guy's got almost 200 yards in the first half. You are making him look like the Heisman Trophy winner!"

Young usually knew when Michigan was running the ball ahead of time. He told his players: "When number 21 is in there, think run; when number eight (backup tailback Chris Howard) is in there, think pass." He decided now that he had to go to a "Bear" defensive front for the remainder of the game, bringing eight players to the line of scrimmage to stop Biakabutuka. That way, maybe Michigan would be forced to pass. It was almost as if he would beg them to pass.

Hollis knew Hoying would see more blitzes in the second half since they had worked for Michigan in the first two quarters. As the coaches had preached all week, protection would be the key. Hoying had been sacked three times for a minus 31 yards, with sacks ending the first two possessions.

"Guys, we can't get in third-and-10 when we have to throw the football," Hollis said. "Now we have been a second-half football team all year. They haven't stopped us. We've stopped ourselves. We've got a full season hanging in the balance here."

Cooper gathered the team and gave one last try to ignite a fire in his players. "We've got the ball first, now let's take it and score," he said. "We haven't blocked them. Now block their ass! Don't let this ballgame slip away from you. What's the score? Does anybody know the score? That's right, it's ten to nine. One thing that is missing out there is emotion. Now let's go out there and win this game!"

As the team walked out, nose guard Luke Fickell said, "This win will last a lifetime." It would, but for whom?

On the first play from scrimmage, Hoying's eyes followed Glenn the entire way and he underthrew him. Cornerback Charles Woodson, who was playing high school football in Freemont, Ohio, a year earlier, intercepted. On the play, Dudley had broken wide open down the middle of the field but Hoying had never looked his way. Biakabutuka then carried six straight times to set up a two-yard touchdown sneak by Griese to increase the lead to 17-9.

Ohio State's offense, so potent throughout the season, was going nowhere now. Hoying was running for his life. Receivers were dropping passes. By the time Hollis relayed the call to the huddle, the 25-second play clock was running down before each play, making it nearly impossible for Hoying to check off to a better play. The first three possessions of the second half ended: interception, punt, punt. Near the end of the quarter, Vrabel made the defense's biggest play of the game — a play an All-American would make. He knocked a pass up into the air, intercepted it and rambled to Michigan's 27.

Hoying then passed over the middle to Dudley in a play reminiscent of the huge completion at Penn State seven weeks earlier. George scored on the next play, OSU's first touchdown in Michigan Stadium in six years, but was stopped short on a two-point conversion attempt. Heading into fourth quarter, OSU trailed 17-15.

But the momentum never swung.

The defense couldn't stop Biakabutuka and the offense couldn't sustain its drives. The Wolverines sandwiched two touchdowns around two straight three-and-out series for Ohio State. It was now 31-15 with only 7:55 remaining. Michigan's band was blaring "The Victors," Ohio State fans had their heads in their hands and another miserable day in Ann Arbor had arrived for the Buckeyes.

Hoying suddenly got protection and got hot, completing seven consecutive passes — the last a 19-yarder to Tillman for a touchdown. He threw to George in the right corner for a two-point conversion to make it 31-23. The drive used only 1:22 and suddenly, there was hope.

But Michigan ate up all but the final 2:01 thanks to a crucial gain of 13 by Mercury Hayes on a reverse on third-and-10. When the Buckeyes finally regained possession, thanks to Vrabel's second sack of the game, Hoying converted one fourth down with a seven-yard pass to Tillman. Inexplicably, he had been ordered to spike the ball on the previous down, third-and-three, illustrating the panic that had set in. A 15-yard pass to Dudley moved the ball to Michigan's 34. Still, a touchdown and two-point conversion for a tie still would have sent Northwestern to the Rose Bowl.

Again, for some reason, Hoying was ordered to spike the ball on first down. With 1:14 remaining, there was plenty of time to score from the 34-yard line. Ohio State even had one timeout remaining. Instead, first down had become a wasted down the offense would later need. Two incompletions later, on fourth-and-ten, Hoying threw high to Glenn. Woodson jumped behind him, took the ball away and headed toward the pandemonium on the Michigan sideline. Hoying had passed for 286 yards but had been intercepted twice by Woodson. The final pass had capped his worst game of the season.

All that remained was for Griese to kneel down twice. In a cruel twist of irony, ABC showed Northwestern's players and coaches celebrating the defeat in Evanston, Ill., holding roses aloft and hugging and high-fiving. Their dream had been realized.

For the Buckeyes, theirs had died horribly and suddenly.

All the goals, which made every minute of sweat and pain since the previous season ended somehow make sense, were gone. Just like that. As Michigan and its fans celebrated, several Buckeyes stood motionless. Some refused to move off the bench. Some cried. After five minutes or so, they moved like mummies up the tunnel to the locker room. It was the same tunnel in which the Wolverines hopped, skipped and celebrated the entire way two years earlier. Now they were doing it all over again. Some even taunted, and for George, it was too much to take. When someone hollered "you're no Heisman winner," he lunged at a Wolverine before being pulled back by administrative assistant Larry Petroff.

Finally, all the players had made it back to the locker room. Following the Lord's Prayer, it was the first time since the Citrus Bowl loss to Alabama a season ago that the Buckeyes did not sing "Across the Field."

"You're eleven and one," Cooper said. "I know how you feel. I feel the same way, but we have to go play Tennessee in the Citrus Bowl."

"F- that," several players bellowed. "F- the Citrus Bowl."

Psychologically, it probably wasn't the best time to bring up the Citrus Bowl, considering the heartbreak was just beginning to sink in. Cooper acted as if he didn't hear their response. After all, he realized their hurt. "You can go down there and get ready to play or you can go down there and let them beat your ass," he said. He then walked away to do his postgame radio show. He was angry. Angry that his players had let themselves down and angry that they had let him and the coaching staff down. In a way, he almost felt betrayed that they hadn't played better.

By the time Cooper finished his radio show 10 minutes later, most of the starters still were in shock. While several second-team players walked slowly to and from the showers, Matt Finkes sat silently and still, his helmet still covering his grief-stricken face. Tears streamed behind his face mask. Fickell stood in front of his locker and just stared ahead. His eyes were glazed over. Hoying sat in the middle of the room, staring at the floor. Dudley stared ahead, looking stunned. They had not removed any part of their uniform, almost as if they were hoping for one more quarter. One more chance. None of them could believe it. How could they have lost, especially now with so much at stake?

George was overcome with grief. First he sat on a trainers' table and cried. After a few minutes, he limped over to the offensive linemen's lockers and hugged each. When he came to center Juan Porter, the two hugged for several minutes as their tears dropped on the other's shoulder. He wailed, as Spencer and then Griffin tried to console him. It was no use. Nobody had practiced or played harder during the season than George, and now, nobody would grieve harder, either.

By now, it seemed the eyes of every player in the room were filled with tears. And somehow, while their collective hearts were breaking, they had to face the media and explain it all. Were they overconfident? Did they underestimate Michigan? Who had the answers? How long would they live with this pain, with what would become a horrible memory?

"It's something I'll live with the rest of my life," Hoying said. "There's no Rose Bowl, no Big Ten championship, and I am a senior. I am not sure I'll ever get over this."

"How do I feel?" Springs said, repeating a question. "Horrible. It's like a bad dream. I am still in shock."

"You just can't put it into words," Bellisari said. "Everything you've ever dreamed of — crushed in 60 minutes of football."

The aftermath was ugly. The defense, the third-ranked defense in Big Ten, had entered the day allowing 124 rushing yards per game. Biakabutuka had gained 125 yards after his sixth carry. He would finish with 313 yards on 37 carries — the second-best rushing day in Michigan history. Throughout the game, would-be tacklers bounced off of his hips and thighs as if he were Jim Brown. They let him run by them as if he were Gale Sayers. And they had been faked and juked by him as if he were Walter Payton.

It wasn't just one or two players. It was Ohio State's best. At one time or another, Vrabel, Springs, Kelly, Gwinn, Bellisari and Miller all hit Biakabutuka and bounced off like a grade-school kid trying to pull down his father in the back yard. "Worst display of tackling I've seen," Young would say later. "We just couldn't tackle the guy."

The real Heisman candidate, George, had his 11th consecutive 100-yard day and had become the school's single-season record-holder with 1,826 yards, gaining 104 yards on 21 carries. But he had carried only eight times in the second half and not at all in the fourth quarter.

"There's two things you must do in this conference," Cooper told the media. "You must stop the run, and you must be able to run yourself. We didn't do either."

When Cooper reentered the locker room following his press conference, Geiger was there to greet him. "First-and-goal twice and we couldn't get it in," Geiger said. "That killed us."

"I know," the coach said. "I know."

A CBS reporter somehow worked his way into the locker room and brazenly told Cooper the network wanted a live interview. "You need to go get Lloyd Carr, don't you?" Cooper said, combing his hair. A few minutes later, he walked outside and granted the interview.

Each player grabbed a pizza on the way out of the locker room, even though few felt hungry enough to eat. Cooper met Helen and daughter Cindy by the busses and kissed each. "Come on, let's get on the busses," he said. "Let's get out of here."

The scheduled three-hour bus ride would be a funeral on wheels of sorts. As the caravan moved slowly away from Michigan Stadium, Wolverine fans taunted and waved good-bye. Others screamed obscenities. Some players tried not to notice. Some couldn't help but look.

Team psychologist Chris Carr sat alone, but he was the only person qualified who could have helped ease the pain. "It feels like the loss of a loved one. It hurts. It will hurt for a while — a week for some and forever for some others," he said. "I would just tell them to put it in perspective. It's tough to deal with. One way for them to deal with it is talk to someone who feels or has felt a similar loss. Someone who understands. I don't expect many of them to come to me, but I think I could help them."

It took nearly 20 minutes for the four busses to crawl to the highway, where bumper-to-bumper traffic awaited. The trip would be even longer now. As a beautiful sun set in the West, the nightmarish day was turning into a nightmarish night. For the next four hours, all the pain had to be absorbed and dealt with. The big plays that never happened had to be rehashed in their minds. What if? Why hadn't? How did we fail? What went wrong? The suffering would be twofold — from not only what occurred in the hours before, but from what wouldn't happen in the future. Northwestern would play in the Rose Bowl, what was supposed to be *their* Rose Bowl.

Those were the thoughts that would drive them crazy for a long time to come. They had envisioned singing the most rousing version of "Across the Field" ever, the ensuing locker room celebrations, the party on the bus trip home and the one that would last a month in Columbus, preparing for USC, and walking into that picture-perfect setting in front of 105,000 fans in Pasadena on New Year's Day. Perhaps the thoughts of what wouldn't happen hurt the most.

"I kept picturing pulling into Columbus and having thousands of people greeting us — all of them holding roses," one player mumbled, staring at the floor of the bus. "It's all gone now. It's all gone."

———————◆———◆———————

Fifteen minutes before midnight, Cooper walked into WBNS' studios to tape his weekly show. He was greeted at the door by a few television staffers who didn't know quite what to say, but they tried their best with their condolences.

"There must have been 100 missed tackles," the coach said, shaking his head. "We just can't get a break. What other year does Northwestern go unbeaten in the Big Ten? You know what the biggest play of the game was? That first play of the second half when Bobby threw it to him. They told me Ricky was wide open. Was he?"

The questions were endless and yet, nobody had any real answers for Cooper until Sunday's usual film review. It seemed like he just wanted to talk to somebody to ease the pain. He walked upstairs where producers of his show popped a highlight tape of the game into the VCR. Of course, there were mostly Michigan highlights.

On the first broken tackle on Biakabutuka, Cooper jumped forward, "Holy shit! Look at that missed tackle. Put your head in front of the guy and make the tackle!" He still was coaching, through the screen as if the offending player would hear him and correct his mistake. After he reviewed the tape, someone asked how he would inspire his players to rebound for the Citrus Bowl, where they were about to play three times in four years and where they surely didn't want to play again. "Just work 'em hard," he said. "That's the only way I know to bring 'em out of it."

Cooper and sports anchor Mike Gleason walked down to the set to tape the show. A red light appeared and Cooper began, "We played today like Illinois played against Eddie George two weeks ago. We couldn't tackle. It's probably as poor a job of tackling as any team I've ever been around."

During a commercial, a producer asked about the coach's family.

"My family?" Cooper said. "Ah, you know. Sometimes they take it harder than me. It really is hard on them."

When the taping had been completed, Cooper didn't waste any time — he headed for the door. "I hurt, my coaches hurt, everybody hurts," he said. "But I really feel bad for these seniors. They will never have another chance to go to the Rose Bowl. I will get another chance."

The loss ensured that it would be nine years since he had been to Pasadena himself, and never while coaching at Ohio State. His record against Michigan now was 1-6-1 and he would be reminded of that for another year. He climbed in his car and sped away. It was 1:15 a.m. But would he sleep?

The answer: very little. Cooper and his son took a four-mile jog around the Woody Hayes Center Sunday afternoon. It always was a sound way for the coach to relieve stress, and stay in shape at the same time. John Jr. tried his best to console his father, but what could he say?

"We didn't talk much football," John Jr. said. "He always holds it in pretty good. He acts like he is not hurting, but I know he is. That's the thing — some people think he's not hurting because he hides it."

Young was the first to the office, already having graded the tape when Cooper walked in at 2:30 p.m. No other coaches were in the building, which was unusually dark and quiet for a Sunday. "I don't know how those other coaches can stay away from the office," Cooper said. "I've got to get in here and find out what went wrong."

Cooper and Young wondered aloud about the team's ranking. How far would the Buckeyes fall? The answer was to fifth, dropping behind Florida (a 35-24 winner over Florida State), Northwestern and Tennessee. The coaches discussed the aftermath in the morning newspaper. Michigan players, and even Carr, had said that Glenn's comments during the week had fired them up, especially the "Michigan is nobody" line.

"I don't think those things have any effect, coach, but we still shouldn't be giving them something like that to fire them up," Young told Cooper.

"I know, I know," Cooper said. "You know how reporters badger them until they say something. I warn these guys about it all the time."

Fact was, following the Indiana game, Cooper had instructed his players to say only nice things about the Hoosiers. He never mentioned doing the same for Michigan, but still, Glenn should have known better. It had been his first season dealing in depth with the media, and he paid for his inexperience. The entire experience was about to become another painful lesson in the painful life of Glenn, who had dropped three passes in the game. For the next few weeks, he would be grilled over the airwaves on radio talk shows and by letters to the editor. The situation also was about to prompt Geiger to take a serious look at the relationship between the athletic department and the media.

A few minutes later, Pagac entered his office and popped the game tape into his machine. Young walked in to watch the tape again, almost as self-administered punishment. "We've got guys playing in a fog," Young said. "Gosh dang it, it just looks like they forget everything we went over all last week."

Almost immediately, the coaches noticed improper alignments — Vrabel and Finkes had lined up too wide at times, leaving a huge gap inside. And Miller had lined up too far inside at times, making it impossible for him to contain on Biakabutuka's cutbacks. "If we had just noticed it yesterday..." Young said. "We had a special season going and it makes you sick to let it just slip away."

Cooper walked back to his office, took a shower and picked up the telephone. He wanted to find a partner to hunt deer the next day. It would be another stress-reliever.

By 3:30, Hollis and a few other coaches had filtered into the building "How's coach doing?" Hollis asked. "Is he taking it pretty hard?"

Cooper walked into Hollis' office and sat down. He watched as one of Michigan's cornerbacks blitzed. "We let this guy cheat here all day, Joe," he said. "I couldn't sleep last night because I was thinking about that."

The offensive tape revealed the carnage and the causes: At times, offensive linemen failed to pick up Michigan's blitzes; at other times they did, and Hoying rushed a throw or scrambled anyway and at times he didn't see open receivers. When he did see them, they dropped more passes than they had in the previous 11 games combined.

At 4 p.m., the entire staff gathered one more time before they would hit the road for recruiting. Naturally, the mood was solemn. As they took their usual seats, hardly a word was spoken. Geiger sat near the head of the table and listened as Young explained, "They aren't that good, and we aren't that bad. But what you can you do now?"

Geiger nodded and turned to the staff: "I just wanted to come over here and thank you. I appreciate you. I know you are hurting. We will do the bowl trip first-class, families and all. Whatever you need to get this football team ready, you'll get."

A few coaches thanked Geiger and he walked out. It was exactly what the coaches wanted to hear. It appeared Ohio State's days of skimping on expenses were over. They had just hoped to do the Rose Bowl first-class, instead of the Citrus again. Cooper told his staff he wanted the same bowl practice schedule as in years past. They would leave for Florida on Dec. 18 for a pre-camp before traveling to Orlando five days later. He lectured them to "crack down" on their players' academics. "If we don't, almost ten kids won't be eligible for the bowl," he said.

"Well, I looked at the game a couple of times, and we stunk it up," he said. "It's almost like we were scared to make a mistake."

Bill Conley took over, pointing to five large boards behind him. They included names of recruits, aligned by position and pecking order. A black star next to a player's name stood for the blue-chippers to which the Buckeyes would offer scholarships. "Find out about their grades and know their parents' names," Conley said. "That is crucial."

The coaches went through the names one-by-one and discussed their strategy. As they discussed one fast running back, Cooper interrupted, "We had better start concentrating on offensive linemen instead of skilled people. We didn't block yesterday. We don't have any bodies to plug in at left guard right now. You had better get on the phone and get a junior-college guy."

On one recruit, Young said, "He's visiting Michigan this weekend. He may commit to them this weekend after what happened to us yesterday."

"Guys, we are right on the verge of having a great class," Conley said. "If we work our asses off, we will get one."

"We've got to start keeping these good Ohio kids at home," Young interrupted. "Michigan beat us with some good Ohio players yesterday."

This had to be the worst possible day in a coach's life and it showed. The pain from losing a conference championship, Rose Bowl trip and possible national championship — all to the school's archrival — and now the thought of hitting the road to recruit was tearing up their insides. By the looks on their faces, it appeared each had arrived home to find that their wives had left them and when they reached down to pet their dogs, they had been bitten on the hand.

Conley had one idea he thought may spark some emotion. He still wanted to plan a staff party for Dec. 9 when the Heisman Trophy was announced. George and Cooper already were booked for New York.

"What do you think Eddie's chances are now?" Conley asked.

"I think it's between him and (Nebraska quarterback) Tommie Frazier," Cooper responded. "I don't think the Florida quarterback (Danny Wuerffel) will pull enough votes. This thing may be so close, we just won't know."

Strength coach Dave Kennedy suggested that Cooper should inquire if the team could see new sights or plan new activities in Orlando this time around. "It's just that they have seen the same things down there," he said. "They need to see or do something different." The request had come from George, who acted as team spokesman when he met with Kennedy earlier in the morning.

Hoping to avoid a repeat of 1990 when OSU lost to Michigan with the Rose Bowl on the line and then slept-walked through a Liberty Bowl loss to Air Force, Cooper gave final instructions. He wanted a motivated team in Florida. "I don't want to see anybody hanging their heads around here," he said. "We played like shit and we got beat — that's all there is to it. Let's get our daubers up, too. We can't let the players see us hanging our heads. The Citrus Bowl will be as good as we make it. For those guys who are complaining about going there again, just tell them they could have controlled that by beating Michigan."

With that, the coaches stood up and walked out slowly. Cooper's words made sense and they knew it, but like the players, they needed time to get over the heartbreak. The reality was that this probably won a wound that wouldn't heal completely — given a day, a week, a month or even a lifetime.

21.

Welcome Back, Mr. Heisman

Once a lazy, unmotivated kid from Philadelphia who liked nothing better than just to sit and watch television, Eddie Nathan George was about to begin the whirlwind tour of what the nation's best college football player experienced each December.

In Columbus, he received the Walter Camp Player of the Year Award on Dec. 4. He also was named the Big Ten's Most Valuable Player. The next day, he flew to Dallas to receive the Doak Walker Award as the nation's best running back. Then he flew to Orlando to appear on ESPN's award show two nights later. There, he was named the Maxwell Award winner while teammate Terry Glenn won the Biletnikoff Award as the nation's finest receiver. On the same night in Houston, tackle Orlando Pace became the first sophomore ever and the fourth Buckeye to win the Lombardi Award, joining Jim Stillwagon, John Hicks and Chris Spielman.

The next day, George flew to New York as one of five finalists for the biggest of them all, the Heisman Trophy.

He was joined by Nebraska's Tommie Frazier, Florida's Danny Wuerffel, Iowa State's Troy Davis and Northwestern's Darnell Autry. The media and long-time Heisman observers speculated that the vote would be closer than ever, with a three-man race between George, Frazier and Wuerffel, who had made a late push in his final three games.

Experts wondered how the loss to Michigan and Biakabutuka's shadow over George two weeks earlier would affect his Heisman chances.

Cooper made the trip with his wife Helen and daughter Cindy. On their way to the Downtown Athletic Club, the three happened to ride the hotel elevator with an accountant from the firm that counted the Heisman ballots. "Give us a hint," Cindy asked the man. "Did the winner play in the Kickoff Classic?" The man answered, "I can't say, but maybe his coach was there."

Before the ceremony, George told the media, "It feels like pregame. I wasn't at ease all last night and all today." He had spent a few hours that morning at St. Vincent's Hospital on Staten Island with the other finalists visiting sick children, before polishing his acceptance speech in case he needed it.

Once the television production of the event began, ESPN's Chris Fowler introduced him as "Ohio State's inspired leader. He drove his teammates each day in practice, he drove defenses backwards with brilliant running."

As past OSU Heisman winners Howard "Hopalong" Cassady, Vic Janowicz and Archie Griffin watched from the audience, George told Craig James that he had learned discipline and his work ethic at Fork Union Military Academy where his mother had sent him. When asked if he considered himself the front-runner, he said, "I don't know...I am just glad to be here."

Twenty minutes later, after all five candidates had been introduced, Frank Powers, the president of the Downtown Athletic Club, walked behind the podium to announce the winner's name. Frazier sat on George's left, Wuerffel on his right. "On behalf of the officers, governors and members of the Downtown Athletic Club, it is my pleasure to announce the winner...Eddie George of Ohio State."

George bowed his head into his hands, as Wuerffel wrapped his arm around him and Frazier patted him on the back. As Ohio State's newest Heisman winner hugged his mother, a faint chant echoed off the walls of the Downtown Athletic Club. "Eddie! Eddie!" It was as if he was back in the giant horseshoe again, running wild against Illinois.

"Glad this is over," George said, before thanking Cooper, his mother, running backs coach Tim Spencer, and strength coaches Dave Kennedy and Dave Langworthy as well as the offensive line. "I am overwhelmed by everything right now. I did it."

As his teammates began practice two days later back in Columbus, George appeared on "Good Morning America." Following the team's workout, the assistant coaches changed into tuxedos and headed to the airport to fly to New York to make the Heisman banquet. They returned that night, but George and Cooper remained for another day. When it finally was time to return to campus on Dec. 13, his newest trophy didn't make the trip without a minor injury. A finger on the famed bronzed stiff-arm had been ripped off from the X-ray machine at New York's LaGuardia Airport.

Part of George's work ethic that resulted in his tour in the first place was displayed every day when he called Kennedy in Columbus. Each time he checked into a different hotel, he would give Kennedy a rundown of the exercise equipment that existed and Kennedy would prescribe a workout routine. He wanted to be in top shape for the Citrus Bowl. "Now that," Kennedy said later, "is one special kid."

In the end, the Heisman vote wasn't as close as some had expected. George finished 264 points ahead of Frazier and 473 ahead of Wuerffel when the 920 ballots were counted. All but one ballot had been received. Sadly and ironically, the 921st ballot had belonged to Les Horvath, Ohio State's first Heisman Trophy winner who died 25 days earlier.

In the course of one month, after losing a championship, history will show that the Buckeyes also had lost one legend and yet gained another.

———————————— •◆ ◆• ————————————

Nine days later, on Dec. 18, Griffin had played nine holes of golf before the team arrived in Vero Beach, Fla., where he and Cooper had arranged for a five-day camp at the spring-training home of the Los Angeles Dodgers. Even though George had displayed a carefree attitude before the winner was announced, Griffin saw the typical George intensity when the two spoke of the Heisman Trophy.

"He wanted it, he really wanted it, I could see it in his eyes," said the only two-time winner of the award. "But none of these kids who win it realize what it means until years after they win it. It takes a while."

George realized that, too.

"It really hasn't hit me yet," he said. "Someday, I guess, I will realize what it means, and it will sink in that I am a Heisman Trophy winner."

Minus backup safety Che Bryant who was declared academically ineligible, the team arrived at Dodgertown that afternoon, following the flight from Columbus and a two-hour bus ride. George, Glenn and Pace had arrived from Los Angeles following the taping of the Associated Press All-American team with Bob Hope. George headed for his room. "I am exhausted," he said. "I was on both coasts, going with two or three hours of sleep each night. It was fun, but you have to go through it to see what it was like."

An hour later, the team would welcome their new-found celebrity back to the practice field. On his first practice carry as the Heisman Trophy winner, he ran a sweep to the right against the second-team defense and collided gently with a defensive back. "Stay off him!" Vrabel shouted from the sidelines, "Don't touch Eddie!" Fickell joined in, yelling, "Don't hit Mr. Heisman!"

The jocularity actually was a positive sign to the coaches, since it appeared the three-week hangover from the devastating loss finally had lifted somewhat, even though the questions would never disappear. Why were they out-played by Michigan? Were they out-coached, too? Were they overconfident, under confident or just right? Did they look ahead to the Rose Bowl? Did they not take Michigan seriously enough since the Wolverines had lost three times?

"We didn't look past them," guard Jamie Sumner said. "But I think we thought we were so good, we would go out there and play well like we did all year. We call the offense 'The Machine' and we kept thinking The Machine would get it done. At the half, it was 10-9 and we thought The Machine would do it. We were so confident in ourselves. I mean we have three of the best football players in the country on this offense.

"I still feel crushed. There's not a day that goes by that I don't think about it. I thought about it all the way coming down on the plane. It will stick with me the rest of my life."

One assistant coach believed Cooper, despite his 1-6-1 record against the Wolverines, still didn't realize the intensity or the importance of the rivalry. "After all these years, he still doesn't get it," the coach said. "He doesn't understand Ohio State-Michigan. You'd think it would sink in when we lose to them every year, and everybody gets all over his back about it."

Receivers coach Chuck Stobart admitted he saw glimpses of signs of a team that hadn't focused on Michigan.

"The week of the game sort of reminded me of the '69 game," he said. "Woody was overconfident that week, and I guess so were a lot of the people around here. I didn't see the focus on Michigan like it should have been. People were focusing on the Rose Bowl and this and that, but not on Michigan. I noticed it, but how do you stop it? How do you change it? I don't know. I know one thing, Michigan focused on us. They didn't have anything else to worry about but us."

Cooper had discovered the idea of holding a pre-bowl camp from Joe Paterno, who had taken Penn State to Melbourne, Fla., in 1993 before whipping Tennessee in the Citrus Bowl. The Buckeyes tried it the next year, but still lost to Alabama in the bowl game, Cooper's fifth loss in six bowl games at Ohio State.

Dodgertown was spacious, plush and the players and coaches could walk to meetings and practices.

But leaving Columbus before Christmas wasn't a popular decision with everyone. If the Rose Bowl was on the line, that would have been another matter. But it was a third Citrus Bowl in four seasons and training an extra week while spending Christmas Eve and day away from home wasn't something that had the players jumping with joy.

"I really don't think too many guys want to be down here this early," one player said. "Now if it was the Rose Bowl, it would be fine. But we've been here three times already. Tennessee's coming in on the 26th. Why couldn't we? The Citrus Bowl is a good bowl, but we've been to it three times. By about the 28th, we'll just want to play the game and go home and Tennessee will be fresh. We'll be tired and they'll beat us."

The night of the Michigan game, Cooper had said there was only one way to bring his players out of a funk — to make them practice twice a day and work as hard as possible to prepare for the Citrus Bowl. When the assistant coaches got wind of his plans, they gathered, agreed they had to convince him otherwise, and then approached him. They needed to ease off the players, and make the entire trip to Florida fun. Otherwise, they would wear down mentally and physically, leading to a possible subtle rebellion.

"We all got together and went to him," Hollis said. "He wanted to go twice a day and grind their ass. Obviously, our approach (a 1-5 bowl record) the last five or six years hasn't worked, so why not change? That's why we have to shorten our practices, go with shorts and no pads. We've got to make it fun."

Cooper relented and changed his mind.

By the time the team arrived in Vero Beach, he had scheduled non-mandatory team outings at the beach, although the weather was colder than normal, at the shopping malls, at an Orlando Magic game and at a Jai Alai fronton. And he gave them plenty of free time. He had heard his coaches' message loud and clear.

Following a light workout after their arrival, he gave them the schedule: "Tonight is a free night. There's a game room over here. Every other night we will have something planned for you. We'll have a lot of meeting time for you. Tomorrow we will practice twice, and then just practice once in the mornings after that. Take a nap when you want to and get your rest. We will make this fun, but let's get ready physically and mentally. We are not going to end this damn season the way we played up at Michigan! We all know that."

Griffin knew, too, that the players needed to have some fun or this would turn into another miserable bowl game for Ohio State. The hangover from the Michigan game was just that strong. "I've felt that bad only two other times in my career," Griffin said.

"The loss to UCLA at the Rose Bowl (Jan. 1, 1976) and the (Bengals') Super Bowl loss to the 49ers (1982). Those three will stick out as long as I live. You just never forget them. You never get over them completely."

Most players had their own depressing memories of the Michigan game. They were images of failure — the plays that went wrong, the Wolverines taunting them in the tunnel, and the complete despair in the locker room after the game. "You know what I'll never forget from that day?" Sumner explained. "The busses were pulling out and I looked out the window and saw this lady wearing a Michigan sweatshirt. She was holding a rose. She shook her head, and threw the rose over her shoulder as if to say, 'Here it is, you don't have it, there it goes.' I will always remember that as long as I live."

Hoying took the loss harder than most. In August, he had referred to how Ohio State quarterbacks were judged when they were gone — did they lead their team to the Rose Bowl? His final chance, which appeared so bright and promising for three and one-half months, had been blown away in three horrible hours in Ann Arbor. "It was devastating to him," Hoying's father Vern said. "It was as disappointed as he's ever been in his life. There is no chance ever to recover it. He went back to Columbus for three or four days and we didn't even talk to him. He took the phone off the hook and just stayed sort of secluded."

Unlike George, he didn't have a case full of awards to lessen the sting. Although he won the Vincent dePaul Draddy Award from the National Football Foundation as the nation's top scholar athlete, he had been repeatedly snubbed on All-American teams. He had thrown for a school-record 3,023 yards, a school-record 28 touchdowns and completed a school-record 63.4 percent of his passes. Nevertheless, Nebraska's Frazier, who passed for less than 1,300 yards, won the Johnny Unitas Golden Arm Award.

"Maybe they should call it the Golden Leg Award," Hoying said. "On the next level, it doesn't matter anyway. When you have to so many great players, it's tough to get everybody on those (All-American) teams. I was disappointed, but I'll move on and go from here. I can't do anything about it. It's all a matter of perception."

Hoying was happy for George, but he still felt neglected by the school's sports information office which had decided after the second game to push George for the Heisman. The decision had paid off handsomely, although the campaign was very low-key and dignified, so it would have been difficult to second-guess it. However, Hoying felt he wasn't being promoted for other awards and All-American teams, so as not to distract from George's run at the Heisman.

"Eddie had a better junior year so he was going to get more hype coming into the season," he said. "I know how much I was involved in this offense, and that's all that really matters."

Hoying's father wasn't as diplomatic. He believed his son, who had a 30-6-1 record as a starter, deserved better.

"Honestly, Bob's never been one to look out for himself," he said. "But he feels the sports information office turned their back on him. They came right out and said, 'Hey we are promoting someone else.' That affected how he was left out for post-season awards. Steve Snapp consciously made a decision not to promote Bobby, and I never talked to Steve about it, but I know Bobby was disappointed in how it came about. On the other hand, he's happy Eddie's got the Heisman."

With the Heisman, Maxwell, Doak Walter, Walter Camp, Biletnikoff and Lombardi Awards secured, there probably had never been such a decorated team in the history of college football. Still, Cooper knew the trophies and awards wouldn't beat Tennessee. That's why he felt his team needed the work in Vero Beach.

"We just want to get them back into a rhythm, back into sync," he said. "We need to get back to when we played good. We are not going to come down here and kill them. We want short, more intense practices. We got a chance to finish second or third in the country, and that's what is at stake."

Giving the players something new to work on also was part of their effort to improve the mood and chip away at the depression left from the loss. Hollis had planned to use the no-huddle offense and an unbalanced line, moving Orlando Pace to one side next to another tackle, often during the game. When Hollis met with the offensive linemen for the first time, he wanted to let them know where he was coming from. "We can't practice for two weeks and not make you think," he said. "With these new things, we can stimulate you a little. We can try and take away the boredom. We want to change things up for you a little."

Hollis, too, had his diversions. As always during December, top assistants were making their pitches for head coaching jobs. Hollis and Young searched, and Harris rebuffed. California's athletic director had called Harris. "Told him I wasn't interested in being one of eight to interview," Harris said. "I told him that unless they were really, really serious about me, that I would stay at Ohio State. My family likes Columbus and we just finished our house. And it's tough to win at Cal."

A few weeks earlier, Young had flown to Honolulu to interview for the University of Hawaii's vacant job. "Flew out there, the plane was packed, interviewed the next day and flew home for Friday's practice," he said. The athletic director called him the following Monday to tell him that the job had gone to someone else.

By the time the team changed and walked to the field for its first practice in Florida, Cooper had heard that Kansas' Glen Mason, an Ohio State graduate who had always wanted the job Cooper possessed, had been hired as Georgia's new head coach. That would soon get Hollis' and Young's attention, because another job was now open.

"I am going to call Kansas tomorrow afternoon," Hollis said. "I will go for that one."

So would Young.

"I probably will put my pitch in for the Kansas job, but I won't get it," he said. "I keep putting my nose out there to get bloodied. They aren't going to hire me. I mean, who am I to them? They don't know me. You really have to know someone close to the school to get a job."

The next morning, after a 6 a.m. workout, Young stuck his head in Hollis' office and joked, "Yessir, I had just had a good workout because I need to look good for that interview at Kansas."

Hollis laughed. The two had talked a long time ago about the possibility they would someday throw their hats in the same ring, and now was the first time it had happened. "Bill and I told each other at the beginning of the season to not let each other affect the other as far as looking for jobs," Hollis said. "He's my best friend. It is a little awkward. But whatever happens, happens."

At times like this, Cooper found himself in the middle. He couldn't recommend one over the other.

"I want Bill and Joe to get head coaching jobs, but I have told them that I can only do so much," he said. "I know the athletic director at Kansas real well and I talked to him. But he asked me about the guy at Toledo. What does that tell you?" Cooper believed Young and Hollis needed to take lesser head coaching jobs first, do well and then progress to a head coaching job at a larger school. "The jobs they are going for are always good jobs," he said.

———◆—◆———

Glenn and cornerback Shawn Springs were considering leaving the program, also, to enter the NFL draft. Glenn was sure he was leaving, although he hadn't told the coaches, while Springs wasn't so sure.

Glenn still felt used and betrayed by the media for emphasizing his comments before the Michigan game. Following the game, in which he dropped a few passes, he was ridiculed on radio talk shows and by letters-to-the-editor in Columbus.

It seemed fans needed a scapegoat for the loss and Glenn unwillingly provided one. The whole episode soured the athletic department's attitude toward the media as it prepared for the Citrus Bowl. In fact, Geiger wanted practices closed to the media because of it. "It got all messed up as far as I am concerned," Glenn said. "They really blew what I said all out of proportion. What I meant was that we, as a team, shouldn't put Michigan up on a pedestal. It came out that I said they were 'a nobody.' I got criticized in the papers, people saying things like 'He should have tried to catch the ball with his big mouth.'"

The issue wouldn't help the coaches when it came to keeping Glenn for his senior season, but his mind was already made up.

"I have some goals in life and playing at the next level is one of them," Glenn said. "I want to help my little sister out and I need to support her. To be honest, I am probably coming out. I hate leaving all my friends behind. Anthony (Gwinn) and Buster (Tillman) are very close to me and if I stayed, I could spend another year with them. But I've got to make myself happy and support those who depend on me."

By all indications, Glenn had every reason to enter the draft. Most scouts thought he would be taken in the top 20 picks of the first round. "I am thrilled with what I am hearing," he said. "I've even heard top-five."

At one practice, after Glenn dropped a pass, Cooper joked, "I wouldn't think the Biletnikoff winner would drop a pass. What happened to bending you knees? Freddy would have caught that."

Cooper may have sensed he didn't have many chances left to rib his star receiver.

Springs' outlook wasn't as certain nor as rosy. The cornerback probably wouldn't have been taken in the first round, and yet, he believed otherwise. "I am hearing the top-15 (picks of the draft)," he said. "I am thinking about it. I will make up my mind after the bowl game."

Neither Glenn nor Springs had communicated their thoughts to any of the coaches, who in turn, hadn't asked since early November.

"Terry has told me he doesn't want to leave, but I haven't talked to him in a while about it," Cooper said. "I will after the game. He would be a first round pick, but would he be a top-three or top-four pick?"

Glenn wasn't the only player feeling used by the media, Bobby and Tommy Hoying and Vrabel did, too. Following a scuffle at a night club in Kent, Ohio, in which they were present, the incident was given top priority on the Columbus television stations' news broadcasts. The news reports indicated Vrabel had beaten up a man.

"Man, was that blown out of proportion," Bobby said.

"Mike wasn't even involved in it," Tommy Hoying said. "None of us were. Mike's friend beat the shit out of the guy, and we never did anything. Then it's all over the news that we're involved in it. Can you believe that?"

Following the morning practice on the team's second day at Dodgertown, Cooper told the team, "We're rusty this morning. It's what I expected. I want to see us get our intensity back and have fun at the same time. Get your rest tonight. Take a nap between practices if you want. There's a game room over there, play some games."

It was the only day he would require two practices. Beginning on Dec. 20, one two-hour practice each day would be enough. He was trying to lighten the mood and he was sticking to the promise he had made to his assistants.

When it turned colder, dipping into the high 50s, he joked to his players, "You can have some time today between lunch and practice, so go get in the pool if you want."

Still, he tried to motivate them. After practice the next day, he asked the seniors to stand in the middle of the huddle. "Now this is the last shot for these guys here. It's their last bowl game," he said. "It's their last chance to win a bowl game. It's the last chance for them to win a game for Ohio State. Think about it for them. Let's win it for them."

Fickell and backup offensive lineman Dan Gibbons got into a fight, one of the few scuffles during the season, at one practice. "I was clowning around, having fun, but I think he got a little mad about it," Fickell said. "It was just fun." Others thought it was the perfect remedy to loosen the mood. "I think that really helped the mood," team doctor John Lombardo said. "That lightened things up a bit. They needed it."

Each day, as word spread that the Buckeyes were in town, the number of onlookers at practice increased, until there were at least a hundred fans watching the final practice. The assistant coaches, proponents of closing practices, tried not to let the throng make them paranoid even though they had installed some new twists for Tennessee.

"I guess I worry about it more than I should because its a neutral place," Hollis said. "Coach Cooper doesn't worry about it, and he's been in the business a lot longer than I have. But yes, I am a little paranoid."

At breakfast on Dec. 23, the team's final day at Dodgertown, Cooper let his players know that the Southeastern Conference owned a misconception about Big Ten teams. "It's the fast guys, against the big, slow guys," he said. "That's the SEC's perception of the Big Ten, isn't it?"

Cooper had a more personal incentive. He grew up close to Knoxville. The Volunteers were his first love when it came to football. He saw his first game at Neyland Stadium. And he had been turned down at Tennessee once as a player and several times as a coach. For him, it would be a personal grudge match. "I wasn't good enough to play for them or coach for them," he said as the final practice in Vero Beach was about to conclude. "So sure, it would be nice to beat their ass. They have redneck fans, obnoxious fans. I don't have many relatives that live there anymore, but I know a lot of people that are Tennessee fans."

A few minutes later, as he called them together, Cooper accomplished what he had intended. "We've had good practices here," he said. "It's all been real good except the weather."

When the week was over the players had been put through six productive practices. The weather had been colder than normal. The players had a little fun, improving the mood gradually to where they joked and laughed loudly at team meals. George had caught up on his sleep. The game plans were in, and neither Hollis nor Young had heard from anyone at Kansas.

Two days before Christmas, on a bright, sunny day with the temperature in the 60s, everyone climbed aboard the busses following lunch and headed north to Orlando.

"Tomorrow," Hollis said, "all the coaches will be happy. The families get here."

22.

A Wet, Miserable Conclusion

Christmas in Orlando.

If the players would have been told on Nov. 24 that would be their fate — again — they would have not believed it. But here they were a month later, their bodies near Disney World and their minds and thoughts near Disneyland. They should have been the Big Ten players in Pasadena, not Northwestern.

"You know what keeps going through my mind?" one player said. "Each day, I keep wondering what we would be doing today in California. Would we be at Disneyland? What was Los Angeles like? What sights would we see? I can't get the Rose Bowl out of my mind. In all honesty, if we aren't there, I would rather be home right now."

Psychologists have contended for decades that depression usually hit the susceptible over the holidays and with the Buckeyes, they were more susceptible than most since the loss to Michigan. They were away from their families, living in a hotel, practicing for a second-place bowl without the newness or excitement that was supposed to surround a bowl trip. They had come to know every nook and cranny of Orlando almost as well as High Street itself. They were familiar with every festivity, with every theme park.

But at least they were together.

By the time they returned to practice the day after Christmas, they were entering their eighth day away from Columbus. They had six more to go.

Except for backup safety Damon Moore, who had broken a team rule involving gambling. It was well-known that several of the players liked to play cards with their per diem expense money on the line. It was no big deal. But apparently, Moore had crossed the line somehow. When Cooper discovered what happened, Moore was removed from practice, driven back to the airport and sent home.

Following practice, he told the team: "Now Damon Moore is heading home on a flight at 1:55. You all know what happened. Now guys I've been hearing some of you have been gambling. Stop it. Don't gamble! Some of you guys, you need to clean up your act. You are looking awful. I have lectured you over and over again. Now guys we need to get focused. We have come down here too many times and got beat. We need to beat their ass. We need to win this one."

When the coaches walked away, George gathered the offense. It had been a pathetic practice, after having Christmas Day off, and the Heisman winner wanted to voice his displeasure. As he had done throughout the season, when he felt it was needed, he chewed everyone out.

Minutes later, he told a few reporters, "We need to pick ourselves up and wipe off the dust and keep fighting. I want the good feeling of hugging and celebrating in my final game. It hasn't happened to end any season yet. We always have that awful feeling."

It had been typical Eddie George, the side of him that fans never saw. He would be a millionaire in a few months. So would Glenn, Dudley and perhaps even Hoying. But he didn't want to mail it in and go with the flow just because he wasn't playing in the Rose Bowl. If only every other player had felt the same way, Tennessee wouldn't have stood a chance.

"This is definitely one of the very biggest games of my life," he said. "It's the last game of my collegiate career. It's a great matchup, and it should be great game. I am not going to sit back and cry about the Michigan game. It's over, but nothing in the world can help you get over it."

Just then, Shawn Springs, finished with an interview of his own, walked over to interrupt George. "Yeah man, now that Eddie won the Heisman, he's changed," he said with a typical Springs smile, winking at a reporter. "He won't talk to me. Eddie and I used to be tight. Now he doesn't want you around unless you've won an award."

Springs, of course, had been joking. George barely smiled and continued the interview. He still had been hot over the poor practice. He wasn't alone, however.

"We were all mad about it," Sumner said. "It was the first day back and guys had been out late the last two nights, letting loose. That was our first day off since we got down here."

Still, Sumner said the team had a better attitude toward practice than it did a year earlier, leading to the 24-17 loss to Alabama. "Last year we had a lot of guys who were looking at making money at this time," he said. "They were trying to make it through practice without getting hurt. Everyone else saw that. Football is a team game and you always are going to have guys who are looking out for themselves, but the team comes first. It was frustrating to be around those guys last year. I don't see any of that now. Bobby, Eddie, Ricky, Terry — all those guys will be millionaires and they are out here busting their hump every day in practice. They are running hard every day and doing what they have to do to make us successful and that rubs off."

If any depression or sadness existed other than what derived from the loss to Michigan, Sumner said, it was because almost every player had a nagging injury or two. Especially the men in the trenches. Pace had a shoulder that kept him from practicing for two days. Sumner and Eric Gohlstin had aching shoulders, too. LeShun Daniels had one hand wrapped in a cast.

"I think the mood is bad not because we are down here but the mood is bad because we are beat up," he said. "It's frustrating because we aren't healthy. It's a long season and at this time of the season, we all have nagging stuff. We're tired too."

Cooper, however, didn't notice if any problems with the mood or attitude of the team existed. When asked by a few Orlando reporters if there had been a lingering effect from the loss to Michigan, he scoffed. "I don't see any effect from it at all," he said. "I think the players have bounced back from it. I think what helps is that we have been here so many times that the players have seen all these attractions and we don't make them mandatory. That way, they focus more on practice and meetings."

The possibility of the Kansas job had closed as shockingly as it had opened, when on Christmas Day, Glen Mason had reversed field and decided to stay rather than become head coach of Georgia. Georgia Athletic Director Vince Dooley then hired Marshall Coach Jim Donnan, leaving an opening that appealed to Hollis, but not Young. Hollis called the Marshall athletic director to throw his hat into the ring.

"He said he was interested, wanted to talk to a few people, and he would get back to me," Hollis said. "I told him not to let my name out if he wasn't dead serious about it. He asked for my phone number here, so if that means anything..."

Hollis had asked Cooper to call on his behalf. The job was a good one, a position that Cooper felt would have been more attainable for one of his assistants. Officials at Marshall, a long-time Division I-AA powerhouse, had planned to move to Division I-A (major college) the following season. "The thing is, I don't even know how much money it would pay," Hollis said, riding back to the team's hotel following practice. "I am not even sure if I would want the job, but I would like to hear what they have to say."

The next day, at the Citrus Bowl kickoff luncheon, university president E. Gordon Gee sat next to Vrabel, with Finkes and several members of the school's board of trustees at his table.

"It was great to see Michigan get beat last night, wasn't it?" Gee asked, referring to the Wolverines' loss to Texas A&M in the Alamo Bowl. Vrabel and Finkes nodded. "Mike, how good is Northwestern? Could we beat them?" he asked. Even the president, it seemed, was thinking of the Rose Bowl.

"I don't think they have as good a team as we do," Vrabel responded. "Athletically, they are not that fast. But hey, they beat Michigan and we didn't and that's what counts."

Later, Gee, who appeared at practice and in the locker room following games often, said, "I like to be around these players, so they feel comfortable around me, and we get to know each other. Some of these presidents at other schools never see them or act as if they care about them."

Minutes later, Cooper took the podium and joked of the allegiance and following of Tennessee's fans. Cooper had been an assistant at Kentucky when he had faced his boyhood favorites for the first time. However, he had never coached against them in the 19 years since he had become a head coach. He spoke, looking over at Tennessee's section of the audience: "When we went to Knoxville, I knew we were in trouble when they played 'Rocky Top' and three of the officials stood at attention (laughter). We sent our captains to the field for the coin flip, we called heads, the coin landed on heads, and the referee said 'Let's make it two out of three' (laughter). Then we took the opening drive right down the field, sent our field-goal kicker in and he kicks it right down through the middle of the goal posts. The referee called it no good. I said, 'No good? What's wrong?' He said, 'It was too high (more laughter).'"

Gee, who had hired Bill McCartney when he was president of Colorado, said he felt redemption when the Buckeyes won their first 11 games during the season. He had stuck by Cooper for the most part, even in the face of widespread criticism.

When the coach left the podium, Gee leaned over and whispered, "In 1991 and again in 1993, I took a lot of heat when I extended his contract. But as the president, I, and along with Andy (Geiger) have to stay above it all and do what's best from a clear perspective."

One thing was certain, even if he had any doubts about his head football coach, Gee believed he had the best athletic director possible. Geiger had worked wonders at Stanford and Maryland before coming to Ohio State. In one year, he had corrected many of the previous administration's errors and misjudgments. The department had been dragged down in recent years by an old-school approach, rather than progressive thinking and action.

"I realized I had to fire the previous athletic director (Jim Jones), but I had to wait for the right time," Gee said. "When he messed up the NCAA investigation (of the basketball program), that was the right time.

"So then I called some people around the country that I knew and asked for a list of the top-five athletic directors. Andy was on everybody's list and at the top of most."

———— ·◆· ◆ ·◆· ————

Cooper's jokes hadn't meant that he was in a good mood about everything. As had happened before the Michigan game, one of his players apparently had publicly predicted a victory over Tennessee. The incident took place at a basketball game in Dayton, backup tight end John Lumpkin's hometown. There, Lumpkin, who would miss the game with a fractured foot, had bumped into Tennessee wide receiver Andy McCullough, also from Dayton. What actually was said between the two, only the players themselves knew, but what had appeared in a Knoxville newspaper was a different matter. A story reported that Lumpkin had predicted a 47-7 Ohio State victory. The *Columbus Dispatch* also ran a similar story, without asking Lumpkin for his version.

Following practice that day, Cooper pulled Lumpkin up in front of the team and told him to explain the situation to his teammates. Lumpkin turned to them and said, "It didn't happen. We were at a basketball game and he said 'We're going to kick your ass.' I said, 'F-that. It ain't going to happen.'" The team broke into laughter, but Cooper wasn't laughing.

He interrupted Lumpkin and started screaming at his team: "Now John here predicts we are going to beat them 47-7 and it's the headline in today's Knoxville paper and it's in the Columbus paper. They are playing this up in Knoxville. Let me tell you, they are going to use this against you. I am catching all kinds of crap — 'Why can't we control our players?' I am pissed off about it. I am really pissed off! You ought to be, too. This is the same thing that happened before Michigan. You guys are too damn nice! You need to get mad. Now we have been down here before, and we haven't won yet. Quit jacking around and get serious. Let's do things right for a change and get focused."

When the team walked off the field, one player remarked, "That's what he should have said before the Michigan game."

Actually, Cooper probably was more angry at the Columbus newspaper than he was at Lumpkin. After all, it had been two kids joking around at a basketball game, not a serious comment made at an official press conference. Later, he said, "That was the poorest journalism I can remember. To write a story like that and not even quote the guy and that's our local paper. That makes me so mad."

A few minutes later, when he walked out of the locker room to speak to a few Ohio reporters, he gave short, abrupt answers to their questions. When someone asked about injuries, he snapped, "You'll know who's playing and who's not when the game starts. That's all I am going to say about injuries."

Two days before the game, Gee appeared at practice. Cooper interrupted the session so he could address the team and thanked the president for coming. "I should be thanking all of you, for how you've represented this university," Gee told them. "What a great feeling you've given 11 million Ohioans this year. I am not going to stand here and try to motivate you to go out and beat Tennessee. I just want you to know that we appreciate you." Gee introduced his wife, and the players applauded again. Then he brought a familiar face into the circle, introducing New York Yankees owner George Steinbrenner.

Steinbrenner, who lived in nearby Tampa, said, "You know, the Yankees have great tradition but everybody points to us. Everybody wants to beat us. They get up for us. That is like the Ohio State University. Everybody points to beat Ohio State. It's a burden you carry, but you should be very proud to carry. I saw you play several times this year and I can't remember any football team where players earned as many awards as you did. At the Downtown Athletic Club that day, we sure had our fingers crossed. You are a great, great football team. I think you will show the SEC how great the Big Ten is on New Year's Day. I wish you good luck." Steinbrenner also had introduced his wife, who was an Ohio State graduate.

After he walked to the sidelines when practice resumed, he said, "You can tell these are great kids. They applauded when the president and his wife were introduced. I've seen many teams sit there with their mouth open like they were bored. Not these guys."

Once the practice concluded, it was Cooper's turn. "To reiterate what Dr. Gee said, as a staff, we are very proud of you," he said. "But let's finish it off. From now until the game, it's all mental. Now there will be a lot of confusion at the hotel. Stay out of the lobby. All the fans will be asking 'Is the team ready?' and all that kind of stuff. Get in your rooms and get your rest."

They surely would need it.

Tennessee, like themselves, had finished only one loss away from being unbeaten and having a shot at a national championship. The Volunteers, behind sophomore quarterback Peyton Manning, had clobbered Alabama 41-14 and had scored more than 40 points five times, but also had lost 62-37 to second-ranked Florida and had ended the regular season by struggling past Kentucky 34-31 and Vanderbilt 12-7.

Manning had passed for 2,954 yards and 22 touchdowns while the Volunteers also had a 1,000-yard rusher in Jay Graham. Young didn't know if they would spread the field with three and sometimes four wideouts, or try to ram it down his defense's throat after what Michigan and Biakabutuka had accomplished a month earlier.

One thing he knew, without Che Bryant (ineligible) and Damon Moore (sent home), he was running out of bodies in the secondary.

"We are in big trouble if we get an injury during the game," he said, adding that he would have his defense play a zone most of the day and keep everything in front of the defensive backs. "We need a touchdown out of special teams. I am worried about it. We feel our offense will move the ball on their defense, and their offense probably will move the ball on our defense.

"We need to run a punt back, block a punt or something like that."

Hollis wasn't as concerned. After all, his offense had averaged 490 yards and 38 points per game, possessed almost perfect balance, and had the Heisman Trophy winner in the backfield. At the same time, he had a beat-up offensive line and an out-of-shape fullback.

In one meeting, he said, "I want to throw to the fullback in the flat, Georgia did successfully against them, but I worry about who to throw it to. Nicky's not motivated. He's talented, sure, but we can't accept the way he practices. He just doesn't bust his ass. He's going to get winded in the game."

It was the same problem the coaches faced with Sualua back in August. Still, four months later, he wasn't in good physical condition.

Hollis also planned to use a no-huddle offense early in the game. He also wanted to confuse Tennessee's defense, which was small but very quick relative to Big Ten standards, with an unbalanced offensive line. "We feel we are more physical than them and we can run it on them," he said, "but we'll mix it up like we have all season."

Before the team's pregame dinner on New Year's Eve, Cooper stopped to talk with a Columbus television reporter. "We need to win one of these games," he said. "We've been down here two or three years, and we haven't won yet." Asked about the forecast of heavy rain, he said, "I hope it rains. I really do. I think it might help us, since we've played in so many bad-weather games this year."

Once the cameraman and reporter departed, Cooper said, "I feel good because we are better than Tennessee. We should win this game."

Cooper looked up to the balcony, where fans stood waving and taking pictures. The lobby had been more crowded as the game neared, with alumni and fans mobbing the players for autographs and pictures. The coach didn't like it. "That would be the one thing I would change," he said. "I wouldn't stay where the alumni were. There are too many distractions here. Eddie's not the only one who can't walk through the hotel, none of us can." He turned around to grant a picture request for some fans, and headed to the team's walk-through practice outside a ballroom.

When it was finished, he told the team, "Tomorrow morning, we'll just let Eddie walk through the lobby, and everybody else can sneak through without being noticed."

When the players finished dinner, they headed out to see the movie "Sudden Death." By the time the clock struck 12, ringing in the New Year, they were tucked away for bed check.

The morning of Jan. 1, 1996, brought weather even the Buckeyes hadn't seen during the season. It didn't just rain. It *poured.* By the time the team busses reached the Citrus Bowl, an inch of rain had fallen already, and the sky was dark. This would be an all-day rain in Central Florida.

One hour and 15 minutes before kickoff, Cooper and a few players wandered onto the field to check out the footing. Matt Finkes planted his bare foot into the grass, as water submerged his toes. "Everybody was telling me how well the field was draining," he said. "It's full of water."

Young, for one, wouldn't feel a drop. For the first time, he would head upstairs to watch the game from the press box. It was Cooper's idea, part of the aftermath from the disaster at Michigan.

"He just felt we needed an extra pair of eyes upstairs," Young said. "It is because of the adjustments we didn't see or make in the Michigan game. With this rain, I just hope one of our (defensive backs) doesn't fall down and give them an easy one. That's what really scares you."

When Cooper finished his walk through the rain, he noticed one of his relatives gesturing to him from the stands. The kid was wearing a Tennessee jacket. After a brief conversation, he headed into the locker room. "That's one of my nephews," he said. "None of my relatives asked me for any tickets, because they knew they wouldn't have gotten any from me." Most all of his kin were diehard Volunteer fans, adding to his desire to win the game.

Following pregame warm-ups, as the players headed into the locker room, George bellowed, "What a beautiful day to play football."

As the downpour showed no signs of letting up, Young instructed his defense in one corner of the room: "It's an ideal day to knock the football loose. There will be turnovers today. Just keep your feet and make the play. All day, let's keep the pressure on them. If you get the chance to knock Peyton Manning's ass out, knock him out!"

In the other corner, Hollis told his offense, "Bobby, we don't want to throw a pass with a soggy ball. Ask for a dry ball. In weather such as this, turnovers will be the difference. Right now, the weather won't affect us one iota. We will pass and run. Remember, in the third series, we're going with the no-huddle. Be ready. Let's finish the year out in style and hang a bunch of points on the board."

When Young and Hollis finished, Cooper gathered the team and asked for the seniors to come to the front of the room. "Now go out there and play like you are capable of playing," he said. "If you do, this will be no contest. I don't want to hear that damn 'Rocky Top' all day long. Kick their ass! We are better than Tennessee! You seniors, we are going to win this game for you guys. You have been the heart and soul of this football team. You are the first football team in the history of this great school that can win 12 games. They will always remember you for what you did last, and they will remember you for winning 12 games.

"I want those damn hillbillies to be talking about how good the Buckeyes are!"

For the first quarter, that may have been what the hillbillies, and Cooper's relatives for that matter, were thinking. Central McClellion had given Young his wish, blocking a punt on Tennessee's second series. Two plays later, George cut away from a tackler and dived into the end zone from two yards out to make it 7-0.

Cornerback Ty Howard, who already had made two helmet-jarring hits, laid another on running back Eric Lane late in the second quarter. Howard's helmet went flying, Lane dropped the ball and Howard recovered at Tennessee's 24-yard line. George carried five straight times until the Buckeyes faced a fourth-and-a-foot at the two-yard line. Hoying probably could have sneaked easily for the first down, but Hollis and Cooper agreed to let George dive over the top.

Instead, the offensive line was pushed back and Volunteer tacklers swarmed George before he ever got off the ground.

After Tennessee punted, George let the first of his three dropped passes slip off his fingers, this one on a perfectly executed screen that would have resulted in a large gain. It resulted in a punt, and the Volunteers took over at their own 20 with only 41 seconds remaining in the half.

To this point, Young's defense had played as well as it had all season. In seven possessions, Tennessee had gained only 96 yards and six first downs. Ohio State defenders were hitting Tennessee hard, but Springs had paid for one solid shot with a shoulder injury. He left the field, gone for the day, forcing freshman Antoine Winfield into his place.

On the next two plays, it appeared as if Biakabutuka had suited up in Volunteer orange just to haunt the Buckeyes again. Graham hit the middle of the line, broke a tackle and darted outside for 11 yards. On the next play, he found a hole over left guard, started up the middle as Kelly and Gwinn dove helplessly at this feet. Graham broke into the clear and sloshed his way downfield. Howard, the only tackler with a chance, had a poor angle and couldn't catch him. The 69-yard play had turned what should have been a 14-0 Ohio State lead into a 7-7 game at the half.

The team stormed into the locker room.

"What the hell happened?" George screamed to no one in particular. "What happened?"

Cooper vented his frustration at the offensive line, which was being beaten repeatedly by Tennessee's smaller, quicker defensive front.

"You guys are making me look like shit out there," he yelled. "We would have kicked the field goal down there, but I had confidence in you guys to go for it, and you make me look like shit!"

He walked away.

Young wanted to reassure his defense, which had lost confidence in itself at Michigan, that Graham's run was not going to be the sign of things to come. "Let's go out and stop them and let them know that was a fluke play," he said. "You are 30 minutes away from 12 wins. It comes down to who wants it."

Hoying had been erratic in the half, completing only five-of-14 passes for 61 yards. He had been intercepted once.

"Bobby," Hollis asked, "is the ball a problem?"

"It is sometimes," the quarterback answered. "It's hard to throw a spiral."

Hollis realized then that the offensive line and George would have to pull the game out. The weather was too lousy to rely on a consistent passing game. "We've got to block!" he told the linemen. "We are going to have to grind them and get after their ass. Block! It's nothing to nothing."

The coaches had suspected Tennessee's players, since they weren't slipping much, were using illegal shoes with three-quarters inch cleats. The NCAA limits the cleats to one-half inch.

"Check their shoes! Check their shoes!" Petroff had told the Big Eight officiating crew. Once when Tennessee receiver Joey Kent slid out of bounds at the Ohio State bench, one of the Buckeyes' equipment managers held his foot to inspect the cleats. They were too long, but officials never made the Volunteers change footwear.

Nevertheless, Young's defense stopped Tennessee in three plays to start the second half, but a questionable roughing-the-punter penalty had given the Volunteers a first down. On the next play, Manning threw high and deep toward Kent, who was blanketed by Winfield. Suddenly, Winfield, who had replaced Springs, turned the wrong way and fell as Kent came back for the football. The result: an easy 47-yard touchdown that gave the Volunteers a 14-7 lead.

The offense moved the ball on each series in the third quarter, but could not sustain a drive. Brent Bartholomew, playing 15 miles from where he had grown up, punted from Tennessee's 40 and then from Tennessee's 43. On the second, his ball was about to roll dead in the slop at the two-yard line, but Finkes slid into it, knocking the football into the end zone for a touchback.

Later, facing a fourth-and-a-foot again, Hollis ordered Hoying for a quarterback sneak. It gained the first down. If only he had done that earlier, and Ohio State had taken a 14-0 lead, the game may have been different by now. Finally, Hoying's short passes and George's gutsy running moved the offense to the Volunteers' 32-yard line. Hoying dropped back and noticed Ricky Dudley running wide open down the middle. He hit him in stride, resulting in a touchdown to tie the game two plays into the fourth quarter.

The play teased coaches because Dudley had broken free often late in the season, and at times, Hoying had elected to throw to Glenn instead. It had happened on the first play of the second half at Michigan. Since his huge catch to set up the game-winning touchdown at Penn State, Dudley had caught only 18 passes over the final six games. The 6-foot-7 tight end towered over most linebackers, he ran like a wide receiver and he would surely be a high-round NFL pick. Yet, after 11 games, he had only 32 receptions for 469 yards.

If anything, it illustrated how good Glenn had become. Whatever Hoying threw his way, until the Michigan game that is, he seemed to find a way to come down with it. Of his 57 receptions, 17 resulted in touchdowns. So it was natural that Hoying would rely on him in the clutch.

Manning answered Hoying's throw by completing four passes as the Volunteers moved 59 yards to set up Jeff Hall's 29-yard field goal to make it 17-14.

With only 9:24 remaining, time was running out on Ohio State's chances to win the school-record 12th victory.

George then lost a fumble, but the defense held.

On a fourth-and-one at midfield, with 5:13 remaining, Hollis called for an option to the right, despite the fact that his offense rarely practiced the play and had run it only a few times the entire season.

Hoying ambled down the line and pitched the football off the helmet of backup fullback Matt Calhoun, but the defense held Tennessee on three plays again.

On fourth-and-two on the next possession, Hoying panicked and scrambled into a sack when Dudley was wide open over the middle.

The defense, however, never gave up as Vrabel tackled Graham for a four-yard loss, forcing another field goal that made it 20-14. With one final chance to pull out the game and provide a happy ending to the season, Hoying passed 12 yards to Glenn, five to George and 14 to Dimitrious Stanley. As Stanley tried to break a tackle, he fumbled the wet ball at Tennessee's 38-yard line and linebacker Craig King recovered.

That was the end.

The offense had been so brilliant, so unstoppable as the team rolled to 11 wins. It had bruised its way over Boston College, rallied against Notre Dame, Penn State and Wisconsin and simply blew away Iowa, Illinois and Indiana. Then after the disaster at Michigan, in which the offense and defense played equally as poorly, the defense had saved one of its better games for Tennessee's explosive offense. The Volunteers totaled only 15 first downs and 327 yards, but 116 had come on their only two touchdowns.

The offense, however, had lost three fumbles, thrown an interception and had failed to convert two crucial fourth downs. The offensive line, so bruising early in the season, had been pushed around by Tennessee the entire day.

"I am still proud of you," Cooper told the team. "You played a good football team down here today. They coached harder and played harder, but hold your heads up high."

Cooper, now owning an embarrassing 1-6 bowl record, walked into the coaches' locker room. "There will be a lot of second-guessing," Hollis told him.

The scene that followed was as glum and as sad as most good-byes could possibly be. Hollis walked around the room, hugging his seniors, Dudley, Hoying, and Sumner. "It's been fun," he told Hoying. Hoying hugged George, as tears filled the Heisman Trophy winner's eyes again, as they had five weeks earlier.

Hollis had been correct. When Cooper returned from the media room, shaking his head in disgust, he said, "All they wanted to ask me about was the option."

Hollis took the blame. "We hadn't run it much, sure, but that's why we called it," he said. "We didn't think they would expect it. It was a bad call by me because we are not an option team."

For the earlier fourth-down failure, which could have changed the course of the game, he blamed the offensive line. "We couldn't get a dang six inches," he said. "If we get that first down, we are in the end zone with a 14-0 lead."

With that, Hollis tied his tie, put on his coat and headed toward the bus.

Cooper's misery had been agitated by a few fans above the entry to the team's locker room. As he neared the tunnel following the game, they let loose with a stream of obscenities, calling him everything but his given name. After a heated exchange that included his son John and a nephew from Tennessee, Cooper made it safely into the locker room. "Those fans from Tennessee can be brutal," someone said. Cooper turned and corrected the statement, "What do you mean? Those fans were *ours*!"

The scene was not only a sad, but a symbolic moment for the head coach. He knew all along, even when the team was 11-0, that his popularity could change with any minute, with any loss. He even said so over and over again. And here, following a devastating loss at Michigan and a depressing, lethargic effort against Tennessee, it culminated on a dark, miserable day in Florida.

Twelve months and three weeks following his meeting with Geiger, when he stormed out of the athletic director's office, he was back where he had started. Was he unwanted by his own university and its fans?

After meeting with the media, Cooper returned to the locker room to change into some dry clothes. The assistants had dressed and headed to the team busses by now. He was alone in his misery. "We had a good one going, a great one going," he said of the season. "We just couldn't finish it off."

The journey that had started in the August heat of New Jersey had ended in the warm rain of Florida. It had been exhilarating at times, leaving the players and coaches to realize they were living a dream season. A once-in-a-lifetime season. But somehow, some way, it didn't last. And when the five months were history, they had experienced the ecstasy of winning 11 games and the glory of becoming the second-ranked team in the country. Now, all they felt was the heartbreak and misery of losing two final football games, which had obliterated the goals and dreams that they would never receive another chance to realize.

Most of the players probably didn't realize it, perhaps some did, but a cruel irony was occurring as they filed out of the locker room just before 5 o'clock. The rain poured on their shoulders as they boarded the busses for a trip to the Orlando airport. Three thousand miles away, on another coast in a beautiful setting and in sunshine, the Rose Bowl was kicking off.

It was supposed to be their game, their moment to remember forever, the greatest three hours of their lives. Instead, they faced what surely would be a reflective but miserable flight home to Columbus.

It was all over now.

Four months of fun and glory — it was what they always would want to remember. Five final weeks of pain and heartbreak — it would be what they would forever want to forget.

Afterword

Two days following the loss to Tennessee, the Buckeyes finished ranked sixth in the Associated Press poll — six positions higher than they had started the season in August, but four positions lower than they had spent the final month of the season.

On Jan. 8, defensive coordinator Bill Young, whose roots were in Oklahoma, accepted the same position at the University of Oklahoma. The move ended a 16-year working relationship under Cooper and an eight-year stay in Columbus.

"It's a really tough decision," Young said, "one of the toughest things I've ever done, having to leave a place like Ohio State and John Cooper. You just don't know how tough. I've been with that man for 16 years. I never thought I would leave here for a lateral move. If it wasn't in that particular area of the country, I wouldn't even have considered it."

As he headed to New Orleans for the NCAA coaches convention, Cooper planned to promote linebackers coach Fred Pagac, who graduated from Ohio State and has coached with the Buckeyes for 18 seasons, to defensive coordinator.

The head coaching job at Marshall went to another candidate, leaving Hollis to return for his sixth season at Ohio State.

Terry Glenn was set to announce he would pass up his senior season in order to become eligible for the NFL draft. Bobby Hoying, Ricky Dudley and Heisman Trophy winner Eddie George continued to work out and prepare themselves for the NFL draft.

By all indications, Bill Conley and the staff were on their way to their finest recruiting class yet, with 22 oral commitments by Jan. 10. Walt Harris would get the quarterback he wanted in Mark Garcia, the junior-college player from Modesto, Calif., who would transfer to Ohio State and be ready for spring practice.

Cooper?

Having accepted the fact that his finest team had failed to achieve their goals and dreams, he went about his business preparing for his 20th season as a head coach, what would be his ninth at Ohio State.

With 16 of 22 starters returning for spring practice, Cooper's Buckeyes would begin working once again to make that elusive trip to the Rose Bowl.

About the Author

Jeff Snook is a 1982 graduate of The Ohio State University. He has covered college football for 13 seasons, and has also written *The Year of the Gator*, a book about the University of Florida's 1993 SEC championship season. He resides in West Palm Beach, Fla.

Split the Uprights with Masters Press!

Masters Press has a complete line of books that cover football and other sports to help coaches and participants alike "master their game." All of our books are available at better bookstores or by calling Masters Press at 1-800-9-SPORTS. Catalogs available by request.

Coaching Football
Tom Flores &
Bob O'Connor
Trace the development of the game from the past to the present to the future and include the latest innovative plays.
$14.95, ISBN 0-940279-71-1

Conditioning for Football
Tom Zupancic
Helps coaches and players develop a program that improves performance and safety with unique methods of motivation.
$12.95, ISBN 0-940279-77-0

Youth League Football
Tom Flores &
Bob O'Connor
Presents drills and coaching suggestions for every position on the field, while emphasizing that you football's main objective is fun! Part of the Spalding Youth League Series.
$12.95, ISBN0-940279-69-X

Football Drill Book
Doug Mallory
Includes offensive and defensive skill drills and overall conditioning tips.
$12.95, ISBN0-940279-72-X

All-Pro Recipes: Great "Chefs" of the NFL
Features favorite recipes from more than 100 current and former NFL stars. It's a cookbook with delicious recipes, and more cooking tips; and a sports book with a brief biography and photo of the recipe's originator. Also includes a glossary of cooking terms and equivalency chart.
$14.95, ISBN 1-57028-058-4

Call Toll Free 1-800-9-SPORTS To Order